Decision Making for Educational Leaders

SUNY SERIES, EDUCATIONAL LEADERSHIP

Daniel L. Duke, editor

DECISION MAKING FOR EDUCATIONAL LEADERS

Underexamined Dimensions and Issues

BOB L. JOHNSON JR.

and SHARON D. KRUSE

STATE UNIVERSITY OF NEW YORK PRESS

Published by
STATE UNIVERSITY OF NEW YORK PRESS
Albany

© 2009 State University of New York

For information, contact
State University of New York Press, Albany, NY
www.sunypress.edu

Production, Laurie Searl
Marketing, Anne M. Valentine

Library of Congress Cataloging-in-Publication Data

Johnson, Bob L., 1956–
  Decision making for educational leaders : underexamined dimensions
and issues / Bob L. Johnson Jr. and Sharon D. Kruse.
      p. cm. — (Education leadership)
  Includes bibliographical references and index.
  ISBN 978-1-4384-2915-1 (hardcover : alk. paper) —
  ISBN 978-1-4384-2916-8 (pbk. : alk. paper)
  1. School management and organization—Decision making.
  2. Educational leadership. I. Kruse, Sharon D. II. Title.
  LB2805.J635 2009
  371.2'07—dc22   2009008523

10   9   8   7   6   5   4   3   2   1

To my parents, Bob and Marie Johnson,
particularly Dad, a *wise* and *seasoned* decision maker
BLJJ

To my parents, Stan and Ruth Youth,
who taught me much about decisions and choices
SDK

Contents

Part I
Decision-Making Theory and Theorizing

Part II
Context and Contextual Issues in Decision Making

Part III
The Decision Maker: Logic, Intuition, Data Use, and Skill

Part IV
Conclusion: Underexamined Issues in Decision Making

Tables and Figures

Preface

This volume represents a collaborative response to specific needs and frustrations we have experienced over the years in teaching graduate courses on decision making to aspiring and practicing educational leaders. It represents our effort to frame and teach decision making as an activity that occurs—more often than not—in a context defined by uncertainty, limited information, competing interests, and variables beyond the decision-maker's control. In it we have sought to reconcile the rational, institutional myths that have historically defined our thinking about decision making with the way decisions are actually *experienced* and *made* in organizations.

Given this conceptualization and the centrality of decision making to the leadership endeavor, the specific topics examined here address issues that we see as underaddressed, inadequately addressed and/or scattered in a sporadic, fragmented fashion throughout the leadership literature. Not only have we made an attempt to address what we see as an important set of "underexamined" decision-making issues in a single volume, we have sought to do so in the context of educational leadership. Though far from exhaustive in our identification and examination of these issues, we hope that readers find what is presented as useful *and* that this volume fills a niche in the educational literature and leader-preparation programs.

There are three targeted audiences for this volume: (a) graduate students with aspirations for a formal leadership role, (b) leader-practitioners seeking a deeper understanding of the decision-making process, and (c) scholars in the field of educational leadership. It is envisioned that this volume will serve as the primary or secondary text in a master's level course in leadership or in an advanced decision-making seminar in educational leadership. The importance of decision making to the leadership endeavor also makes this volume attractive to students/practitioners in other professional schools and fields: public administration; business administration; hospital administration; nursing administration; etc. Although the public school sector and organization define the context of this volume, much can be gleaned from a comparative study of the decision-making process across multiple sectors, public and private.

We have made a conscious effort to provide relevant, case-based examples throughout the volume. This was done in order to provide concrete examples of those theories and abstract concepts described in the narrative. An important conceptual skill for the reflective practitioner is the ability to move up and down in levels of abstraction when reading a text or conversing with others. While the goal of theorists is to pitch working theories at higher levels of abstraction so as to increase the scope of explanatory power (for example, one might offer a theory of decision making applicable for leaders in any and all organizations), the leader in the field is preoccupied with immediate problems of practice at lower levels of abstraction in his or her specific organization (that is, how to solve the parental revolt over excessive student fees faced by Steve Combs, the instrumental music teacher at Oak Ridge High). We have pitched this text at a level of abstraction that allows us to address the decision-making process in various educational organizations. With the concrete examples provided in each chapter, however, we have also made a conscious attempt to illustrate the applicability of our ideas and lead readers through multiple levels of conceptual abstraction. We are of the opinion that leadership preparation programs in education do a less than adequate job inculcating this important cognitive skill. This skill facilitates the learning process by helping students access literatures pitched at levels of abstraction beyond that of educational organizations—specifically the larger social science literature, a rich and at times abstract literature.

Writing a book is an interesting and challenging endeavor. Among other things, it assumes that the author (in this case, authors) has something of substance to say to an audience that has an interest in hearing. Indeed, this may be presumptuous on our part. For those who lack such an interest, this assumption places the author in the position to *woo* potential audiences in a manner similar to the romancing of the learner described by Whitehead (1957). In addition, those academics experienced in book writing—for that matter, sustained writing in any genre—quickly experience the challenge of translating the complex web of thoughts that exists in one's mind into the sequence of words that become the text. Much like moving between languages, there is that indefinable something that gets lost in translation. We have anticipated and experienced both challenges in this project. Realizing that education is the art of knowledge utilization, we hope that this book proves inviting and useful for those who read it, and that it not only contributes to the understanding of the decision-making process, but facilities in the development of decision-making skill. We assume full responsibility for the commissions and omissions of our work and hope that readers will allow the ideas presented here to provoke dialogue on the decision-making process. We also hope that this book encourages further dialogue on *how* to teach this important skill-set to educational leaders in a way that authentically reflects the realities of leadership and organizational life.

Acknowledgments

Much thanks to the College of Education at the University of Utah and my chair Diana Pounder for granting me the sabbatical that provided the much needed time to plan and write this book. Thanks also to those graduate students in my courses and doctoral seminars who heard, read, received, discussed, questioned, and challenged many of the ideas expressed in this volume . . . on *multiple* occasions. These interactions help me distill and clarify my thoughts on a variety of fronts. Particular thanks to my graduate assistant, Michael Owens, who over a period of several years listened to me talk about decision making, organizations, the academy, and life in general.

Finally, special thanks to my wife, Carol, and children, BJ and Katie, for their patience and love. They've heard more than they probably care to about such things and have patiently allowed me to voice my excitements and frustrations with being an academic at a research institution.

—Bob L. Johnson Jr.

A *Faculty Improvement Leave* awarded by The University of Akron for the Fall 2007 semester supported the writing of this book. The support of the department of Educational Foundations and Leadership and the College of Education in the application of leave materials is greatly appreciated. Jane Beese, who read early versions of the manuscript as well as provided final editing, deserves many thanks for her ability to turn work around in record time without complaint and with great skill. No book that addresses schools can be written without the stories and reflections of countless teachers, principals, superintendents, and other school personnel, the ongoing willingness of these professionals to formally and informally talk with researchers cannot be under estimated.

Finally, it goes without saying that my earliest introduction to decision making was provided to me by my parents, Stan and Ruth Youth. They along with my sister Susan Youth and brother Brian Youth offered important lessons about what making choices meant and the ways in which decisions matter.

—Sharon Kruse

PART I

Decision-Making Theory and Theorizing

CHAPTER ONE

Introduction: Leadership, Decision Making, and Underexplored Issues in Decision Making

Who needs another book on decision making? How can yet another volume on such a familiar, well-worn topic be justified in an already crowded field? How presumptuous. What can be said that has not already been said? What value-added contribution can justify the efforts of those who think they have something new to say?

No doubt, such responses typify the initial reactions shared by many who—*like you*—have picked up this volume to investigate its contents. Long before we officially launched this ambitious project, we pondered these and other questions at length. We have returned to them many times since. What justifies the addition of this volume to an already crowded field? *What* new insights about decision making can be shared with educational leaders that have not been shared? These are legitimate questions that we hope to reasonably address in this volume.

ON THE PERSISTENCE OF DECISION MAKING AS TOPIC OF INTEREST

A cursory review of the literature on decision making reveals a vast, multidisciplinary literature. Whether searching Google online, perusing the catalogue of one's favorite library or plodding through ERIC or SSI using carefully chosen descriptors, one is quickly struck by the breadth, depth, quantity, and persistence of this literature. Much has been written. There is much to be read. The sheer volume of the decision-making literature is in many ways telling. Its proliferation underscores the centrality of decision making to individual and collective life.

At the individual level, Heidegger (1962) and Jaspers (1968) remind us that life is about the decisions we make day-by-day, moment-by-moment. Each of us is the sum total of past decisions. These decisions in turn determine the future we eventually create. Less philosophical yet as important is the role decision making plays in defining the many social collectives of which we are part. As the dominant structural feature of society (Scott, 2002) formal organizations provide *the* principle mechanism for realizing ends that lie beyond the abilities of the lone individual. Organizations of various shapes, sizes, and purposes surround us. Much of the social activity of life is *organizational* activity. As organizational participants, we not only make decisions that affect the organizations we inhabit, we are influenced by the decisions made by coworkers in these organizations. We influence and are thus influenced.

Individuals and organizations are likewise vulnerable to decisions made by organizations of which they are *not* a part. A decision by the U.S. Department of Energy to build a research facility in Salt Lake City affects many individuals and organizations both positively and negatively. As homeowners, the influx of labor- ers will increase the value of our property. A decision such as this threatens the environmental concerns of Utah Green Peace. Universities in the area are excited about the research opportunities the new facility will create for them. Local school districts bemoan the potential loss of millions of dollars in future tax revenue. While these individuals and organizations are far removed from the making of the actual decision, all are affected by it. Each reacts and responds as interests dictate.

For the dominant coalition that controls the decision-making process in an organization (Cyert & March, 1963), the decisions produced by it are conse- quential for the effectiveness, efficiency, and life of the organization. A rushed decision by school leadership to hire a science teacher with a mixed track record in a district with Ivy League expectations can lead to outcomes that are conse- quential for all stake holders. A decision by a district curriculum team to change the methods used to teach numeracy at the elementary level may or may not lead to increased learning for all students. High-stakes decisions such as these under- score the importance of decision making to individual and collective life. The sheer volume of the decision-making literature is indicative of this importance.

The nature of the decision literature also draws attention to the complex- ity of the decision-making process and the extent to which the nuances of this process continue to elude our understanding. While there is a great deal that we know about the decision-making process, there is much that remains unknown. Decision complexity and uncertainty appear to covary: as the complexity of a decision problem increases, the uncertainty of the decision-making process associated with it likewise increases. These unknowns create the demand for more information, greater insight, and increased clarity. The vastness of the literature on decision making reflects this unmet demand. This literature is further indicative of our ongoing quest for uncertainty reduction. A paraphrased Jewish proverb cleverly captures the essence of this perpetual search: "It is the glory of the gods to conceal a matter; it is the lot of humans to search it out."[1]

The persistence of decision making as a topic of interest in professional schools likewise explains in part the proliferation and multidisciplinary roots of the decision-making literature. Preparing leaders is an interest shared by many

---

1. Proverbs 25:2

professional schools. Whether offered in the area of public, hospital, business or educational administration, courses in decision making are defining curricular components of these schools. Having skilled decision makers in an organization is an indispensable ingredient of organizational success. Effective leaders are defined and distinguished by their decision skills. Decision making is perhaps the lowest common denominator of leadership exercised in all settings. For Barnard (1938), Simon (1976), and others (Thompson, 1967; Weick, 2001, 1995), decision making lies at the heart of leadership behavior. Leadership is synonymous with decision making. It is *decision making in action*.

The importance of decision making to leadership and organizational life is such that organizations can be described as rational attempts to control and channel decision premises. For Simon (1976), the leadership challenge consists of making decisions that direct the decisions of organizational participants. As Simon noted, "decision-making is the heart of administration" (1976, p. xlviii). It is in this sense that leadership and administration may be defined as decision making. The prominence of decision making in leadership provides an adequate justification for its inclusion as a front-and-center topic of study in professional schools. The centrality of decision making to the administrative endeavor coupled with its elusive character offers yet another reason for the continued interest in and proliferation of the decision making literature.

OUR PURPOSES

Underexamined Decision-Making Dimensions and Issues

With these thoughts in mind, our over-arching purpose in the chapters that follow is to explore a set of underexamined dimensions and issues associated with the decision-making process. These dimensions are as follows: (a) the art of theory use in decision making; (b) the organizational context of decisions; (c) the political dynamics of decision making; (d) the inferential leaps and causal assumptions of decision making; (e) the role of intuition in decision making; (f) data-driven decision making; (g) the role of emotions and affect in decision making; and (h) making the *tough* decision. The work world of educational leaders and the organizations they inhabit define the specific contexts for this exploration. While this broad exploratory purpose provides the rationale for the name given to the volume, it raises a number of questions that beg further clarification. Anticipating what we hope are the most important, we make use of a question-and-answer format to elaborate further the specifics of this overarching purpose.

The eight dimensions examined in this volume have as their focus the larger decision-making process. It is this common focus that binds them together. Though treated separately and presented in a serial-type fashion, each highlights an important dimension of this process. All are seen by us as critical to decision success or failure. Our experience suggests that the importance of these dimensions is less obvious and even puzzling to many decision makers, particularly students. This is perhaps due to society's preoccupation with the microeconomic model of decision making, a hyper-rational model that ignores or de-emphasizes the importance of these factors in the decision process. Based on our professional judgment, each of the eight topics is central to most decisions educational leaders are called on to make.

The decision to describe these dimensions as "underexamined" and "underexplored" is based on our collective judgment. This judgment is informed by three factors: (a) the reality of these dimensions and the extent to which they define the decision-making process; (b) the lack of systematic, prolonged attention given to these dimensions in leadership preparation programs in education; and (c) the relative attention—or *inattention*—given to these dimensions in the theoretical and empirical work being done in the field of educational leadership. Our experiences as leader-practitioners, researchers, and professors in leadership preparation programs at the master's and doctoral levels lead us to these conclusions.

In describing these dimensions as *underexamined* we are not claiming that they have gone *unexamined*. This distinction is significant. As will be seen in each chapter, others in our field have addressed one or more of these issues in various contexts. Most have been examined here and there, some more than others. What we hope distinguishes our work from other decision-making texts is our effort to: (a) consciously label these dimensions as such, (b) pull them together for examination into a single volume, and (c) explore the nature and essence of each and underscore their importance to the larger decision process. Until raised for conscious and systematic reflection, most of these dimensions fly below the radar of many educational leaders. As a result, the role of these dimensions in the decision process remains underappreciated.

These dimensions are certainly not exhaustive, nor are they the most important. The decision rules used to guide our choices were far from arbitrary. Though informed, they are not to be taken as definitive. Our dual hope is that we have successfully provided a reasonable justification for labeling these dimensions as such and have offered substantive examinations of each that validate our judgments. We have in no way sought to be exhaustive in identifying nor examining all issues related to the decision-making process. No comprehensive view of decision making is assumed here. We also recognize that others might include or exclude some or all of the dimensions we have highlighted in this volume *or* even prioritize them differently. Such is the nature of work both in the academy and professions where reasonably intelligent people disagree over a number of issues—you say potato, I say po*tah*to; you say tomato, I say to*mah*to.

Inferences drawn from two related literatures provide the theoretical bases for this volume: (a) the broader administrative science literature; and (b) the narrower educational leadership literature on decision making. The administrative science literature is an eclectic and at times messy literature. As such, it is an aggregate of multiple knowledge domains and literatures (e.g., leadership, decision making, supervision, administration, planning, budgeting, organization theory, politics, etc.). Because there is no hard-and-fast consensus as to what these components are and the weighting to be given each, the components of this aggregate are neither static nor fixed. Nevertheless, this aggregate exhibits a loosely coupled quality that yields a modicum of logical cohesion (Johnson, 2004b). The foundational work of Barnard (1938), Simon (1976), March (1965, 1988, 1994), Cyert and March (1963), and Weick (1979, 1995, 2001) exemplify its eclectic nature. This literature provides the broader base for this volume.

The decision-making literature in educational leadership and administration provides the narrower base for this volume. Similar to that of other executives, the work of leaders in educational organizations revolves around decision-making activities. The work of theorists such as Mintzberg (1973), Wolcott (1973), Cuban (1988), Leithwood and Steinbach (1994), and others corroborates this (Boyan, 1987; Blumberg, 1986; Blumberg & Greenfield, 1980; Gronn, 2003; Hoy & Miskel, 2001; Hoy & Tarter, 2004; Johnson & Fauske, 2000; Martin & Willower, 1981; Sergiovanni, 1995). The distinctiveness of this literature rests on the fact that it examines the decision-making processes used by educational leaders in educational organizations. One notable feature of this literature is the absence of work that examines decision making from the perspective we have defined above. We have been unable to identify a single volume, book chapter, or refereed publication that examines decision making from the vantage point of underexamined issues for educational leaders. It is this perspective that we suggest distinguishes this volume on decision making. While it is this larger purpose of exploring a set of underexamined decision dimensions or issues that defines the niche for this volume, there are other ancillary purposes that we seek to address.

THEORETICALLY GROUNDED DESCRIPTION OF DIMENSIONS AND ISSUES

With an eye to practice, it is likewise our intent to provide a theoretically grounded description of these dimensions or issues. We are well aware of the history, frustrations, and debates for and against the use of theory in our field over the last fifty years (Campbell, 1960; Halpin, 1966; Culbertson, 1973; English, 2003; Greenfield, 1975; Griffiths, 1978; Murphy, 1992). These debates notwithstanding, we value both theory and the systematic logic associated with the theorizing process as useful ways of thinking. A formal theory is a systematic attempt to explain something. It consists of a set of interrelated concepts, assumptions, and relationships that are used to describe, explain, and at times, predict a phenomenon of interest. A theory is an attempt to describe what *is* (descriptive). In describing theories and the theorizing process as such, we highlight several features of these important concepts.

Consistent with the ideas of Dewey (1933, 1938), we learn little from experience unless we reflect on it. The kind of theorizing of interest to us is succinctly captured in the concept *praxis*, a concept that is used and misused in a variety of ways. To understand *praxis*, one must move beyond the theory-practice dichotomy that has dominated the social sciences and view both as twin moments of the same activity dialectically united (Freire 1973; Habermas, 1973). *Praxis* is an experiential and reflective way of knowing in which articulated theory arises from *praxis* to yield further *praxis*. It is practice informed by theoretical reflection and, conversely, theoretical reflection informed by practice. *Praxis* provides a means for keeping theory and practice together as dual and mutually enriching activities defined by human intentionality.

Theories and the theorizing process are thus grounded in the world of data. Theories are not something we impose on the data, rather they are explanations that arise from and are tested by our experiences with it. Theories are tested, validated and refined (or invalidated and rejected) in the life-world of data experience. A given theory is judged to be valid or invalid to the extent that is isomorphic or aligned with lived experience. When viewed in the context of *praxis*, a theory is the product of our efforts to make sense of the world as we experience it. The dynamics of this interpretive process are indeed complex and vary across individuals. They are also value-laden. We recognize and appreciate this complexity.

Given that individuals and groups experience the world differently, competing theories of the same phenomenon are to be expected. Of greater importance for the critical thinker are: (a) the extent to which these competing explanations are grounded in the data of experience; and (b) the extent to which the logical moves from data to explanation have been articulated in a way that adequately captures the richness and complexity of the phenomenon itself. Judgments between competing explanations are informed by these and other logic-criteria. This ongoing process of sense-making leads us to suggest that all theories are relative, partial, and in the process of becoming. All theories are products of a specific context, culture, time and place. Hence, they are relative. Given that theories are noninclusive, less than comprehensive in what they seek to convey, they are also partial. The continual revision-refinement process associated with theorizing suggests that all theories are partial and in the process of becoming.

Finally, we suggest that developing and testing theories are not only defining activities for educators in the academy, they are defining activities for educators in schools and classrooms committed to the refinement of craft wisdom. In the pursuit of this wisdom, the theorizing outlined above provides a means for increasing the *efficiency* of one's thinking (Dewey, 1933, 1938; Weick, 1989). In our interactions with the world, all individuals theorize—some more systematically, efficiently and formally than others. To say that theorizing is the sole concern of professors and researchers is to misunderstand *how* we think and learn (Bruner, 2006; Dewey, 1933, 1938; Sternberg & Pretz, 2005). The theorizing which undergirds our examination of topics in this volume provides an efficient though not infallible means of thinking that is consistent with the approach of reflective practitioners (Argyris & Schon, 1974; Schon 1983, 1987, 1988) in various roles across many types of educational organizations. It is also our intent to provide a theoretically grounded description of these dimensions with an eye toward empowering the decision-making practice of educational leaders.

Provoking Thought on the Dynamics of Decision Making

A third purpose identified for this volume is to provoke thought on the dynamics of the decision-making process. This provocation is intended to assist readers in *complicating* (Weick, 1978) their thinking about the decision-making process. Rather than reduce conceptual horizons on the topic, our hope is to expand these horizons. Toward this end, we have consciously tried to avoid suggesting that decision making is a neat, symmetrical mental activity that rests on a definitive knowledge base. While there is much that we know about this process, there is much that remains unknown.

Ricoeur's (1976, 1981) insights on the hermeneutic process (that is, how individuals construct and interpret meaning from experience) are useful for conveying this important educational purpose. Ricoeur (1981) has written about the text world that is created when an author commits his or her thoughts to writing. Whereas prior to writing, a writer's thoughts are under his or her control, once committed to text thoughts take on a life of their own. They are less under his or her control than before. The text is free in that the writer has let it go; gesture, intonation, and context have fallen away. The reader has no choice but to accept it as it comes. In this sense, the text stands between the author and reader.

As readers separated by time, distance, and a personal relationship with an author, we can never be absolutely sure of what an author is fully intending to convey. We are left to operate in the world of the text and face its demands.

While the past experiences we bring to the text aid us in sense-making what we read, differing experiences across readers ensure variation in interpretation. Thus, as readers we can never be absolutely sure what an author means. We are rarely in a position as readers to conclude that we have drawn out the full, rich variegated meaning intended by the author. Conversely, the author cannot control how readers will interpret the text and the meanings they will bring to it.

This is certainly the case as you read and hold this book in your hand. Now that we have committed our ideas on decision making to writing, the thoughts in this and the chapters that follow now stand independent of us. They are no longer directly under our control. They are being mediated to you *via* this text and as such are open to a variety of interpretations and meanings. We cannot be sure that what we intend to convey is being interpreted by readers in ways that reflect the fullness, precision and, subtle nuances of our intent. The text is mediating this conveyance. Neither can be control how readers are interpreting what we have written. Such are the limitations of communication and the complexities of the hermeneutic process.

With these thoughts on interpretation as context, Ricoeur (1981) has identified three life-worlds associated with a text: (a) the world *behind* the text; (b) the world *in* the text; and, (c) the world *in front of* the text. Distinguishing and determining the meaning of each provides further insight into the complexity and generative potential that surround the interpretation process as one reads. Having read a text, it is the generative potential and possibilities that come from the reader's provoked imagination that are of interest to us. As noted above, an important purpose of this volume is to provoke thought on the dynamics of the decision-making process.

For any given text, *the world behind the text* refers to the original intent of the author. What *exactly* did the author mean when she or he wrote this text? Regardless of how I am reading it, what was the author's *original* intent? What is she or he trying to say? According to Ricoeur (1981), literalists informed by the historical-critical perspective are inordinately preoccupied with seeking to recover and reconstruct the world *behind* the text.

This perspective is personified in the search by conservative ideologues to determine the original intent of the U.S. Constitution. Though a noteworthy endeavor, the deaths of the original framers coupled with the time, distance, and culture that separate us make this recovery impossible. We are unable to talk with the constitutional framers. We are several steps removed from them. The relationship we share with them is a *mediated* relationship. All that exists are texts that mediate the meaning of the Constitution for us. Hence, there will always be debates about original intent. Much like the search for the Holy Grail, constraints such as these make the search for the original intent an unending search. The full life-world *behind* a text is unavailable to most readers. So it is with most texts; so it is with this text. Time, physical distance, and the absence of a personal relationship with us, make this search somewhat elusive for you.

There is also *the world found in the text*. This world consists of the assumptions, interactions and reality created by the author. It emerges from the actual story line of the text itself. This story line is a world created by the author. It often (though not always) consists of places, settings, occurrences, and actions that do not exist in the "real world." An excellent example of the world *in* the text is found in the children's book, *Alice in Wonderland* (1865). In writing this story, Charles Dodgson (a.k.a. Louis Carroll, 1832–1898) masterfully creates a world *in* his text: *Wonderland*. In so doing, he sets aside the "real world" as we know it. *Wonderland* is a world distinct from our world. It is a fantasy world in which animals (e.g., the rabbit, turtle, and gryphon) and playing cards (the King of Hearts) talk. The constraints of reality have been suspended. The work of the Oxford Inklings provides additional examples of vivid life-worlds *in* the text (C. S. Lewis's *The Lion, The Witch and The Wardrobe* and J. R. R. Tolkien's *The Hobbit*).

To be sure, the life-world created *in* this text is far different from the fantasy worlds of these British authors. Our intent is to examine decision making from the perspective of the educational leader and in the context of educational organizations. While there are generic challenges and behaviors that define leadership (Mintzberg, 1973; Pfeffer, 1981; Simon, 1976; Yukl, 2002) in all organizations (Mintzberg, 1979; Scott, 2002; Thompson, 1967; Weick, 1995), the life-world in this text is that of the educational leader. The theories, behaviors and examples provided *in* this text seek to recreate the realities of this world. Having noted this, it is our hope that the ideas presented in this book are accessible to scholars and practitioners in other fields interested in the decision-making process.

In addition to the worlds behind and in the text, Ricoeur (1981) speaks of *the interpretive world in front of the text*. This is the life-world generated *within* the reader by the text as she or he reads it. It is a function of the experiences, knowledge, and cognitive abilities the reader brings to the text *as* she or he interacts with it. This complex interaction is *generative* in that it evokes imagination, new insight, and heretofore unknown possibilities for the reader. These in turn become the practical datum for reflection on the topic at hand. The life world of reflection that occurs in front of the text is neither supervised nor monitored by the worlds *behind* or *within* the text. Rather it is provoked or animated by these and as such remains *in front of* the text at the interface of text and reader. This interaction provokes ideas, thoughts, and insights that often go *beyond* the text. In this sense, this world animates and propels the imagination of the reader.

Though the cognitive processes associated with the sense-making that occurs as the reader interacts with the text are complex, it is something that is experientially familiar to most. Stumped as an educational leader about what to do with a student whose behavior is a problem from year to year, you persist in your patterned responses to him. These responses are deeply ingrained and border on the habitual. Frustrated by the lack of success, you make an appointment with the counseling director of the district to seek advice. The meeting is long yet productive. Upon leaving, she shares a book with you; one that she claims has been of great help to others. The book consists of twenty real-life case studies by experienced administrators on how to work with and motivate challenging students. The book describes successes and failures. You are engaged and fascinated by what you read. While no single case in the text is congruent with the specifics of your situation, reading the book provokes new insights for you. The experiences, knowledge cognitive dispositions you bring to the text as you read it combine to lift you out of the box of your imprisoned thinking and generate new imaginative possibilities for responding to the student. This dynamic is something that most professionals have experienced at one time or another. As we read, our interaction with the text generates new ideas, new insights and unseen ways of seeing and thinking. It is an example of what Ricoeur refers to as the sense-making that occurs in the world *in front of* the text.

It is just this phenomenon—*the world in front of the text*—that defines an important purpose for this book on decision making. This work does not represent an exhaustive treatment of the decision-making process. Our purposes are more modest than this. Beyond exploring a set of underexamined dimensions, our hope is that the topics explored in this volume will generate for the reader new possibilities and insights into the decision-making process *that go beyond* what is presented here. The imagination that is provoked as one interacts with a text creates liminal learning moments for the reader. Such moments become rich opportunities for seeing what was before unseen, seeing anew and generating new insights. As you interact with the text, we encourage you to allow the material to serve this important generative function.

Realizing that the world that emerges in front of the text for individuals varies from reader to reader, we often remind students in our classes how important it is that each read and come prepared to discuss a given week's reading with the class. Rather than being punitive with those who choose to do otherwise, we remind them that no two individuals interact with a text the same way. The knowledge, experiences, and cognitive style that each brings to the text means that no two students will experience the world in front of the text in exactly the same way. By choosing not to read or fully engage the text, individual students rob the larger class of the generative insights that are unique to each reader as she or he interacts with the text. It is these generative insights that enrich the individual and group learning process. It is our hope that in reading this volume, you will allow it to serve this important generative function in your own learning. Allow it to lead you *beyond* what is discussed in this and subsequent chapters.

ENCOURAGING THE DEVELOPMENT OF DECISION-MAKING SKILL

The final purpose we have identified for this volume is to inform and encourage the development of decision-making skills among potential and practicing educational leaders. In identifying this purpose, we are well aware that skill development consists of more than knowledge acquisition. Among other things, it involves dialogue, reflection, theorizing, experimentation, practice, trial and error, and success and failure. Research in the physical sciences suggests that structural engineers learn as much or more in from design failures than successes (Petroski, 1985). Building on the generative insights experienced as one interacts with the text and the *praxis* approach to thinking and doing described above, readers are invited to use the ideas explored in the chapters that follow as means for improving their own decision skills. *Praxis* suggests that the improvement of decision-making skill calls for intentional, reflective thought when deciding.

DECISION MAKING AND THE WORK OF EDUCATIONAL LEADERS

A decision is a *conscious* choice made between *two or more* competing alternatives. This choice can be made by an individual or group. While various theorists have sought to model this process (Hoy & Miskel, 2001; Simon, 1981, 1976; Weick, 1995), decision making is not the robotic affair that traditional economics would have us believe. Microeconomics has embraced an exaggerated, romantic view of human rationality that is unwarranted: an omniscient decision maker with well-defined decision preferences (*what we want*) who knows exactly what is to be decided (*what is being decided*), what decision alternatives are available (*what is possible*), and the cost-benefits ratios associated with each alternative (*what each costs*). Although a handful of decisions lend themselves to this hyper-rational approach, most decisions are made in the midst of unknowns. These unknowns are consequential for the decision-making process. When coupled with the limitations of human cognition, unknowns increase the potential for error in the decision-making process.

Like leaders in other organizations, the work of the educational leader is defined by decision making. The decisions educational leaders are called on to make occur in social systems that are complex and contingent. The educational community is populated by diverse constituencies, all of whom hold expectations for the school (Cusick, 1992). As a result, numerous and at times conflicting demands are placed on the individuals who lead them. These expectations underscore the value-laden nature of administrative work.

The work of the educational leader is also people-intensive. School administrators are continually engaged with others. A typical administrative day consists of a number of brief, fast-paced interactions, some of which are intense. Much of the work of educational leaders focuses on helping others solve problems. These problems often become their problems. Given the centrality of their role as decision makers, educational leaders are vulnerable to the eccentricities, foibles, and humorous dynamics common to organizational life (Willower, 1991). They are frequently the focal point of gossip and grapevine talk in and around the formal collective. In sum, the work world of the educational leader is a world conducive to conflict (Pfeffer, 1981), politics, and occasional loneliness. It is a role defined by decision making.

Our experiences with educational leaders suggest that most are committed to doing good things for those with whom they work. Most are people-centered. Most enjoy the pleasant surprises and variability that come with each new day. Most find satisfaction in knowing that what they do contributes to the well being of students and society. *But having a good heart is not enough.* Not all educational leaders are equally competent. Some are less than competent. More importantly, most are not as competent as they *could* be.

Beyond good intentions, there are two crucial challenges that appear common to all educational leaders: (a) determining *how* to make difficult choices wisely; and (b) determining *how* to create a more desirable, improved state of educational affairs within the organization. The two are related. Careful consideration of these challenges leads one to conclude that successfully addressing each is a function one's skills as a decision maker. Yet decisions that lead to the realization of desired intent do not just happen. Effective decisions are the fruit of the decision-making processes that precede them. Just as fruit varies in quality, so do decisions. For educational leaders, effective decision making involves *deliberate* thought and *deliberate* choices, choices informed by the best *available* data and ideas. These ideas and the logic behind them empower leaders to efficiently make sense of the seemingly chaotic stream of organizational life in the decisions they are called on to make. But how does the ambitious leader come to and appropriate these ideas? Consistent with our stated purposes above, it is here that the methods and content of systematic inquiry prove beneficial to the leader's search improved decision-making skill.

The essence of science is its method. In an effort to describe how humans think, Dewey (1933, 1938) refers to this method as *the method of inquiry.* It consists of several defining activities that are animated by cognitive dissonance or felt difficulty: (a) problem identification and formulation; (b) the development of explanations for the problem; (c) the search for confirming or disconfirming evidence to test, reject and modify competing explanations of the problem; and (d) the move to eliminate cognitive dissonance through problem solving. Consistent with our discussion of theories or theorizing above, this method of inquiry described by Dewey is the logic of theorizing. It is also the logic of the decision-making process.

The use of this method by educational leaders to problem solve is described by Willower (1991) as the blending of science and art. The *scientific* use of the method consists of one's knowledge, skill, and facility in using this method *and* the knowledge produced by it. Using this method to systematically investigate leaders and their work, concepts have been developed that are especially useful in the decision-making process: *social system, formal and informal organization, culture and subcultures, conflict,* and *equilibrium*—to name a few. Concepts such as these are useful in sensitizing leaders to a wide variety of social and organizational phenomena. Scanning the decision environment, educational leaders can use these as efficient sense-making tools to facilitate the decision process. We suggest that leaders who utilize such concepts solve problems more effectively than those who do not. Each of these concepts is a product of Dewey's method of inquiry. A working knowledge of this method and the fruit produced by it define the *scientific* side of problem-solving.

By contrast, the *artistic* side of the problem-solving consists in the problem solver's intuitive and adaptive use of this method to a specific decision. Knowing *how* and *when* to systematically approach a decision, knowing *what* concepts or theories to use in the sense-making process and *when* require artistry on the part of the decision maker. The educational leader should not rely on one or a few concepts or theories. Rather, the astute decision maker must have a skeptical familiarity (Weick, 2001) with an array of theories and concepts that allow for the viewing of a scenario from multiple angles. The complexities, contingencies, and information gaps of decision scenarios in the day-to-day world of the educational leader, work against efforts to apply a one-size-fits-all approach to decision making. Navigating and orchestrating the specifics of a given situation, framing it from a variety of perspectives using select concepts and theories accentuate the creative, artistic side of decision making.

The personal needs, bias, and presuppositions that leaders bring to decisions are part and parcel of the human condition. Together they inform the scientific and artistic approaches individuals exercise in the decision-making process. These realities underscore the need for educational leaders to be *reflective* and *reflexive*—that is, self-aware and critical (Mead, 1934)—in the decisions they make. Deliberation is critical to leadership that does justice to the decision-making process. It is also essential for realizing the valued outcomes society has for education. Such an approach is consistent with the notion of *praxis* and—though not infallible—is superior to dogma and recipe. The specific dimensions of the decision-making process examined in this volume are approached systematically with a commitment to Dewey's method of inquiry. At the same time, these issues are approached with an eye to the uncertainties and ambiguities that define the work of leaders in educational organizations, work that requires both science and art.

OUR EXPLICIT AND
NOT SO EXPLICIT ASSUMPTIONS

Several assumptions are apparent in what has been read and what is to follow. Rather than have others second-guess our approach to decision-making, we choose to make these explicit. The topics to which we attend and the perspective adopted reflect our predispositions and biases as scholars. This is not to say that the concerns we highlight are unique to us. Nor do we suggest—as Locke's radical empiricism would have us believe (Locke's *egocentric predicament*)—that these predispositions prevent us from describing phenomena in ways that can be recognize and understood by others (Miller & Jensen, 2004). In an effort to *situate* ourselves, we articulate our assumptions and invite the reader to evaluate the validity of each.

Leadership Is Decision Making

As noted above, we assume that the essence of leadership *is* decision making. It is *the* defining activity, the lowest common denominator to which leadership can be reduced. The centrality of decision making to the leadership role provides an important justification for this and other volumes on the topic. Decision making lies at the heart of leadership.

A Decision Is a Conscious Choice

Second, we assume that a decision is a *conscious* choice. While one might argue that some of the choices we make are unconscious, the focus of this book is on those choices that are *consciously* made. A conscious choice may be as simple as choosing not to decide. A superintendent's decision *not* to act on a media *faux pax* committed by one of her principals is an example of consciously deciding not to decide/act.

Two or More Competing Alternatives
Required for a Decision To Be Made

As is likewise noted above, we assume that a decision involves a choice between *two or more* competing alternatives. A situation that does not present the decision maker with at least two alternative courses of action does not qualify as a decision. Based on a required end-of-year review, a principal can decide either to reappoint or release a teacher from his or her current assignment. If such options are not available, the principal has no decision to make. The very word *decision* suggests that at least two known, competing courses of action are available to the decision maker.

ALL DECISIONS ARE MADE IN A CONTEXT, NO TWO OF WHICH ARE IDENTICAL

We also assume that all decisions are made in a context. This context consists of a set of actors and a host of social, political, cultural, and economic factors that constrain or facilitate (or both) the decision-making process. A decision cannot be considered apart from its context. Further, we assume that no two decision contexts are the same. While there are contexts that share remarkable similarities, the specifics of each are unique (Simon, 1991, 1993; Weick, 1995, 2001). The contextual particulars of a personnel decision made in one school are different from a similar personnel decision made in another. Though the subject matter of the decisions is the same, the particulars of each context mean that the decisions cannot be approached in exactly the same way. The contexts dictate otherwise.

MOST DECISIONS ARE MADE IN THE MIDST OF UNKNOWNS

We also proceed on the assumption that in most situations (*not all*), the decisions educational leaders are called on to make are facilitated and constrained by a host of known and unknown variables. Of those variables that are known, many may lie beyond the immediate control of the decision maker. Others remain contingent. The uncertainty created by this state of affairs has major implications for the decision-making process. Chief among these is the realization that for most decisions, the educational leader is neither omniscient nor operating in the absence of constraints. We are well aware of this. As noted above, the myths and limitations of the rational, omniscient decision maker have been examined and exposed (March, 1994; Scott, 2002; Simon, 1976; Weick, 1995). We situate this volume in a view of decision making that appreciates the uncertainties, complexities, and contingencies that surround most decisions. More often than not, the educational decision maker is a *constrained satisficer* rather than an *omniscient optimizer*.

ROUTINE AND NONROUTINE DECISIONS ARE DISTINGUISHED BY THE DECISION CONTEXT

Frequently made decisions rooted in contexts that are familiar and well known lend themselves to preprogrammed, routine decision procedures (Simon, 1981; Weick, 2001). Sickness, for example, is a frequent occurrence among students in all schools. As a result, it is not surprising to find that routinized decision procedures exist for dealing with students who are sick and need to leave for the day. On the other hand, there are decisions that are defined by contexts that are full of unknowns. Such contexts are difficult to read and analyze. Decisions such as these call for approaches that are less routine, approaches that allow for flexibility and discretion in dealing with the uncertainties embedded in the context.

Decision Subject Can Be Distinguished from Decision Process

In reflecting on the decision-making process, we assume that it is possible to differentiate the subject matter of a decision from the processes and procedures used to arrive at that decision. Stated otherwise, there is a difference between *what* is being decided and *how* the decision is actually made. Simon (1981) refers to the former as *substantive rationality* and the latter *procedural rationality*. The primary focus this book is on procedural rationality: on the logic, processes and procedures that define the decision-making process. Regardless of what is being decided, it is this rationality that is common to all decisions.

Effective Decision Making Consists of More Than Mere Knowledge Acquisition

Consistent with the importance we place on theorizing as *praxis*, we assume that competence in decision making consists of more than mere knowledge acquisition. Knowledge of the decision-making process is a necessary yet insufficient component of effective decision making. Competence in decision making is also a function of one's *cognitive habits*. As Weick (1995) reminds us, training leaders in decision-making is an exercise in habit training; it is more like training athletes than scholars. In the context of decision competence, this training focuses on internalizing *the habit* of searching for procedural and contextual patterns in the decisions faced. This search is informed by one's knowledge of the decision-making process, a knowledge that provides clues as to *what patterns* to look for and *where*. The topics examined in this volume highlight and explore some of these patterns. The search for such patterns is habitual for the effective decision maker.

ORGANIZATION AND OVERVIEW OF
TEXT AND DECISION DIMENSIONS

A loose, organic quality binds the chapters of this volume together. The common theme across all is decision making, both as an object of study and a skill to be honed. As a means for organizing our thoughts, we have chosen to structure the ten chapters of the text into four larger sections. Broadly speaking, the sequence and flow of these sections is from *theory*, to *theory in use*, to *theory in action*—from an examination of the more abstract and theoretical abstract aspects of decision making to the more immediate, concrete dimensions of the process. Each focuses on the procedural rationality of the decision making.

While this scheme provides a reasonable means for sequencing the ten chapters, its validity should not be pressed too far.

Part I is titled *Decision-Making Theory and Theorizing*. It consists of two chapters linked by a common concern with decision-making theory and theorizing. Whereas the present chapter seeks to provide a theoretical approach and justification for what follows, chapter 2 examines how theory can be used to inform the decision-making process. How effectively do professional schools teach students to theorize about how theories of decision making can be used to improve decision skills? The disconnect that exists between what is taught in many leadership preparation programs and the day-to-day realities of organizational life reflects a collective insensitivity to the importance of developing the abilities of leaders as theorists, artists, and in the art of theory use. In what we think is an important yet underexamined topic, we suggest that there is an underappreciated artistic element associated with theorizing and theory use. It is incumbent upon professional schools to help practitioners develop and refine their abilities as street-level theorists concerned with improving decision skills.

As implied by its title, *Context and Contextual Issues in Decision Making*, Part II examines two sets of issues that define the decision-making context in educational settings. Chapter 3 focuses on the organizational context in which decisions are made. It defines and explores the multidimensional nature of this context and its influence on the decisions leaders make. Using frameworks and concepts from the organizational theory literature, this chapter examines unique features of schools as human service organizations. Decisions are not made in a vacuum. Much of the decision-making literature reflects a superficial understanding of the organizational perspective and an incomplete grasp of the fundamental character of school organizations. A basic understanding of these features and how they shape the larger decision context is beneficial to those who would seek to strengthen their decision-making skills.

Chapter 4 offers a description of the political context in which decisions are made. Political dynamics define an aspect of social life that many choose to discount. Yet these dynamics are real and ever present. After reviewing the literature, we offer a working definition of politics for educational leaders: politics is that set of activities and strategies used by organizational participants to influence decisions that allocate scarce, but valued resources within the organization. To ignore these realities is to invite disaster. Our intent in this chapter is to address these and other political dimensions that define the larger decision context.

Part III, *The Decision Maker: Logic, Intuition, Data Use, and Skill*, focuses on a range of issues and skill-sets that educational leaders must address if they are to improve their decision-making efforts. All we feel have been underexamined; most stand in need of further exploration. After examining the meaning and implications of the call for increased data-driven decision making, chapter 5 explores two underexamined yet critical elements of the decision-making process: the working, taken-for-granted causal assumptions that educational leaders bring to the decisions they make *and* the inferential leaps made as leaders iterate between data and decision. Both focus on the logic of decisions. Both spring from the uncertainties inherent in limited, incomplete, and equivocal decision data. We suggest that there is a need to increase our collective awareness of these process issues and how they frame our approach to decisions.

We then move to explore an oft discussed yet infrequently examined decision topic in a chapter titled, *The Intuitive Decision Maker in the Information Age*. Intuition is frequently evoked as a basis for action in decisions defined by high levels of uncertainty. Using Gladwell's work *Blink* (2005) as a point of departure, we examine the meaning of intuition and the role it plays in the decision-making process. We suggest that decision choices attributed to intuition may in fact be informed by ephemeral or well-developed knowledge that only appears to be intuitive. By attending to the more intuitive aspects of decision-making process, it appears that individuals and organizations can benefit in distinct ways.

Chapter 7 provides a systematic look at data-driven decision making aimed at school improvement. A central focus in this chapter is decisions relating to student-learning and school-reform initiatives. Following a discussion of data types, data collection and data analysis, attention shifts to the pitfalls of data-based decision making. Meaningfulness of data-use within the school setting comprises a substantial focus of the section with attention directed toward appropriate data-analysis techniques and practical applications of findings.

Related yet distinct from the chapter on intuition, chapter 8 focuses on those affective and dispositional aspects of decision making faced by educational leaders in the decisions they are called to make. Attention to the dispositional aspects of quality leaders has become the focus of a new and growing literature. These include such things as perseverance, willingness to live with ambiguity, the lack of closure, criticism, as well as developing a thick skin. Of particular interest in times of crisis, the dispositions with which a leader approaches problem definition and decision making have the potential to influence the success of eventual responses and a leader's reputation within the larger organization.

The final chapter explores the character, qualities and strategies associated with the making of difficult decisions. While all decisions have consequences, the scope and consequences associated with the variety of decisions the educational leader is called on to make vary. This chapter examines that subset of decisions known as the *tough* decisions. What distinguishes tough decisions from other decisions? How should such decisions be approached? These and other questions are addressed in this chapter.

The final section considers the ways in which the knowledge and skills explored in this text can be used to improve the decision skills of educational leaders. Three recurrent themes are identified and discussed. In addition, we explore ways in which leaders can think about prioritizing the decisions they are called on to make. Thinking about decision-making priorities offers us a way to integrate the ideas that underscore this text while still providing the reader foundational understandings about sense-making in organizations.

ON APPROACHING THE TEXT

One can approach this text in multiple ways. As noted above, all chapters and topics addressed are bound together by a common focus on the decision-making process. We have organized it in a way that is conducive to a sequential, beginning-to-end read. The chapters can also be read independently of each other in a stand-alone manner. Regardless of how it is used, we suggest that this text be read alongside a primer in decision making. We have not taken the time to provide an expanded and exhaustive definition of decision making. Nor have we outlined a generic, detailed model of the decision-making process. Given our primary focus on underexamined issues and dimensions, we have left this to others. In an effort to cover our bases on these two fronts, we have provided a reasonable working definition of decision making and describe several theories of the decision-making process.

As you read the chapters that follow, we encourage you experience the text in several ways. Whitehead observes that the curriculum of education is life (Whitehead, 1957). An important educational task is to learn to read and discern the experiences we have in the world. This task consists of reading both ourselves and the world in its playfulness *and* realizing that what immediately meets the eye does not exhaust all that may be there. In an effort to learn to read and discern more effectively the complexities embedded in the decisions leaders are called on to make, we encourage you attend to the three instructional dialogues available to you. As noted above, the first dialogue is that which occurs in *the world in front of the text*. It is the dialogue generated within you *by* the text as you read it. Your side of the dialogue consists of the experiences you bring to text. There is much that can be learned from this dialogue. The second is that dialogue which occurs between you and those reading the text with you. There is also much that can be learned from others and their experiences. For those using this text in a course, the third dialogue is that which occurs between students and the instructor. We encourage you to be aware of these instructional dialogues. As importantly, we encourage you to engage and take advantage of these dialogues as you work through and beyond this text.

CHAPTER TWO

Theories, Theorizing, and the Art of Theory-Use in Decision Making

The literature on decision making is voluminous. As most students in professional schools can attest, the range of decision theories is matched only by the number of flavors found at one's favorite ice cream shop. We have many varieties from which to choose: a flavor to satisfy every taste, a theory or combination to match one's cognitive or dispositional interests. One reads of economic decision theory (March, 1988, 1994), administrative decision theory (Nutt, 1984), optimizing, satisficing (Simon, 1976), incrementalism (Lindblom, 1993), consequence-analysis (Willower & Licata, 1997), the garbage-can theory (Cohen, March & Olsen, 1972), and the conflict-minimization model of decision making (Janis & Mann, 1977) to name a few.

Initial attempts by students in leadership programs to mentally sort through these theories can be daunting. More often than not this sense-making results in sensory-overload and frustration. Student responses are somewhat predictable. Three lend themselves to caricature.

For those with a more pragmatic orientation, there is the obligatory response of kneeling before the shrine of abstraction that is the ivory tower (the academy). Because such theorizing is pitched at a level of abstraction removed from the day-to-day realities of school, these students have little patience for what they perceive to be a useless game of mental gymnastics. They are unconvinced and remain unwilling to be convinced. Instrumental in their motives, these students know well their role in the ceremonial dance. To earn the degree, they feign interest in the literature and commit to memory those theories required by the instructor. This knowledge is paraded out for display as needed to signal that they have indeed learned something. Once the course ends or the degree is earned, these theories are quickly discarded as irrelevant. The tune is a familiar one.

In contrast to the unconvinced, there are those who reflect a more docile and reflective response. These students are eager to explore the literature on decision making and are willing to seek insights to improve educational practice. Yet with a sophomoric naïveté, they succumb to one of two temptations: *theory mystification* or *theory reification*. Enamored with the institutional mystique of the academy, certain students find themselves awestruck at the display of intellectual rigor in what they read. The depth and detail of information in this literature lead them to conclude that mastery can only be achieved by a few. Convinced as neophytes that they will never be able to achieve this complexity, their impressionable psyches lead them to mystify both theories and theorists. With expectations for themselves lowered, they persist in hopes of gleaning a few morsels to inform their ongoing professional development. Unfortunately, this mystification prevents students from taking full advantage of these theories as analytic tools.

Then there are those who succumb to the temptation of theory reification. These students make the mistake of viewing a given decision theory immutable. In doing this, they impute to the theory a life of its own and view it as something that stands over against them to be rigidly received and applied. Though initially excited with the newfound theory and its insights, these students quickly experience frustration as they realize the particulars of their context fail to match those of the theory. Theory reification prevents them from understanding the tentative, in-process, flexible quality of theories. It also prevents them from seeing their own role as *theorists*. Viewed in this manner, theory reification places them in a cognitive prison that inhibits rather than empowers thinking.

CONTEXT AND PURPOSE

To be sure, these caricatures do not capture the responses of all students to this literature. Not all succumb to these temptations. Our experiences in departments charged with preparing educational leaders, however, suggest that a critical number do respond to theory and the decision-making literature in these ways. Such responses raise a number of questions about leadership preparation programs and the knowledge and skill-base on which they rest.

Much has written on the knowledge-base reflected in leadership preparation programs (Johnson, 2004b). Ours is an eclectic, conceptually-messy field. As with other types of administration—business, hospital, and public administration—it is rooted in what Barnard (1938), March (1965), and Simon (1976) refer to as *administrative science*. While this descriptor reflects the theory-practice tension inherent in professional fields, it remains suspect on two fronts: Are we educators, administrators, or leaders? Is this activity a science or an art?

The field of administrative science draws from a variety of sources. As such, it is an *aggregate* of multiple knowledge domains and literatures, for example, leadership, decision making, supervision, administration, planning, budgeting, organization theory, and politics (Cyert & March, 1963; Simon, 1976; Yukl, 2002). Because there is no hard-and-fast consensus as to what these components are, this aggregate is neither static nor fixed. Yet in principle there remains a loose, organic coherence to it that in turn defines many preparation programs (Johnson, 2004b).

Equally important in this debate are questions regarding *how* this knowledge- and skill-base are conveyed to students in professional programs. The dominant professional training model found in most universities reflects an entrenched positivist epistemology. Separating knowledge from practice, this hyper-rational epistemology gives privileged status to scientific, technical knowledge and to those who master it (Hughes, 1965; Schon, 1987; Eisner, 2002). With this knowledge as *the* educational referent, problems of practice are framed in hyper-rational terms and addressed through the application of research-based theory and technique. This hyper-rational approach is consistent with what Weber (1946) refers to as *technical rationality*. Professional competence is defined as the mastering and successful application of privileged knowledge to instrumental problems of practice.

Of special interest here, however, are the important components of successful practice that are de-emphasized or ignored by this epistemology and the educational implications that follow from it. These include such issues as the following: (1) distinguishing with greater clarity one's *knowledge* of the decision making literature from one's *skill* as a decision maker; (2) decentering theories and recentering students, skill-development, and the process of *theorizing* as *the* points of departure in professional education; (3) acknowledging the artistic, intuitive, and tacit knowledge aspects of professional practice and legitimizing these as serious objects of study (Polanyi, 1967; Howells, 1995; Smith, 2001); and (4) attending anew to the process of *synthesis* and the skill and artistry associated with it in addressing problems of practice (Dewey, 1933, 1938; Eisner, 2002).

Epistemological and methodological debates coupled with recent theoretical developments in the social sciences have provided us with a broader range of analytic tools with which to frame and address the training challenge. New frames and perspectives allow for new ways of seeing, thus generating new questions for investigation. Using these ideas and the decision-making literature to provide a context for discussion, the purpose of this chapter is to provoke thought on a set of professional competencies and issues that have been largely ignored or underexamined in the field of educational leadership.

There is room for improvement in professional preparation programs. The disconnect that exists between what is taught in many programs and the day-to-day realities of school life reflect an insensitivity to the importance of developing the abilities of students as *theorists*, *artists*, and in *the art of theory use*. We suggest that there is an underappreciated artistic element associated with theorizing and theory use and argue here that it is incumbent upon professional schools to help practitioners develop and refine their abilities as "street-level" *theorists* and *theory validators* (Lipsky, 1978). As a bread-and-butter component of the professional school, decision theory and skill provide a natural context for examining these issues.

LEADERSHIP AND ADMINISTRATION AS DECISION MAKING

Reduced to the lowest common denominator and consistent with the arguments made decades ago by Barnard (1938), leadership and administration are about decision making.[1] Whether prompted by a problem or perceived opportunity, decision making lies at the heart of managerial behavior. The importance of decision making to leadership and organizational life is such that organizations can be described as rationalized attempts to control and channel decision premises. For Simon (1976), *the* leadership challenge consists of making decisions that structure and direct the decisions of organizational participants. The *anatomy* of an organization is found in the distribution and allocation of its decision-making functions, its *physiology* in those organizational processes that influence the decisions made by organizational participants. As noted in the preface to his classic volume, "decision making is the heart of administration" (1976, p. xlviii). It is in this sense that administration may be defined as decision making.

Similar to that of other executives, the work of leaders in educational organizations revolves around decision-making activities. Mintzberg's (1973) in-depth study of managerial behavior led to the identification of four decisional roles enacted with great frequency by leaders (note, one of the five managers he observed was a school superintendent): entrepreneur, disturbance handler, resource allocator, and negotiator. Wolcott's (1973) ethnographic study of Ed Bell and March's (1978) review of literature provides detailed accounts of the decisions faced by educational leaders. Seeking to capture the managerial imperative of leadership practice in schools, Cuban (1988) argues that teachers, principals, and superintendents make multiple yet similar kinds of decisions at different levels of the organization. These decisions are associated with three distinct roles performed by each: the instructional, managerial, and political role.

A sampling of the literature examining the actual work of superintendents and principals paints a picture of educational leaders making multiple decisions throughout the course of the workday (Griffiths, 1969; Blumberg & Greenfield, 1980; Martin & Willower, 1981; Blumberg, 1986; Boyan, 1987; Sergiovanni, 1995; Johnson & Fauske, 2000). These decisions vary in scope, complexity, and intensity. They range from the routine and familiar to the nonroutine and unfamiliar, and focus on a variety of topics: strategies for school improvement, hiring new teachers, teacher evaluation, budgets, student suspensions and

---

1. We are well aware of the ambiguous nature and contested use of the concepts leadership, administration and management. This debate notwithstanding, these distinctions are seen as inconsequential for the argument made here. We have thus taken the liberty to minimize these distinctions in this context.

expulsions, dealing with parents and the community, managing the environment and ordering of custodial supplies.

This literature substantiates the central role of decision making in leadership behavior. The prominence of decision making provides an adequate justification for its inclusion as a front-and-center topic in the professional school. This prominence likewise provides a justification for questions regarding how decision making is actually taught to educational professionals. Before reflecting on how this has traditionally been done, an examination of two strategies for sorting and sense-making the population of decision theories found in the literature is in order.

MAKING CONCEPTUAL AND PRACTICAL
SENSE OF DECISION THEORIES

The decision-making literature is a transdisciplinary literature with roots in many fields (Simon, 1991, 1993). Though of unequal quality, books on decision making are readily accessible. One need only visit a bookstore or an airport to see that the topic provides a foundation for a robust publication, talk, and training industry. The widespread availability of this literature and level of abstraction at which it is pitched underscore the importance of decision making to social life.

As noted above, theories of decision making also abound. Motivated by an innate desire to maximize utility, these explanations represent attempts by theorists to manage the uncertainties and risks that would frustrate this desire (Simon, 1976, 1981; Weick, 1979, 1995; March, 1988). Two heuristics are available to help students initially sort and sense-make these theories. The first is a familiar one. It provides a means for sorting the population of decision theories into one of two categories: normative or descriptive.

The normative theory of decision-making seeks to explain decisions from the perspective of the omniscient decision maker and how decisions *should* be made (Simon, 1976, 1981; March, 1988). As personified in traditional microeconomic logic, it describes decision making under optimal conditions. This theory assumes consensus among decision makers and few if any decision unknowns. Complete information is assumed regarding the decision topic, decision preferences, the ranking of these preferences, and the cost-benefit analysis of decision alternatives. As part and parcel of the institutionalized rational myth that in Western thought, the classic theory of decision-making continues to enjoy an exalted place in the professional school curriculum. So entrenched is its influence that March (1988, p. 2)—using a clever tongue-in-check analogy—refers to it as the "orthodox doctrine and dogma" of decision-making. Yet this hyper-simplistic view of decision-making is as myopic as the hyper-rational assumptions on which it rests. Its inadequacies have given rise to another set of decision theories.

Descriptive theories of decision-making seek to explain how decisions are *actually* made. Building on his critique of economic rationality, Simon (1976) was among the first to articulate a descriptive theory of decision based on the reality of a "bounded" or "limited" decision rationality. Others have since followed substantiating Simon's claim that decision rationality is less coherent than classic decision theory would have us assume. Sources of decision incoherence include but are not limited to the following: the cognitive limitations of decision makers; the narrow attention-structure of decision makers; incomplete or invalid information available for decision; the ambiguities and political contests surrounding decision preferences; the ambiguities and political contests surrounding the means adopted to achieve decision goals; and the ambiguities of the causal assumptions on which decision are based. For most descriptive theorists, the realities of bounded rationality call for a *satisficing* rather than an optimizing approach by decision makers. Satisficing refers to the efforts of decision makers to find the first workable solution given the limitations and constraints of the decision context.

The ideas of Simon provide a conceptual foundation on which many theorists have built. As noted in the opening paragraphs of this chapter, there now exists a theory or combination of decision-making theories to match a variety of cognitive and dispositional interests. Initial attempts by students to sort through these theories are challenging. The details and distinctions of each are difficult to keep separate. More often than not the result is more confusion than clarity.

Thompson's (1967) description of the decision process provides the basis for a second heuristic for distinguishing theories of decision at a general level. He identifies two "major" dimensions of the decision process (1967, p. 134). Dimension one consists of *decision preferences* and the level of consensus, which exists for these preferences. Consensus regarding the preferred decision outcomes cannot be assumed. As expressions of value, decision preferences are often contested or unknown. These contests account for the political element found in many decisions. Using this logic, decisions marked by agreement on end-state preferences are less susceptible to politicization than those marked by disagreement. Where there is agreement on organizational goals, political contests regarding these goals are nonexistent.

Thompson's second dimension focuses on *decision means* and the clarity that exists regarding these means. What means can be used to realize decision preferences? To what extent are these understood? How well are the cause-effect linkages that define these means known? Whereas questions regarding decision preferences deal with issues of *substantive rationality*, that is, *what* do we want to do? Discussions of decision means raise questions about *procedural rationality*, that is, *how* will we do it? For any given decision, knowledge of the means needed to realize decision preferences can vary from known to unknown. This element of the decision-making process accounts for the level of technical certainty or uncertainty that defines a decision.

Considered together, Thompson's dimensions can be used to define the broad context of a decision. Both are variable. Dimension one highlights the political elements of the decision process, dimension two the technical elements. When juxtaposed, these dimensions of decision making offer a heuristic for contextualizing and comparing various theories of decision making. This juxtaposition is captured in Figure 2.1. The variable *decision preference* is depicted on the x-axis and the *cause-effect* dimension on the y-axis. Though presented in Figure 2.1 as dichotomous, each variable can take on a range of values between the extremes noted: *consensus-dissensus; known-unknown.* Combining these dimensions of the decision process, an infinite number of decision contexts are possible. We suggest that the variety of descriptive theories found in the decision-making literature can be explained by the variety of decision contexts reflected in the juxtaposition of these dimensions. Using this heuristic, we will contextualize and briefly contrast four well-known decision theories found in the literature.

Thompson's ideas can be used to provide a vivid contrast between those theories of decision that make extreme assumptions about rationality and the role it plays in the decision process. We refer to these here as the *hyper-* and *hypo-*rational families of decision theory. Those contexts characterized by a high level of consensus on decision preferences *and* a high degree of technical clarity around decision-means call for a computational approach to decision making. The classic or economic theory of decision making with its hyper-rational assumptions can be used to explain decisions made in contexts such as these.

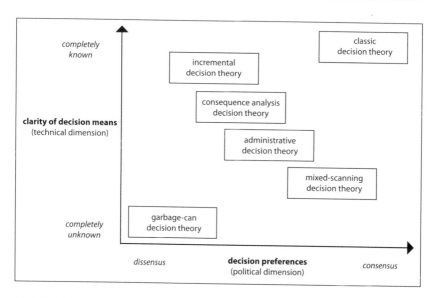

FIGURE 2.1. Dimensions of Decision and Decision Context

This theory of decision making can be placed in the upper right quadrant of Figure 2.1.

Conversely, those contexts characterized by a low level of consensus regarding decision preferences *and* a low level of technical clarity around decision-means lend themselves to explanations that de-emphasize the role of rationality while emphasizing the role of chance, fate, and ambiguity in the decision process (e.g., the garbage-can decision model). *Hypo*-rational decision theories such as these assume little or no clarity around decision preferences and means. The garbage-can theory of decision (Cohen, et al., 1972) can thus be placed in the bottom left quadrant of Figure 2.1. Using Thompson's model, the features of the decision context define the conditions under which these extreme theories of decision making are valid.

Though more problematic to classify, decision theories that are inconsistent with the extreme conditions of rationality assumed by the classic and garbage-can theories can be distinguished by the emphasis placed on political *or* technical elements of the decision-making process. For example, numerous stakeholders with conflicting decision preferences call for an approach that will allow decision makers to maintain a critical level of stability in the social system. Incremental decision theory explains decision behavior in such contexts (Lindblom, 1959, 1993; Wildavsky, 1979). Politics and the political process are its defining features. Within the context of Figure 2.1, the center of gravity for theories of decision that emphasize the political dimensions of the decision process is in the general area of the upper left-hand quadrant. It should come as no surprise to learn that incrementalism has its roots in the political science and budgeting literatures.

In contrast to Lindblom's incrementalism, Etzioni's (1986, 1989) mixed-scanning model places greater emphasis on the level of technical clarity that defines the decision context. It offers a description of decision behavior in conditions of complexity where there is a critical level of agreement on decision-ends yet where knowledge of means-ends relationships are unknown or incomplete, that is, *how* will these ends be realized? This theory of decision making has its roots in the field of medicine. As such, it reflects both the hopes and technical limitations of that field: A critical level of agreement exists that the goal of medicine is to facilitate the healing process; however, knowledge of how this goal can be realized is limited and incomplete for many diseases and ailments. Emphasis on the technical uncertainty surrounding decision-means places this theory somewhere in the lower right-hand quadrant of Figure 2.1.

The normative-descriptive distinction and ideas of Thompson provide two heuristics for sorting and sense-making the population of decision-making theories found in the literature. In addition to the four noted above, additional theories have been contextualized in Figure 2.1. The placement of these theories represents approximations and exemplifies the sense-making efficiency this heuristic provides. Other heuristics can be used to achieve a similar purpose.

Heuristics such as the two outlined here address important educational needs for students. First, they provide a means for increasing the accessibility theories to students while negating the debilitating deer-in-the-headlights effect that comes as the details of each is encountered. Thompson's ideas in particular help students maintain a forest-level perspective as needed.

Second, understanding the logic behind these heuristics and classifying theories accordingly can help demystify this literature for students. Demystification increases the accessibility of this literature and allows reflective practitioners to appropriate these theories as analytic tools. These decision theories and heuristics also provide the reflective practitioner with a reasonable platform from which to do his or her own theorizing about the decision-making process. This exercise in sense-making facilitates the theorizing of others. Having a means for distinguishing these theories is a critical step in helping students develop their own abilities as theorists and the art of theory use. It is to the process of theorizing that we now turn.

ON THE NEED TO DECENTER
THEORY AND RECENTER THEORIZING

The discussion of the decision-making literature above clearly reveals the value we place on theory as a means for developing and refining our collective thinking. It also reveals our assumptions regarding the utility of theory for leadership preparation programs. These sentiments however are not shared by all. For a critical number of scholars, the theory movement in educational leadership has fallen short of its promises and has brought the field to a dead-end (Murphy, 1999; English, 2002, 2003).

Though somewhat understandable, this dismissal of the theory movement appears to be a premature response to the no-nonsense accountability demands that have increased in education over the past four decades. In making these arguments, these individuals have overstated the case in a way that amounts to throwing out the proverbial baby with the bath water. Yet their concerns should not be dismissed out of hand. It seems wise to speculate on what it is about theory and the theory movement that has provoked this response. We would argue that it is not the failure of theory *per se* to which these scholars are responding, it is the role professors have allowed theory to assume in leadership preparation programs that is of concern.

Theories and theoretical knowledge constitute *the* curricular focal point for many leadership preparation programs. This centering we would argue is problematic in professional fields. It has created a distorted paradigm that equates *knowing about* with *knowing how*. Using the topic of decision making as an example, mastery of the literature on decision making has emerged in many programs as a *proxy* for skill in decision-making. Professors often assume that students who master this knowledge in the classroom will become skillful decision makers in the field. This assumption is highly problematic. Two examples from the arts can be used to undermine its validity. Knowledge of music theory and the ability to identify the notes on the piano do not make a musician. While the knowledge and ability are prerequisites to skilled musicianship, the two are not the same. The artist combines these and other inputs in creative ways to transform these inputs into music. Likewise, a working knowledge of primary colors and the array of brushes available for painting do not make an artist. It is in the skillful synthesizing and combining of these inputs that artistry is expressed. Though related, *knowing about* cannot be equated with *knowing how*.

The distortions inherent in this training paradigm call for a rethinking of how leadership preparation programs are structured and the assumptions on which they rest. One strategy is to reflect on the focus or center of such programs. What is the focal point of these programs? Around what are they centered? Consistent with the ideas articulated above, we would suggest that there is a need to *decenter theory* in our preparation programs and to *recenter theorizing*. Stated differently, there is a need to decenter knowledge acquisition in our programs and to recenter skill development in decision making *and* students' theorizing about this development. This means distinguishing yet relating anew the relationship shared between *knowing about* and *knowing how*. This requires a subtle yet profound shift in the way we think. Instead of discarding the theory movement and its fruits as irrelevant, this shift leads us to embrace it as a means to a greater end, namely skill development. Before exploring the implications of this way of thinking further, it is important to define what we mean by "theory" and "theorizing."

Much of the confusion that exists regarding theory and its place in professional preparation programs can be traced to the multiple connotations associated with it. One useful strategy for understanding the meaning of theory is by describing what it is not. As used in this volume, theory is *not* the philosophical, speculative, impractical, unworkable, ideal or normative. Neither is it a set of values. This is not to say that these connotations are invalid. The existence of multiple connotations underscores the importance of discerning the *intended connotation* of theory when the concept is encountered.

The definition of theory used here is consistent with that found in the research community: *A theory is a tentative, working explanation of something*. It consists of a set of assumptions, concepts, relationships and logic that are combined to explain a phenomenon of interests (e.g., decision making, leadership, motivation, artistry, etc.). Implicit and explicit theories exist for a wide range of phenomena. The working theories an individual holds provide the script for much of his or her behavior. A major goal of research in any field is to articulate and explicate theories that validly describe the defining phenomena of that field. The decision-making theories described above are the fruit of research in this area.

The multiple connotations associated with theory make the concept a cognitive stumbling block for many. It behooves us to facilitate students' understanding of these competing definitions of theory and to help them discern its referent when used. It is likewise important that students approach the literature in the professional school with an understanding that the theories encountered there are *explanations*. Theories of decision making represent attempts to *explain* the decision-making process. As tentative working explanations, these theories should not be reified. Likewise they should not be taken as the focal point of leadership preparation programs. It is the process that leads to the development of these theories—*theorizing*—and the skills associated with it that should be the focus of leadership preparation programs.

ON THE SCIENCE AND ART OF
DECISION MAKING: *THEORIA* VS. *POIESIS*

Decision making is a complex cognitive process influenced by a number of factors (Simon, 1981). Many of these remain elusive and beyond the control of the decision maker. Yet in spite of this, there are number of identifiable skills associated effective decision making. At the risk of oversimplifying, these include but are not limited to the following. The ability to:

- recognize *the need for* a decision (Dewey, 1933, 1938)
- define the *subject of decision* (i.e., what needs to be decided?).
- discern, define, and reconcile competing *decision goals and preferences*
- develop and assess *means-ends alternatives* in the quest to realize decision goals
- identify, analyze, and synthesize the *data needed* for decision
- *read the context* in which the decision is being made
- identify those *contextual factors that facilitate or constrain* the decision process
- *identify and address the variables that can be manipulated* in the decision context
- *accept and manage uncertainty and ambiguity* in constructive ways
- constructively deal with the *lack of cognitive closure* as needed

Much has and could be written on each of these. This list provides a point of departure for thinking about the skills of decision making and the art associated with the use and combination of these skills. It also provides clues as to how these skills and artistry can be taught to others.

For starters, this list highlights the complexity and skill that surround the simplest of decisions. It provides insight into the cognitive processes that occur as the decision maker seeks to impose a manageable (note, not omniscient) level of rationality to a wide range of inputs and stimuli (Simon, 1976; March, 1988; Weick, 1995). Multiple lines of thought converge in search of a workable solution. Consider for example the cognitive processes and multiple factors involved in deciding to suspend a student. There is the analysis and synthesis of information, the finding, sifting, distilling, and recombining of bits and pieces of data (Dewey, 1933, 1938). Several skills are in play as the decision is made. These skills vary across decision makers.

As important, this list reminds us that decisions are not made in a vacuum. Every decision has a context. For example, knowing that the student being considered for suspension is the child of the local superintendent is a critical feature of the larger decision context. Decision context is an important variable that complicates the decision-making process. This context is defined by a host of givens that function to constrain and/or facilitate the decision process. These givens include such factors as the level of uncertainty and risk surrounding the decision, the level of resource scarcity or abundance associated with the decision and time constraints that frame the decision, the extent of decision involvement and participation by others, the intensity of political dynamics, the number of stakeholders and political stakes associated with the decision, etc. Chief among these are the quantity and quality of data or information available to the decision maker.

If decision making lies at the heart of the administration, then information is lifeblood of decision making. The quantity (*amount of*), quality (*reliability and validity of*), and availability (*costs associated with obtaining*) of information are important variables of the decision context. Decision contexts characterized by an abundance of accessible, high-quality information typically present fewer challenges to the decision maker than contexts where data is scarce, of low quality, and difficult to obtain. Just as the skills of the decision maker vary, the complexity of givens that define the context in which a decision is made varies. The quantity and quality of data are but one of these givens that must be addressed by the decision maker.

Of interest here is the distinction we offer between the *science* and *art* of decision making. To be sure, the characterization of decision making in these terms is somewhat risky. The casual, ill-defined manner in which these descriptors are used reflects a familiarity that blinds us to the rich connotations of each. Yet these distinctions have the potential of facilitating our thinking about how the teaching of decision making in professional schools can be improved. We suggest that most of our time is spent on teaching students the *science* rather than the *art* of decision making. This suggestion begs the larger question of how science and art differ.

A brief excursion into the epistemology of Aristotle provides the context for a useful working distinction. Reflecting on how individuals think and come to know, Aristotle argued that the free person has multiple ways of relating intelligently to life (Ross, 1942; Aristotle, 1949). He identified two of these ways of knowing as *theoria* and *poiesis*. Each epistemology is distinguished by the end or *telos* toward which it is directed. Together they provide the basis for a useful science-art distinction.

Theoria refers to the speculative life of contemplation and reflection. It is thinking and knowing apart from engagement. The goal of *theoria* is the development of objective knowledge or truth for its own sake. We contemplate and reflect so that we can expand our collective knowledge. Knowledge is created for knowledge's sake.

Aristotle's *theoria* is an epistemology with which most of us are familiar. As the predominant way of knowing in the West, its legitimacy is reflected in the emphasis given to science (*scientia*–knowledge) and theory in the academy *and* the concomitant de-emphasis given to practice. With the goal of developing new knowledge, the incentive to connect theory with practice is secondary. This epistemology explains in part the bifurcated worlds of theory and practice experienced by many students in our preparation programs. It also explains the research-practice schizophrenia witnessed in professional schools housed at research universities.

A *theoria* epistemology promotes a pedagogy that focuses on the transmission and development of the accumulated knowledge of a given subject. For topics such as decision making, this means helping students master the knowledge, theories and technical-procedural algorithms that define the decision-making knowledge base. We suggest that this accumulated knowledge constitutes the *science* of decision making. As noted above and consistent with a *theoria* epistemology, mastery of this knowledge has emerged as a proxy for skill in decision-making. This is the dominant professional-training model found in many universities.

In contrast to *theoria*, Aristotle described an epistemology associated with art and the creation of artifacts (Ross, 1942; Lobkowicz, 1967). It is a way of knowing inherent in the creation of something and is witnessed as the creator synthesizes or combines various elements to create a desired end. This epistemology is seen in the work of the sculptor, musician, poet, and craftsperson. With a working end in view, *poiesis* involves a series of judgments as to how available inputs can be skillfully combined to realize or create this end.

Synthesis and the knowledge that guides this synthesis constitute the essence of *poiesis*. Working on a painting, poem, or musical score requires that one have the ability to compose qualitative relationships to satisfy a purpose. What a painter paints is the result of qualitatively relating and *synthesizing* a number of colors from an infinite number of relationships. What a composer composes is the result relating a number of notes from an infinite number of tonal relationships (Eisner, 2002; Johnson & Owens, 2005).

Familiarity with music theory and the ability to identify notes on the piano represent one kind of knowledge. This knowledge is an example of *theoria*. The ability to synthesize or combine certain principles of music theory, notes, and a given combination of instruments to create a composition that conveys a desired musical effect represents another kind of knowledge (e.g., consider the musical theme from the Spielberg movie *Jaws* and the fearful emotions it evokes). This knowledge provides an example of Aristotle's *poiesis*. It is related to yet distinct from his *theoria* way of knowing. These contrasting epistemologies provide a working basis for distinguishing science and art, for distinguishing knowing *about* from knowing *how*.

As a way of knowing, *poiesis* has fallen into oblivion since Aristotle's death. Reflecting on how an artistic or *poiesis* way of knowing has been neglected in the West, Sir Herbert Read argued that the aim of education should be the "preparation of artists" (Read, 1944 p. 3).

Read's use of the word "artists" is expansive. It goes beyond the role of painter, dancer, musician poet or playwright to include work not associated with the traditional arts. Read envisioned an educational system that would prepare individuals in all walks of life to be artists, artists who had developed the ideas, sensibilities, skills, and imagination to *synthesize* and *create* well-proportioned, skillfully executed work of various kinds. Whether referencing a cook, surgeon, teacher, engineer, carpenter or decision maker, the highest accolade one can give is to say that he or she is *an artist*. As artists, these individuals are engaged in the act of creating through a synthesis or the combining of elements. This creation is *poiesis*, a knowing through making (Eisner, 2002). For Read, the arts and a *poiesis* epistemology have no monopoly on the artistic.

Seeking to pinpoint those elusive aspects of educational leadership not addressed by the literature of his day, Griffiths (1978) was sensitive to the artistic side of leadership: "There is much in administration that lies outside the scope of theory. The practice of leadership is largely an art . . . much of which lies beyond the reaches of theory as we know it" (1978, p. 82).

This observation by Griffiths is telling. On the one hand, it reflects an appreciation for the artistic side of leadership. On the other hand, it recognizes the influence and adverse effects of positivism on our theorizing: leadership, artistry, and the knowledge associated with it are seen as beyond the *legitimate* scope of science and our theorizing efforts.

Thirty years later this positivist epistemology remains as an entrenched training model in many professional schools. Yet over this same period of time, epistemological debates and developments in the social sciences have provided the field with a broader range of tools that legitimize and frame the examination of this artistry (Schon, 1983, 1987, 1988; Eisner, 2002, 2003). As argued above, professional schools should not confine their attention to questions of how to make better use of theories and research in decision making. They should also attend to the artistry of *how* competent professionals *synthesize* this and other knowledge inputs in making decisions that address the pressing, indeterminate problems of practice.

Science and research (*theoria*) occupy an important though limited space in professional practice. This space is bounded on several sides by artistry (*poiesis*). If its legitimacy as a topic is acknowledged, professional schools can learn much from examining this artistry. To further illustrate the nature of this artistry, two aspects of decision artistry—the art of synthesis and the art theory use—are examined below.

THE ART OF SYNTHESIS AND THEORY-USE IN DECISION MAKING

In light of the conceptualization of artistry offered above—the creative and skillful process of *combining* or *synthesizing* multiple inputs to *make* or *create* an artifact—there are many artistic elements associated with *making* or *creating* a decision. To identify and explore each of these is beyond the scope of this endeavor. For illustrative purposes, only two elements are explored here. Our intent is to provoke thought on the meaning and nature of this artistry and to champion its legitimacy as a focus of instruction in leadership preparation programs.

THE ART OF SYNTHESIS

The first element to be considered is the synthesis associated with the decision making process. Given that synthesis is the process of purposively combining, there is a strong artistic quality to the act of synthesis. Yet synthesis cannot be discussed from its counterpart analysis. Consistent with its etymological roots [Gk: *analien*], *to analyze* means *to break up or apart*. Conversely, to synthesize is *to combine or put together* [Gk: *synthesien*]. Dewey's (1933, 1938) insights into the nature of thinking are useful in distinguishing and relating these two important cognitive activities of decision making.

When faced with a decision, the individual must first sense-make the situation to determine *what is there* before he or she can determine *what might be done*. Much of this sense-making constitutes analysis, a process whereby the leader identifies the data in the decision context. From this, judgments are made regarding the usefulness of this data. This breaking apart and subsequent weighing of data is known as *analysis*. As Dewey notes, "every [decision] is analytic in that it involves discernment, discrimination, and marking off the trivial from the important, the irrelevant from that which . . . points to a conclusion" (1933, p. 130). The cognitive ability, experiences, values, and dispositions of the decision maker influence the analysis process.

Yet decision making involves more than just analysis. It also involves synthesis. Synthesis is the process of combining or piecing together relevant data in a reasonably coherent way. In the context of decision making, the data identified as relevant (as a result of the analysis) are then combined by the decision maker in an effort to determine *what* must be decided. Again Dewey's insights are useful, "Synthesis takes place wherever we grasp the bearing of facts . . . every judgment is synthetic in so far as it leaves the mind with an inclusive situation within which selected facts are placed" (1933, p. 130).

Whereas analysis represents a *picking to pieces* to assess what is there, synthesis is a *pulling together* of that which is deemed important in order to determine what can be done. Analysis leads to emphasis; synthesis to placing. "[Analysis] causes the emphasized fact to stand out as significant; [synthesis then] puts what is selected into a sensible context" (Dewey, 1933, p. 129). Individuals vary in their ability to analyze and synthesize. In addition, the absence of valid and reliable data coupled with the potential for multiple synthesis-combinations of this data introduce uncertainties into the decision-making process.

To be sure, the full complexity of the analysis-synthesis decision processes described above is masked by the linear manner in which we have presented them. It is difficult, for example, to determine when analysis ends and synthesis begins or if they are separate and sequential as opposed to simultaneous activities. Such issues are perhaps best addressed by cognitive and educational psychologists. Of interest here is an attempt to exemplify and explicate some of the artistic elements of decision. Consistent with the working definition of art articulated above, there is an art associated with the act of synthesis in decision making. The ability to synthesize or combine elements in the creation of an artifact—in this context a decision—constitutes the essence of Aristotle's *poiesis*.

The following example provides a useful means for vivifying these abstract concepts. Math achievement scores have declined over the past three years at Oak Ridge High. With the start of a new year only six weeks away, scores from the latest round of testing are in. The news is discouraging. Not only have the scores continued to fall, the drop in last year's scores is precipitous. The principal, June Smitherman, is instructed by district officials to do whatever is necessary to address the issue. Motivated by this mandate and its political implications, June immediately moves to assess the situation. What is happening? What is the problem? Is it something the school is or is not doing? What decision(s) must be made?

As a former math teacher, June realizes the importance of valid and reliable data in the decision making process. She spends several weeks collecting and analyzing a wide range of data with her team: the assistant principal for instruction, chair of the math department, and two veteran math teachers. Included in this data is information on such factors as the math curriculum, teaching methods, teacher evaluations, course assignments, course sequencing, course-taking patterns, course loads, teacher-student ratios, student demographics, faculty and departmental dynamics, and so on.

After five intensive weeks and long hours of analysis and planning, a decision is made. June and the team decide that there is a need to rearrange and standardize the unit sequencing in all math courses, tighten the sequence-articulation of these courses, and spend the first month of each course carefully reviewing with students the material covered in the previous year. An emergency meeting of the department is called two days prior to the start of school to seek further input and approval from teachers. A few objections regarding teaching assignments are raised. With a promise that these will be addressed in an equitable manner, teachers vote to accept and implement the decision.

Two years later the results are in. The first year yielded a turnaround and modest increase in achievement scores. However, significant discrepancies between students remained, particularly between male and female students. The second year witnessed an increase for all students and a reduction in gain-discrepancies across multiple subgroups.

There is much involved in this decision. Two importance features are the analysis and synthesis processes experienced by the decision makers. When faced with declining test scores, June and her team experienced a period of sense-making wherein they sought data to determine what was happening. This search involved the collection and analysis of data. Informed by their own educational experiences and theories of the teaching-learning process yet unsure of exactly what they were looking for, the team focused its initial data-collection efforts on casting a broad net. They soon discovered however that much of this data was superfluous. This conclusion was reached after a prolonged, iterative process of *analysis*—a process of discernment whereby discriminating judgments were made regarding the identification of irrelevant and important decision data. This analysis process was filtered through the lens of the team's experiences, cognitive abilities, working assumptions, values, and dispositions.

As this analysis led to the identification and separation of relevant from irrelevant data, June and her team then moved to identify a reasonable definition of the problem. This working definition emerged as the remaining data was synthesized by the team. Much like drawing a line between multiple dots on a page to create the outline of a recognizable figure, June and her team examined the data for logical links and relationships. A reasonable though inconclusive outline of the decision problem soon emerged. It centered on such issues as unit sequencing, course articulation, and the lapse and discontinuity in learning presented to students by the three-month summer hiatus. Though other ways of configuring the data were possible, this configuration of the data and definition of the problem—both the fruit of synthesis efforts—became *their* working definition. Consistent with the conceptualization of artistry offered above (*poiesis*), this act of data synthesis or configuring can be described as an artistic endeavor. As artists, the team synthesized multiple data points to create a reasonably well-proportioned definition of the problem (Read, 1944).

Beyond this, there was another level of synthesis evident in the decision. Once a reasonable working definition of the decision problem was identified, June and the team faced the challenge of determining what should be done to ameliorate the problem. This too involved the synthesis of a number of disparate inputs. The solution crafted required the team to identify, reconcile, configure and proportion a *select* set of inputs (i.e., synthesize) from a larger population of possible decision inputs. This meant utilizing certain inputs to craft a solution while ignoring others (Weick, 2001, 1995). These inputs included such things as: competing decision preferences; competing decision solutions; facilitating and constraining features of the decision context, for example, time constraints, resource limitations, uncertainty, risk, decision stakes, stakeholders and political dynamics.

As synthesis, this selecting-configuring-proportioning process is likewise an artistic endeavor. An analogy from art is again useful in illustrating this process. If you ask an artist to paint an oil portrait of your family, he has a number of colors, shades, brushes, and techniques from which to choose. He will not make use of them all, only a subset. As an artist, he will select, configure, and proportion these inputs to craft the picture. A similar artistry is inherent in the writing process. While there are an infinite number of words and word-combinations that could be used to communicate an idea, we have chosen to use and synthesize only a subset of these to write this essay. (It is of course left to the reader to make judgments regarding the quality of this artistry).

Thus, as exemplified in this decision example, there are at least two focal points of synthesis involved in the decision-making process: (1) the synthesizing of data that occurs as the decision maker moves to create a working definition of the decision problem, that is, determining *what* must be decided; and (2) once the working problem is identified, the synthesizing of disparate inputs that occurs as the decision maker moves to craft a solution to this problem. There is an artistry associated with each of these. To what extent do educators in professional school acknowledge this artistry? If acknowledged, how effectively do they teach and develop these artistic skills in students?

The Art of Theory Use

A second artistic element worthy of consideration focuses on the use of existing decision theories by educational leaders to inform the decision-making process. The three caricatures of theory-use sketched in the opening paragraphs of this chapter capture how some students respond when introduced to these theories: theory irrelevance, theory mystification or theory reification. These responses notwithstanding, there is much benefit to be gleaned from having a fundamental command of these theories and literature. Mastering this knowledge allows one to complicate his or her thinking on the subject (Weick, 1978). Beyond this knowledge, there is an artistic skill associated with the effective use of these theories as conceptual tools. Knowledge of this literature is a necessary but insufficient condition for the effective use of these theories as conceptual tools to inform skillful decision making. *Knowing about* is related to but not the same as *knowing how*. As one of many potential inputs available to the educational leader as a decision maker, what is about the use of these theories that can be described as *artistic*?

There are at least two ways in which the use of theory can be described as artistic. Before discussing these, recall that the word *theory* here is equated with explanation. A theory is a working, tentative explanation of something. This chapter is concerned with the existing explanations of the decision-making process found in the decision literature.

The dialectical nature of theory-practice relationship should also be noted. Theory begins and ends in practice. The raw data of lived-experience provide the grist for our individual and collective theorizing efforts. The theories abstracted and developed from our experience are then tested, retested and refined in the world of lived-experience. It is through the dialectical interplay of these specific and abstracted experiences that the validity of theory is assessed. Hence, a given theory of decision making is said to be *valid* if the essence of its abstracted explanation assists us in understanding and addressing the high-stakes decision we as educational leaders currently face in our schools.

Useful theories are those which provide explanative power to a wide variety of contexts. The theories of decision making that have emerged over the years have been developed in very *specific* decision contexts. Yet their persistence in the literature can be traced to their ability to explain decision making in a *variety* of contexts. This contextual dilemma of the theory-building process highlights a fundamental challenge for those who seek to use theory as a guide to practice. As Thorngate (1976) reminds us, it is impossible for a theory of social behavior to be simultaneously general, accurate, and simple. The more general and simple a theory is, the less accurate it will be in predicting details of specific contexts.

Those students who succumb to the temptation of theory reification (see opening caricatures above) and seek to rigidly receive and apply the theories of decision found in the literature do not understand the practical implications of Thorngate's postulate. Use of theories in this way can only lead to frustration as students come to realize that the particulars of their school context fail to match those of a given theory. We suggest that we have done an inadequate job of teaching students how to use theories as analytical tools to improve their decision-making skills. This is perhaps due to a failure to recognize the artistry associated with the use of these theories as tools.

This artistry is rooted in the recognition that all theories are *partial, relative*, and *in the process of becoming*. A given theory is *partial* in that it cannot always be inclusive. An omniscient understanding of a phenomenon of interest is elusive. As an explanation, a theory is considered *relative* in that it is a product of a specific context, time, place, and perspective. While there may be similarities across contexts and decision makers, no two decision contexts or decision makers are exactly the same. Given that it should be subjected to continual testing and revision, a theory is *in-the-process* of moving toward full development and explication.

An understanding of this partial, relative and in-process quality of theories should mitigate efforts to reify or mystify theory. Further, this understanding should empower students to *theorize* on how these working explanations can be used to sharpen their own decision skills as they address the immediate decisions of the school workplace. As argued above, this means decentering theory and recentering theorizing in our preparation programs. Stately somewhat differently and in the context of decision making, this means decentering knowledge acquisition of decision theories and recentering decision-making skills and students' *theorizing* about skill development in our programs. Knowledge of the literature and theories on decision making is not to be disregarded. Rather, this knowledge is to be consciously used as a means to a greater end, namely the development of decision skills. In professional schools this knowledge should be embraced as a means to this greater end. Hence the question for both professor and student becomes: How can these decision theories be used to develop decision skills?

The answer to this important "how" question is arrived at through the process of *theorizing*; theorizing is about *explaining*. As importantly, this question focuses attention on the abilities of students as *theorizers*. Given that the process of theorizing involves the synthesis or pulling together of multiple data inputs to develop this explanation, there is an artistic element to it. It is in the role of theorist that the student synthesizes multiple data inputs in search of a workable decision solution. Decisions faced by educational leaders do not always present themselves as neatly-packaged, well-defined problems conducive to clean and tidy resolution through a predetermined decision protocol. Such problems defy technical, algorithmic solutions. Yet these problems are often of great practical and professional concern. With few if any precedents to follow, they call for flexibility of thinking, synthesis, and on-the-spot improvisation as data inputs of various kinds are combined to address the problem at hand. One of these inputs is the decision literature. Drawing from this knowledge, the reflective decision maker creatively and selectively uses these theories to facilitate—not *supplant* (an important distinction)—his or her own theorizing about the decision at hand. What is needed to successfully address the decision? What must I do? As an input, how can my knowledge of the decision literature facilitate my thinking?

The uniqueness of the context coupled with the configuration of the problem may mean that there is no single theory of decision to call upon. Rather, the problem dictates that the decision maker create a hybrid approach which combines his or her own working theories with bits and pieces of a subset of theories found in the larger decision literature. Instead of looking to these theories for definitive answers, the practitioner looks to this literature as an aid to his or her own theorizing and as a means of generating of creative insights into the decision at hand. In this way, these conceptual tools are combined, bent, and shaped to the decision maker's will as the decision is made. This act of combining, bending, and shaping decision theories and other inputs in the move to decision solution reflects *poiesis*. As such, there is an artistic quality to it.

This theorizing and the synthesis process reflected in it are similar to the challenges faced by the theater organist in the days of the silent movie.

Given the genre and plot of the movie, many decisions were required of the organist. Drawing from his knowledge of music theory, musical styles, personal preferences, and his own technical proficiencies, the organist was charged with creating a mood for listeners to match the theme and flow of the story line. His means of doing this was the organ.

The instrument presented to the organist multiple notes, ranks (keyboards), stops and pedals. The challenge: What combination of notes, ranks, stops, and pedals can be used to produce the desired effect? Theoretically, an infinite number of combinations were possible. Yet to produce the desired sound, the seasoned performer knew exactly what notes to play, what stops to use, and what pedals to press to match the mood of each scene as well as the ebb and flow between scenes. There was much artistry in doing this. A working knowledge of a wide variety of musical styles was required of the organist as he moved from movie to movie. Beyond this knowledge, however, was an ability to skillfully synthesize various notes and styles as the situation demanded.

It is in this sense that we suggest that there is an art associated with the use of existing decision theories by educational leaders to make decisions. This art is not a matter of imposing a theory on our decision context. Rather, it is using our knowledge of these theories—whether consciously or unconsciously—to assist me in such things as: (1) sense-making this context (i.e., sensitizing me to what defines this context); (2) identifying those variables in the decision context which can and cannot be manipulated; (3) defining decision goals; and (4) in light of this information, theorizing about how the decision can be adequately addressed.

It is also in this sense that the sense-making heuristic offered by Thompson above represents an exercise in artistry (see Figure 2.1). Given the decision theories with which he was familiar, Thompson related and contextualized these by identifying and abstracting elements common to each. In doing this, he was forced to *theorize* about existing decision theories. One can appreciate the artistry reflected in his effort and the utility found in the heuristic. More thought should be given to this artistry and how it can be effectively taught to students.

CONCLUSIONS AND IMPLICATIONS OF AN ARTISTIC PERSPECTIVE ON DECISION MAKING

How effectively do professional schools teach students to theorize about *how* theories of decision can be used to improve decision skills? To what extent is the art associated with this theorizing recognized and taught? There are perhaps other artistic elements (*poiesis*) associated with the decision-making process beyond the two examined above. Motivated by an appreciation of the importance of artistry to leadership practice, our purpose has been to provoke thought on a set of professional competencies and issues that have been largely ignored or underexamined in the field of educational leadership.

We have pursued this purpose in the context of the decision-making literature and student responses to this literature. Decision making is a bread-and-butter topic in the professional school. As Simon (1976) noted, administration is decision making. The underexamined aspects of decision making highlighted here underscore the need to:

- distinguish with greater clarity yet relate one's *knowledge* of the decision making literature from one's *skill* as a decision maker;
- decenter theories and recenter students' skill-development and *theorizing* about this development as the points of departure in professional education;
- acknowledge the artistic, intuitive and tacit-knowledge aspects of professional practice and legitimate these as serious objects of study;
- attend anew to the process of *synthesis* and the artistic skill associated with it in addressing problems of practice.

Our concern with these issues is prompted by an epistemological monism that has come to define the education experienced in many professional schools. The ideas of Aristotle have been used to unpack and critique this monism. As an entrenched epistemology, *theoria* equates knowledge and skill. Knowing *about* is taken as a proxy for knowing *how*. In the context of decision making, it leads many to erroneously assume that students who master the decision-making literature will be skillful decision makers in the field. Professional competence is defined as mastering this knowledge.

Without discarding the importance of *theoria* as a way of knowing, we have sought to problematize the dominance of this epistemology in professional schools. This we have done by introducing and elaborating a second epistemology identified by Aristotle. *Poiesis* is a way of knowing inherent in the creation of something. This epistemology is seen in the work of the artist as he or she combines various elements to create a desired end. It involves a series of judgments as to how available inputs can be skillfully combined to create this end. *Poiesis* is the knowledge that guides the individual as he or she combines *theoria* to produce an artifact. Synthesis and the knowledge, which guides this synthesis, constitute its essence.

The arts and a *poiesis* epistemology have no monopoly on the artistic. As we have discussed here, there are many artistic elements associated with *making* or *creating* a decision. Yet our experiences as faculty in a field charged with preparing educational leaders suggests that we have done an inadequate job of teaching students how to theorize and reflect on the synthesis processes involved in decision making. How can I synthesize my knowledge of the decision literature (and the theories found in it) to solve this problem I am facing in my district? How can I use this knowledge to improve my own synthesis skills as a decision maker?

While we have been effective at teaching students in our programs the literature on decision making (*theoria*), we have been less effective at teaching them how to make effective use of this literature as decision makers (*poiesis*).

Knowledge acquisition and the skillful use of this knowledge are related yet distinct activities. Hence there is a need to distinguish knowledge as *an end* from using knowledge as *a means to an end.* We have also been ineffective in teaching students how to theorize about this synthesis process. In the role of theorizer, the student synthesizes in order to explain. The ultimate goal of this theorizing is the development of decision skill. The theories of decision making found in the literature provide the reflective practitioner with a working knowledge to facilitate—not supplant—his or her own theorizing.

As noted elsewhere, this failure is tantamount to teaching students to paint-by-number (Johnson, 2004a). The art and needed skill are not just in knowing what colors are available. It is knowing *how* to creatively combine, temper and synthesize these colors to paint pictures. It is in these dual activities of *knowing how* and *theorizing about this know-how* that students become artists. The disconnect which exists between what is taught in many preparation programs and the day-to-day realities of school life reflects an insensitivity to the importance of developing the abilities of students as *theorists, artists,* and in *the art of theory use.* This calls for a decentering of theory and a recentering of theorizing and instruction in theorizing in our programs.

The arguments we make beg questions regarding the end-goal of this artistry. At the risk of sounding verbose, there are several ways to characterize the artistically skilled decision maker. The seasoned professional has the ability to make decisions in the absence of rules or in light of few if any precedents. Given the constraints and unknowns of the decision context, she displays great facility in navigating the decision terrain in the realization of desired ends. In the words of Schon (1987), she is skilled at making decisions regarding the "indeterminate zones of practice." This artistic competence comes into bold relief in unique, uncertain, and conflicted situations. These situations elude simple, recipe, by-the-book solutions, and require judgments in the absence of rules. Such artistry is a high-powered variant of the more familiar sorts of competence exhibited daily in multiple acts of recognition, judgment and skillful performance.

This artistry and concerted efforts to attend to it are key elements missing in the way we think about and train educational leaders. While there is a tacit "know more than we can say" quality associated with it (Howells, 1995; Polanyi, 1967; Smith, 2001), more thought should be given to understanding the artistry of decision making. Further thought should likewise be given to how this artistry can be effectively taught to others. Toward these ends we offer these thoughts for consideration and as provocation.

QUESTIONS FOR REFLECTION AND DISCUSSION

- What was the purpose and primary argument of this chapter?
- In what sense is leadership synonymous with decision making? What does this mean?

- Why are there so many theories of decision making? Why don't we know more about it?
- What is the difference between *knowing about* decision making and *knowing how* to decide?
- Define or distinguish *theoria* and *poiesis*. What are their implications for decision making?
- *What* about the decision making process may be considered artistic and creative?
- What is meant by *the art* of theory use? How can it be used artistically in decisions?
- Think of and identify an activity that requires you to synthesize knowledge in order to do. How do you go about doing this? Why is it difficult?
- Why is it important to know decision theories? How might you appropriate these?
- How might the two heuristics for sense-making decision-making theories in this chapter inform your thinking about decision making? What does Figure 2.1 represent?
- How were you taught decision theories and literature? How were you taught the decision-making skills? Does it emphasize *knowing about* or *knowing how?*
- As a learner and leader, how can you improve your *theorizing skills* as a decision maker?

PART II

Context and Contextual Issues in Decision Making

CHAPTER THREE

Organization as Context:
Decision Making in Educational Organizations

Decision making is a cognitive process that guides human thought and action. Regardless of when, where or by whom a decision is made, a number of common elements define this process. Driven by the need to eliminate the dissonance created by a problem or perceived inconsistency, decision making consists of the following cognitive activities: data search, data collection, data analysis, data synthesis, and multiple inferential leaps (Dewey, 1933, 1938). These activities occur in contexts defined by varying levels of uncertainty and risk.

More often than not, the amount of information available to make a decision is incomplete. The uncertainty this state of affairs creates has implications for the entire decision-making process. For example, decision preferences may be known or unknown. If decision preferences are unknown, the decision maker lacks an organizing referent for decision activities. If decision preferences are known, the decision maker often encounters multiple means or alternatives for realizing these preferences. Incomplete knowledge of how each alternative is logically linked to decision preferences makes the prioritization of alternatives problematic.

The various levels of detail and different amounts of information at the disposal of the decision maker can be mind boggling. Whether the decision is made by a police officer patrolling an Atlanta neighborhood, a consumer contemplating the purchase of a new vehicle in upstate New York, or a principal in rural Wyoming, these and other common elements define the decision-making process. Yet in spite of the potential complexities these present, sound decisions are made daily with little or no thought given to the mental processes identified above.

Decisions are also made in a *context*. Though analyzed and studied by many as if made in a vacuum, decisions are made in a context that influences and is influenced by the decision maker. To appreciate the role of context in the decision process, it is imperative that the concept be delimited in ways that make it useful. Its utility as an analytic tool must be explicated.

Context is a multidimensional concept with numerous connotations. One can describe a decision in terms of its *cultural, social,* or even *political* context.

Viewed from the perspective of resource abundance or scarcity, a decision can also be described in terms of its *economic* context. Of particular interest here is the *organizational* context of a decision. As used in this chapter, organizational context refers to the organizational setting in which a decision is made.

Scott (2002) describes the organization as a formalized social collective. It is a dynamic entity made up of individuals pursuing goals within a relatively formalized structure of coordination and control. All organizations exist in an environment. Organizations such as schools influence and are influenced by the larger environment in which they exist. The relationship shared between an organization and its environment is symbiotic.

A focus on the organizational context of decision making is justifiable on several fronts. Organizations provide the principal mechanism for realizing ends beyond the reach of the individual. Much of the activity in life is *organizational* activity. For these reasons a wide variety of organizations can be found. Not only are we members of multiple organizations, we also feel the effects of many of which we are not a part.

Second, organizations are ubiquitous. As *the* dominant form and venue for social interaction, organizations provide the context for many of society's decisions. Most decisions are made in an organizational context. These decisions and the decision-making processes that create them cannot be fully understood apart from this context.

Third, the decisions faced by educational leaders are made in organizations created specifically for educating people. Although these educational organizations share features common to all organizations, the distinguishing features of schools as *human service* organizations shape the kinds of decisions leaders face and how they address these decisions. The numerous activities that occur in educational organizations—leading, teaching, counseling, decision making, and so forth—take place within this *organizational* context. While experientially known to the seasoned leader, these features and their influence on the decision process have been underexamined in the field of education.

PURPOSE AND PERSPECTIVE

This chapter examines the organizational context in which educational leaders make decisions. We suggest that there is a constellation of organizational features that define the unique character of the public school organization. Our intent is to provide an overview of some of these features and to explore how they define, facilitate, and constrain the decision making process.

The following observations are informed by frameworks and concepts found in the organization theory literature. As a subfield of sociology, organizational theory is concerned with the systematic study of formal organizations (Thompson, 1967; Mintzberg, 1979; Morgan, 1986; Hall, 2002; Scott, 2002).

This literature provides a rich set of analytic tools that are often ignored by educational leaders.

Much of the discussion of decision making found in educational literature reflects an inadequate, superficial understanding of the organizational perspective and an incomplete understanding of the fundamental character of school organizations (Johnson, 2004b). This is expressed in at least three ways. First, it is reflected in the attitudes that many in our field exhibit toward this literature and the lack of perceived relevance it has for our understanding of leadership and educational organizations. Whether unwilling or unable to wrestle with the abstract nature of this literature, or frustrated by the theory movement on which it rests, the press of practice creates for many an impatience that leaves little use for organization theory.

This superficial understanding is also reflected in the undue preoccupation of overly zealous reformers with narrowly defined outcomes and the manner in which these have been abstracted from the organizational context where they occur. Absent is an appreciation of the relationships shared by these and other outcomes with key organization variables. The parts are considered apart from whole, apart from their larger organizational context.

This superficial grasp is likewise reflected in the cut-flower approach through which many concepts derived from this literature are used in policy and practitioner dialogues. One need only point to the concepts *loose coupling*, *structure*, and *teacher autonomy* as examples. As developed by Bidwell (1965), *loose coupling* describes one aspect of the structural features of schools; namely, the link between classroom units and the larger organization. Without an understanding of this concept, many individuals carelessly underestimate the number of structural links that bind classroom subunits with the larger school. Drawing from the organizational theory literature, we suggest that the defining features of schools *as organizations* and the realities of school life provide an important yet overlooked context for understanding decisions made by educational leaders.

SCHOOLS AS HUMAN SERVICE ORGANIZATIONS

Theorists have long sought to identify both the common and distinctive features of organizations. While concepts such as structure, culture, and core technology represent common organizational features (Hall, 2002), numerous typologies have been offered as a means of highlighting distinctions (Blau & Scott, 1962; Carlson 1964; Parsons, 1967; Etzioni, 1975; Scott, 2002). One idea that has received less attention in the literature, yet which highlights the distinctiveness of educational organizations, is the concept of *human service organization* (Hasenfeld, 1983; Johnson, 2004b).

Human service organizations are organizations whose primary function is to protect, maintain or enhance the well-being of human beings. Whether through defining, shaping, or altering personal attributes, the core task of these organizations focuses on transforming people. Organizations such as schools, universities, churches, hospitals, prisons, counseling agencies, and rehabilitation clinics share this defining feature. The National Football League, Macy's, Neiman Marcus, and the IRS do not. Along with other human service organizations, educational organizations are distinguished by the following features. Considered together, these features define the larger organizational context of decision making for educational leaders.

DIVERSE, MULTIPLE, AND AMBIGUOUS NATURE OF ORGANIZATIONAL GOALS

The goals of human service organizations are ambiguous, problematic, and often contested. Toward what end should the organization seek to change the individual? What attitudinal or dispositional outcomes should be sought? These are perennial questions for human service organizations. Many of the client attributes that human service organizations are asked to change cannot be readily observed. Because disagreement exists over outcomes and end-states, human service organizations typically have multiple, vague goals.

The following adjectives have been used to describe the goals of public education in the United States: *multiple, vague, diffuse, complex, inconsistent,* and *multidimensional* (Cohen, et al., 1972; Spring, 2005). As human service organizations, schools seek to define, shape, and alter the personal attributes of society's youth. The moral overtones of these activities infuse the school with value and make education a highly moral and environmentally sensitive enterprise. Individuals and groups disagree as to what the goals of public education are and what the educated student or end product should be. The goals of education are a perennial topic of debate. These disagreements constitute a defining feature of the school organization, one that has wide implications for the public and those charged with educating young people.

AMBIGUITY OF THE DEFINING CORE TASK

The term *core technology* is used in the organizational theory literature to describe two notable organizational features: (1) *the* core task that defines the essence of an organization; and (2) *how* this defining core task is actually performed, that is, how an organization transforms its inputs into outputs (Perrow, 1967; Thompson, 1967; Scott, 2002).

Organizations can be distinguished by the core task that defines them. For example, the defining task of the Boeing Corporation is aircraft production. The defining task of General Motors is automobile production. Likewise, the defining task of Taco Bell is fast-food preparation. The defining task in human service organizations focuses on transforming people. In educational organizations this transformation revolves around the teaching-learning task. Teaching is a task aimed at altering and improving the personal attributes of students. While many supplemental tasks can be found in schools—managing, counseling, and coaching—teaching is *the* core task that defines the essence of educational organizations. Schools are defined by the teaching that occurs in them. This core task gives the educational organization its identity; this core task distinguishes it from other types of organizations.

Core technology also refers to *how* the defining core task of an organization is actually done. As suggested by its etymological root (from Greek *technē*: art or skill), technology is the intellectual know-how, techniques, physical hardware, and sequence of activities used to *skillfully* transform inputs (inanimate or animate) into outputs (Thompson, 1967; Hulin & Roznowski, 1985; Scott, 2002). In this sense, technology refers to *all* of the components and activities noted above in combination, not just to the physical tools used in transformation.

Organizations vary in the level of clarity that characterizes their defining task. The level of task clarity associated with building diesel engines for trucks—the degree to which inputs are certain *and* the means of transforming these into outputs are known and predictable—is much higher than the task clarity of teaching (Perrow, 1967; Rowan, 1990). Engineers at General Motors have identified "one best method" for making engines. This method has been standardized. By contrast, there is no "one best method" of teaching. An instructional approach that works with one student may not work for another. What worked with last year's class of Geometry students may not work with this year's class. The task clarity of teaching—the degree to which the inputs and effects of teaching can be predicted with certainty—is much lower than that associated with building engines. As raw materials and objects of transformation, people represent complex, variable and unstable entities. Knowledge of how to foster change effectively and consistently within them is incomplete.

Various adjectives have been used to describe and define the technology of teaching: *vague, ambiguous, uncertain, ill-defined* (Cohen, et al., 1972). These descriptors are rooted in the fact that the technology of teaching lacks a definitive knowledge base. As human service organizations, public schools are plagued with ambiguities surrounding the technical core (Hasenfeld, 1983). Not only are goals for school organizations vague, but also teachers make use of technologies that are ambiguous and at times unpredictable. These technologies fail to diagnose and solve the learning challenges faced by all students. Core-task ambiguity is a defining contextual feature of the public school organization.

PREDOMINANCE OF CLIENT-CONTROL ISSUES

A third distinguishing feature of human service organizations is the predominance of staff-client relationships in the organization (i.e., what Hasenfeld labels "the functionary-client relationship") and the challenges associated with managing these relationships. The staff-client relationship is a critical determinant of success in human service organizations. Maintaining cooperation with clients who have the ability to resist is a key factor in the quality of this relationship. This challenge is particularly acute in organizations where client participation is mandatory (e.g., public education, prisons). An essential task for leaders and staff in these organizations consists of a series of transactions between clients and staff in which compliance is negotiated. This negotiation is a moral process.

Like other human service organizations, the relationship between school personnel and students is of utmost importance in educational organizations. Waller (1932) has aptly described this relationship as a *fragile equilibrium*. Schools are densely populated organizations. Controlling and channeling student behavior are defining challenges. These challenges are managed using a variety of crowd-control routines and procedures (e.g., strict policies regarding out-of-class behavior, playground activities, student assemblies, etc.).

An example of how the staff-client relationship defines life in schools is also evident in the relationship that exists between the teacher and students. When students dislike a teacher, the motivation to learn suffers. The creation and maintenance of an effective learning environment is complicated by two factors: (1) attendance for public school students is mandatory; and (2) the maturity level of students is such that the educational goals, demands, and values personified in the school's representatives (i.e., administrators and teachers) are often incongruent with student motivations. Because public education is compulsory, a certain percentage of students attend school unwillingly. Much like prisons and other types of "total institutions" (Goffman, 1961; Carlson, 1964), the unselected and captive nature of students creates client-control challenges and an underlying adversarial culture between teachers and some students (Waller, 1932). Simply stated, students are captive clients with immature tendencies (Waller, 1932; Carlson, 1964; Jackson, 1986, 1990; Muir, 1986).

These factors make creating orderly learning environments an ongoing challenge for schools. Teachers must coax, negotiate, and occasionally resort to various "strong-arm" tactics with students. Whether through an appeal to the authority-status of the teaching role or to the bureaucratic rules of the school, these tactics are impersonal and potentially alienating for students. If used in excess, passive resistance can easily escalate into overt rebellion. However, if used with skill these tactics can create an environment conducive to learning (Johnson, 2004b).

The irony of these dual teaching challenges is not the mutual relationship they share. Rather it is the paradoxical and countervailing tensions they create. The teacher must skillfully balance these tensions. Whereas the need to establish classroom order rests on the use of impersonal bureaucratic tactics with students, the need to motivate students rests on the affective, personal appeal of the teacher. Reflected in this tension is the juxtaposition of the personal and impersonal. In dealing with students, the teacher must behave in personal yet impersonal ways. This highlights a basic dilemma in school organizations: the need to motivate students to learn (i.e., the need to solicit student cooperation) while creating an orderly environment in which this learning can occur (i.e., the need to threaten and force compliance as needed while running the risk of undermining student motivation). The environment that exists in a given classroom is a function of the teacher's ability to effectively balance these countervailing tensions. Likewise, the environment that exists in a school is a function of the principal's ability to effectively balance these countervailing tensions with various school personnel. The centrality of the teacher-student relationship in educational organizations and the potential for students to resist make client-control issues a predominant theme in schools. The relationship between student and school is a *negotiated* relationship rooted in *exchange* and mediated by various personnel. The predominance of client-control issues has contributed to the emergence of a strong norm in schools regarding the importance of maintaining order and control. A teacher's effectiveness is often defined in terms of his or her ability to establish and maintain order in the classroom (Johnson, 1997). Principals that maintain a safe and orderly school environment are likewise perceived by others as effective leaders.

NOTABLE STRUCTURAL FEATURES

In the most generic sense, *structure* may be defined as the way an entity is configured, patterned, or arranged. Mintzberg (1979, p. 66) defines organizational structure as "the sum total of ways in which [organizational leaders] divide [the labor of organizational participants] into distinct tasks, and then achieve coordination among [these tasks]." In a similar vein, Scott (2002, p. 8) defines organizational structure as "that set of features that arises as a result of the efforts within the organization to differentiate the labor; and coordinate and control the work."

While these definitions may be criticized as hyperrational, a substantive measure of validity is contained in each. Considered together, organizational structured may be understood be as the ways in which the work within an organization is divided, grouped, coordinated, and controlled. The social patterns that result from efforts to divide, group, coordinate and control the work done in organizations constitute its structure. Implied in this definition are assumptions regarding the assignment of sets of work tasks to individuals, roles or groups and the relating or coordinating of these work tasks toward some larger end(s). One can speak of the following dimensions of structure: differentiation (horizontal, vertical, and spatial), the distribution or constellation of authority, and the level of formalization, also called standardization. One can also speak of the functional, dysfunctional, and symbolic aspects of structure. The normative goal of structure is the realization of increased organizational efficiencies.

Decentralizing Tendencies

As noted above, a distinguishing feature of human service organizations is the extent to which the core tasks that define them are unclear. As raw materials and objects of transformation, humans represent complex and variable entities. Knowledge of how to foster change within them effectively and consistently is incomplete. Returning to our example above, the level of task clarity associated with building diesel engines—the degree to which inputs are certain and the means of transforming these into outputs are known and predictable—is much higher than the task clarity associated with the salvation of souls, rehabilitation of criminals, psychological healing, or teaching-learning (Perrow, 1967; Rowan, 1990). There are more uncertainties associated with the latter than the former.

As with other types of human service organizations, the low level of clarity that surrounds the core task of educational organizations—teaching and learning—means that the structure found in these organizations tends to be decentralized to point of direct and sustained staff-client interaction. It is in the classroom that teachers interact consistently with students.

The importance of the task-clarity variable is rooted in the relationship it shares with organizational structure. Task clarity shares a positive relationship with the structural centralization. While a centralized structure is conducive to tasks that exhibit high degrees of task clarity, such structures work against tasks exhibiting lower degrees of clarity (Burns & Stalker, 1961; Thompson, 1967; Hall, 2002). The uncertainties of teaching call for a decentralized structure that allows for teacher autonomy and flexibility (Bidwell, 1965; Lortie, 1975; Jackson, 1986, 1990). The decentralized structure that typifies school organizations provides teachers with the autonomy and flexibility needed to adapt and adjust to the uncertainties of teaching. Teachers regard classrooms as territory over which they exercise considerable control. They jealously guard their domain.

The structural relationship between classrooms and the larger school has been described as loosely coupled (Bidwell, 1965; Weick, 1976; Meyer & Rowan, 1977, 1978; Rowan, 2002). This looseness represents a structural response to the ambiguities of the teaching-learning task. Yet to say that the structural link between the classroom and school is loosely coupled is not to say that it is decoupled, or in other words, that no single structural link connects the classroom subunit to the school. Not only do multiple structural links connect classroom to school, the number and strength of these vary across and within schools (Gamoran & Dreeban, 1986). Whether expressed in recent accountability reforms such as a prescribed curriculum, required text, teacher evaluation system or end-of-year standardized student-exam, these links place constraints on teacher autonomy.

Teacher autonomy has its limits; it is a *constrained* autonomy (Corwin & Edelfelt, 1977; Gamoran & Dreeban, 1986). The decentralized nature of core-task delivery in the classroom and the teacher autonomy associated with it are defining structural features of educational organizations.

Dual Authority-Control Structures

Like other human service organizations, educational organizations are defined by a dual authority-control structure (Freidson, 2001). On the one hand, schools are *bureaucratic* organizations exhibiting in varying degrees the noted features of bureaucracy: hierarchy, a well-defined division of labor, expertise-based employment and codified policies governing behavior. These structural mechanisms provide a means of coordinating and articulating the work done in classroom subunits across age-grade cohorts and time.

Schools are also *professional* organizations (Scott, 2002). Those working at the core—teachers in the classroom—have been professionally trained, have a professional (or quasi-professional, Lortie,1969) referent group and enjoy a measure of autonomy in the planning and implementation of instruction. The complexity of the teaching task, variability of students, and norms of the teaching profession mitigate the effects of direct supervision and excessive standardization.

Taken together, the bureaucratic and professional character of the school organization represent separate but competing authority-control structures, each with its own countervailing influence. One structure has a centralizing, rationalizing effect, the other a decentralizing effect; one structure encourages a local orientation among school personnel, the other a cosmopolitan orientation; one encourages commitment to the organization, the other a commitment to the profession. Operating at the organization's core, teachers must reconcile the tensions created by these competing control structures. This dual control structure and resultant tensions further define the context of decision making in educational organizations as professional bureaucracies.

A STIMULUS-OVERLOAD WORKING ENVIRONMENT

An additional contextual feature is the nature and character of the work environment which exists in schools as human service organizations. In the day-to-day life of schools, teachers and administrators find themselves subject to numerous interactions of short duration with multiple individuals. Many of these interactions are intense and personal. Time is a scarce resource and paper work is abundant. Frustration is often at or near the threshold level. The frequency and length of meetings are minimized when possible. In sum, school personnel find themselves working in what has been identified as a *stimulus-overload, labor-intensive* working environment (Willower, 1982). This environment is a defining organizational feature of schools.

AN INSTITUTIONAL ENTITY

Schools can also be described as *institutional* entities in highly *institutional* environments. As described by sociologists, institutions are the defining, historically-rooted, value-infused social systems found in society (Giddens, 1987; Rowan, 1978; Meyer & Scott, 2000). Examples of notable institutions include the family, government, religion, the media, the economy, and education. As venues of patterned interaction, institutions play a critical role in defining reality for us. As such, institutions are an important part of our collective thinking. Yet much like the streets we walk, the stores we frequent, and the houses in which we live, they often go unnoticed and are taken for granted (Selznick, 1957).

Institutions personify a socially constructed reality that is objectified and accepted as real by many (Berger & Luckmann, 1966). Institutions are symbol systems and cultural elements that govern life by imposing taken-for-granted values, myths, norms, and structures on society (DiMaggio & Powell, 1983). These elements exert a subtle yet powerful influence. Institutions not only define reality for many but in so doing create expectations as to what constitutes legitimate cultural expressions and forms.

Schooling and school organizations reflect these institutional qualities. Schools are part of the collective mental furniture that defines who we are and what we value. The fundamental features of the school—its practices, organizational form, methods of teaching, reward system, and aims—are deeply embedded in our culture and have an extraordinary impact. Schools and schooling influence how we define and legitimate knowledge, intelligence, beauty, and success. Schooling also influences how we see our place in the world. By its very nature, the institution we know as school *teaches* (Eisner, 2003). The institution of education reinvents the culture in which it exists through the people it produces and reproduces.

The social reality that schools define for us is a reified reality. This reality plays a critical role in defining society's judgments and expectations. Yet much like the fish that is unaware of the water in which it lives, the embeddedness of schools in our culture often means that the values and assumptions on which they rest often go unexamined. This reified, institutional quality of schools is a defining organizational feature.

Examples of the influence of the institutional character of schooling can be seen in the historical forms, routines and methods that define the school organization, *and* the value-infused meanings society attributes to these. Although the low task clarity associated with teaching calls for a decentralized organizational structure, the current classroom structure rooted in historical evolution of schools reflects an excessively rational quality. The institutional myth associated with the utility and desirability of the rational-bureaucratic organizational form provides a context for understanding this.

The current organizational structure of schools is as much the product of the hyperrationalized thinking associated with the scientific management movement as it is of the expediencies of the classroom (Callahan, 1962; Tyack & Cuban, 1995). Faced with the challenge of providing a mandatory education for all, the school organization was consciously modeled on what progressives of an earlier day identified as the most efficient of all organizational forms, *the factory and batch-processing model.*

While distinctions exist between elementary and secondary schools, the structural and process artifacts of this thinking are familiar to all former students: age-graded student cohorts; the egg-crate organizational structure; the one-teacher-one-class division of labor; the whole-group, textbook-based instructional approach; the multiperiod day; 55-minute teaching units separated by a rigid bell schedule; three to four daily preps per teacher; multiple, quick, and at times intense individual student-teacher interactions; extensive paper work; a detailed student record and tracking system; homework, in-class assignments, tests, and report cards (Bidwell, 1965; Corwin & Borman, 1988; Willower, 1985). These and other features have come to define for the American public what it means to *do school* (Eisner, 2003). Similar to other enduring mythical images that define our national identity—for example, McDonald's, Disney World, and the New York Yankees—these features of schooling have been *institutionalized* in the American psyche (Meyer & Rowan, 1978, 1977). Though many of these features have outlived their usefulness, their imprimatur provides the public with a set of criteria by which qualitative judgments regarding the effectiveness of schools are made. This phenomenon speaks to the institutional quality of schools.

There are at least three implications that follow from this institutional characterization of the school organization. First, the structure of schools and the nature of teaching have changed little over the past century. The institutional features of schooling are such an entrenched part of our collective mental furniture that innovations that substantively deviate from this pattern are met with suspicion. Institutionalization has morphed into a cognitive ossification that serves as a roadblock to change and innovation.

Second, the factory model from which the current school structure is fashioned has perpetuated a one-size fits all approach to the organization of schooling (Callahan, 1962; Tyack & Cuban, 1995) *and* an excessively technical-rational view of teaching (Elmore, 1990, 1995; Rowan, 1990). While this model has facilitated educators' attempts to address the logistical and efficiency issues associated with the mandate of educating the masses (a diverse group indeed), it often falls short of facilitating the work done by teachers.

Third, the institutional views of schooling are such that the public views teaching, much like the organizational structure in which it occurs, as a hyper-rational task subject to high degrees of standardization, centralization, and predictability (Johnson, 1997). It is this hyperrational institutional myth that drives much (certainly not all) of the demand for educational reform. Central to this way of thinking is the desire to make teaching an excessively planned and engineered activity. While certain aspects of teaching are routine and repetitive, many of the uncertainties of teaching noted in the previous section elude excessive rationalization. In spite of this, institutional myths of rationality perpetuate a hyperrational view of teaching in the schools' external environment.

With the goal of changing people, human service organizations operate in a value-laden, morally-charged institutional milieu (DiMaggio & Powell, 1983; Scott, 2000). This is a defining organizational feature that influences the decision context in educational organizations.

ENVIRONMENTAL VULNERABILITY

The moral ambiguity surrounding debates over the goals and technologies used in human service organizations underscores the turbulent environment in which they often operate. This environment consists of multiple interests. While consensus among interests may exist at an abstract level, implementation necessitates that human service organizations make normative choices in a society of multiple interests and competing values. An important challenge facing educational leaders in this setting is the management of the organization's environment (Meyer & Rowan, 1977; DiMaggio & Powell, 1982; Scott, 2000).

When used to describe schools, the adjective *public* is significant (Johnson & Fauske, 2000). Schools are domestic (Carlson, 1964) open systems that interact with and are legitimated by the environment. As public institutions, schools are vulnerable to a variety of environmental forces (Scott, 2002). Life for school personnel is a constant interplay between the activities that the school must perform and the organizational accounts that the school must give to its publics (Meyer & Rowan, 1978). Consequently, the skin that separates the school from its environment is at times unbearably thin for school personnel. This environmental vulnerability is a defining feature of the public school organization.

The sources of this vulnerability are varied. As clients and taxpayers, the public has the right to voice demands and offer advice to school personnel. This prerogative highlights a perennial governing tension in public education: Who governs, the public or professional educators (Boyd, 1976; Malen, 1995; Spring, 2005)? Recognizing and effectively managing this tension is an ongoing challenge for educational leaders.

The intrinsic value of those served by the school is also a source of environmental vulnerability. Not only are schools responsible for the growth and development of society's most valued and vulnerable population—children— they are responsible for the growth and development of *our* children. They are not just names and faces in the crowd, they are *our* children. As parents motivated to act in behalf of their best interests, we hold the educational system accountable for its contribution to their success. We expect our children to be treated professionally and responsibly by school personnel. Because of the value of our children to us, violation of this trust will evoke a passionate response.

The intrinsic value of those served by schools introduces a strong emotional component that can easily animate parents to voice demands and supports. This too exacerbates the public vulnerability of schools.

Society's familiarity with schools and schooling also contribute to this vulnerability. Most have been to school. The majority of citizens are themselves products of the public school system. Teaching is unique in that it is a profession in which professional socialization begins at age five or six (Eisner, 2003). At this age students quickly learn what it takes to *do school* and what a teacher does in the classroom. They also learn how to behave in order to succeed. During these years, students spend more time with teachers in schools than with their parents.

This informal apprenticeship breeds a public familiarity with schools. Citizens know what to expect from schools. Though rooted in the past, these expectations contribute to the environmental vulnerability of educational organizations. Most have definite opinions about what constitutes *effective* schools and teaching. Unlike hospitals, high-tech engineering firms, and investment companies that have their own esoteric language and modes of operation, schools lack an *organizational mystique* with the public.

Environmental vulnerability and the continual search for environmental legitimacy are defining features of schools as human service organizations. The zone of public confidence is not without limits; and it must be nurtured and managed. It too is part of the larger organizational context in which educational leaders make decisions.

DECISION MAKING IMPLICATIONS FOR EDUCATIONAL LEADERS

While not to be taken as exhaustive, the following seven features of schools define and distinguish them as *human service organizations*:

1. the diverse and ambiguous nature of organizational goals
2. the low task clarity associated with the organization's core task (teaching)
3. the extent to which client-control issues are a dominant organizing theme
4. the decentralizing tendencies and dual authority-control demands reflected in the organizational structure
5. the stimulus-overload work environment experienced by organizational participants
6. the strong institutional environment in which the organization is embedded
7. the vulnerability of the organization to environmental demands

These features are also consequential for the educational leader *as decision maker*. They place the leader in a context animated by multiple and at times countervailing forces. These forces shape the character of decisions that arise in schools. These countervailing forces also inform how these decisions can be effectively addressed.

DECISION MAKING AND THE AMBIGUITY OF EDUCATIONAL ENDS AND MEANS

There are several implications for decision making that follow from the ambiguity that defines the ends and means of school organizations. First, the decisions that educational leaders are called on to make are situated in *potentially conflictual* contexts. Legitimate disagreements over the ends and means of education exist not only within the larger public, but also among professional educators. The public nature of the educational enterprise makes schools vulnerable to the effects of these conflicts. As the face of the organization to the community, educational leaders are the focal point of demand articulation. As the principal teacher within the school, educational leaders are also the focal point of conflicting teacher demands.

This contextual feature does not mean that conflict is inevitable in schools. However, it does mean that the potential for conflict and the conditions for its emergence lie just below the organization's surface (Pfeffer, 1981). This also does not mean that the potential for conflict need be self-fulfilling. There is no need for educational leaders to invite conflict. At the same time, leaders should not be surprised if conflict emerges. The potential for conflict around these issues is a defining feature of school organizations. Educational leaders must reconcile themselves to this reality.

Second, the ambiguity that surrounds the ends and means of education necessitates the need for educational leaders *to find ways to functionally manage this ambiguity and the challenges it creates*. From a technical perspective, this often means that there may be no single best or right answer for a decision. Yet while one's efforts to find a definitive technical solution remain elusive, there is often a politically expedient answer to be found. Educational leaders vary in their ability to deal with the ambiguities and lack of closure inherent in certain decisions. Leaders also vary in their willingness *and* ability to effectively use politics as a means for dealing with decision ambiguities.

The ambiguity of educational ends and means also means that *the desire to make decisions that consistently satisfy all constituents is ill founded*. While this aspiration is a worthy normative goal, it is an unrealistic goal for the educational leader. Even in the context of smaller, more homogenous school environments, such widespread satisfaction is more the exception than the rule. This realization calls for a disposition on the part of the decision maker that accepts this aspect of decision making, a willingness to live with the fact that keeping all constituents happy all the time is a pipe dream. Educational leaders vary in the degree to which they possess this dispositional orientation.

The potential for conflict, the elusive search for the one-best answer, and the impossibility of satisfying all constituents all the time highlight *the importance of developing a bevy of decision-making skills*. For example, there is a need for educational leaders to develop skill in identifying the potential and actual flashpoints that surround the decisions they encounter. Anticipating these flashpoints can inform a more proactive response. Such information can be used to frame, craft, and implement a decision, thus increasing its chances for success.

This proactive response also calls for two additional skills: skill in discerning decision stakes and skill in predicting how a decision will be received by stakeholders. While decisions should be informed by these expectations, the leader should not always feel compelled to respond to the demands of all. Nor should the leader be held captive to the interests of a few. Furthermore, a commitment to social justice dictates that the leader be sensitive to those constituents who lack the power, ability, or resources to make their demands known. There is a skill associated with demand discrimination. This skill focuses on the ability to determine *what* decision demands should be attended to, *for whom* and *when*.

In highly institutional organizations where goals and means are contested, the success of many decisions often rests on the ability of the decision maker to persuade others of the worthiness of her position. Effective decision making in these situations calls for persuasion and negotiation. Both are essential communication skills. Implied in the word *communication* is the ability to convey one's thoughts through various media, to listen and receive feedback from others, and to discriminate the relevant from irrelevant.

DECISION MAKING AND ENVIRONMENTAL AND INSTITUTIONAL VULNERABILITY

The environmental vulnerability and institutional character of schools focus our attention on additional features of the organizational context that influence the decision-making process. To begin with, *the vulnerability and institutional nature of school organizations must be accepted as givens by the leader. Both must also be strategically managed.* Lest these admonitions seem unnecessary to the seasoned educator, there are those leaders whose actions betray the recognition and acceptance of these dual realities.

Most leaders work in educational organizations that are public. For those who do not, the patrons and markets they serve define the primary audiences on which they depend. As a result, much of their life is played out on a stage before the community. Life for the educational leader may thus be defined as *life on the stage.* Here one's decision performances become objects of careful scrutiny by an audience socialized and familiar with the school institution.

Essential to successful performance is the leader's ability to generate, nurture, and bank the legitimacy capital needed to sustain credibility. This glass-bowl existence is a reality for the leader. Sensitivity to it is heightened as decisions are addressed. Mixing the glass-bowl and stage metaphors, certain decisions create intense public drama. As decisions are made, the leader is engaged in creating and managing a public persona on which the legitimacy of leadership and school are at stake. On the one hand, this contextual feature calls for an acute environmental sensitivity on the part of the decision maker.

On the other hand, it calls for a proverbial *tough hide* and a disposition that is not easily rattled by the voicing of environmental demands.

The environmental vulnerability of school organizations also dictates that the decisions faced by educational leaders be made with the public *vs.* profession governing-dilemma in view. As noted above, a defining tension in American education centers on the issue of control: Is it the tax-paying public who has ultimate governing authority over education *or* trained educational professionals?

To be sure, the full weight of the public-professional tension is not felt in every decision the leader is called on to make. Routine decisions are made daily with little or no thought given to it. Many of these are of minimal interest to the public. From time to time, however, decisions arise that deal with those mythic and institutional aspects of schooling that are sacred to the public. It is around such decisions that the public-professional tension is magnified.

A decision by a superintendent in a larger urban school district to close a high school is an example of this. South High was a institutional fixture in the community dating back to the turn of the century. Its stately, multistoried frame housed the memories of generations of students. With rising maintenance costs, declining enrollments, and growth in the district elsewhere, the superintendent moved to recommend closure. Data supporting this recommendation were carefully prepared and submitted to the Board. These data were technically sound, his initial argument convincing.

Yet over a period of months the superintendent's recommendation would lead to his downfall. Underestimating public sentiment against the proposal and the institutional myth that was South High, his decision elicited a strong negative response. The emotional chord struck within the community animated a series of mobilization efforts. His base of support began to erode and his legitimacy as a leader was eventually called into question. He had underestimated the public-professional tension. Several months later he was fired.

Regardless of when or where it is magnified, educational decision makers must recognize this governing tension. It must also be skillfully negotiated and managed. A provoked public creates challenges for the leader that are difficult to overcome.

The vulnerability and institutional character of schools likewise underscores the importance of institutional myths and precedent in the decision-making process. While the decision maker should not be imprisoned by the organizational forms and methods of the past, these precedents cannot always be dismissed in a cavalier fashion without consequences. Institutional precedents often serve important symbolic functions.

An example of this is seen in the symbolic functions served by the rational organization myth, an idea examined earlier in this chapter. Organizations structured in ways that are consistent with accepted views of rationality—that is, those that exhibit the defining features of Weber's classic bureaucratic form—conform to this myth. As a result, they are seen as legitimate and afforded the resources needed for survival from the environment. Those structured otherwise do not. Stated somewhat differently, the public expects the educational leader to run a "tight ship." The public also expects schools to be "structured" and "orderly." Leadership styles and organizational forms that deviate markedly from these expectations are viewed with suspicion. These expectations explain in part why the open-class movement of the early 1960s (i.e., classes without walls) failed as an acceptable structural form. It was inconsistent with myths of rationality that defined society's perceptions of what it means to "do school." These expectations also explain why some parents remain skeptical about instruction that is not teacher- and text-centered. Instructional approaches that are not, violate accepted environmental myths regarding appropriate structural forms and modes of instruction.

The myth of rational organization perpetuated in the institutional environment presents a unique challenge for schools and leaders. While the nature of teaching and learning call for less bureaucratic, decentralized organizational forms, myths of rationality pressure schools to move toward more hyper-rational structural forms. This places the educational leader in an interesting position as decision maker. He must reconcile the institutional myths of rationality with the organizational realities of day-to-day life in schools. He must signal to the environment that the school he leads is structured in a "rational way" while at the same time buffering the negative effects of this hyper-rational structure from the actual work done in the school. He must project an acceptable facade of structural rationality to the environment while allowing for more functional levels of decentralization and disorganization than this facade conveys.

Meyer and Rowan (1977, 1978) refer to this phenomenon as *decoupling*. There is a measure of duplicity involved in managing this conundrum. When faced with certain kinds of decisions, this duplicity requires the leader to engage in a ceremonial dance in homage to the gods of hyper-rationality. Engaging in this dance signals a symbolic conformity to this myth. In reality, however, the leader pursues more functional courses of action that often deviate from this idea. Legitimacy for self and school rests on one's willingness to engage in this dance as needed. Without this legitimacy, one's effectiveness and influence as a decision maker are not possible.

The environmental vulnerability and institutional quality of schools also means that there are times when decisions made by the educational leader must be morally justified. As human service organizations, educators engage in activities that have long-term consequences on the social, intellectual, and emotional development of students. The instructional effectiveness of a caring teacher can inspire a child to excel as an adult. Likewise, scars made by an insensitive, abusive instructor can have lasting effects far beyond the formal years of schooling.

The long-term moral consequences associated with nurturing and shaping society's most vulnerable population infuse the educational enterprise with a sacred quality. Consequently, decisions that affect how schools deal with students must be morally constrained and justified. How will a decision to move to ability-grouping in math, science and reading affect students' sense of self? How will a one-strike-you're-out discipline policy affect the motivation to learn? The burden falls on the leader as decision maker to demonstrate how a proposed change is in fact in the best interest of students. This demonstration must be sound, sincere, and authentic. It must be morally justified. Otherwise the legitimacy of both leader and organization suffers.

DECISIONS REGARDING TEACHERS, CLASSROOMS, AND INSTRUCTION

The defining features of school organizations examined above also provide a context for understanding leadership decisions regarding teachers, classrooms, and instruction. A fundamental grasp of the relationship shared between an organization's structure and defining core-task is essential to addressing these decisions effectively. What kind of organizational structure will facilitate the work being done by those at the organization's core? What configuration of structural elements in the school facilitates the work done by teachers in the classroom? There are several implications that follow from these kinds of decisions.

Decisions and the Classroom Threshold-Calculus of Teachers

As noted above, the work of teachers centers on efforts to address the fundamental challenges of teaching: maintaining classroom order and motivating students to learn. The learning classroom environment that emerges is a function of the abilities of teachers to negotiate these countervailing challenges. Not only do these challenges define the way most teachers approach students, they also define teachers' perceptions and responses to instructional decisions imposed on them by the others (i.e., the school, district or state level). These challenges function as perceptual filters that assist in identifying and assessing those aspects of a decision that would facilitate or hinder their ability to address these challenges in functional ways.

Evidence of this behavior is seen in most attempts at systemic reform. Teachers tend to assess decisions imposed on them along two dimensions: (1) *How* will this decision affect my ability to maintain order in my class (challenge 1)?; and (2) *What effect* will this decision have on my ability to motivate and teach students (challenge 2)? School-level decisions that undermine teachers' abilities to address the challenges of teaching are typically resisted. This resistance explains in part the conservatism of the teaching profession. However, school-level decisions that facilitate teachers' abilities to address these challenges are often embraced.

This governing logic can also be seen in the way teachers deal with other school influences. As threshold guardians of the classroom (Willower, 1985), teachers scan the school environment for influences that hinder or facilitate efforts to manage the challenges of teaching. To minimize the effects of hindering influences, teachers employ various buffering strategies. These strategies allow teachers to protect the classroom from influences that threaten autonomy and success. To capitalize on the energy and momentum of facilitating school-level influences, teachers employ strategies that allow them to bridge the classroom with the organization. In doing this, their ability to manage the challenges of teaching is enhanced.

The school-classroom relationship tends to become an issue for teachers under negative rather than positive conditions. Teachers' awareness of this relationship is heightened when they sense that decisions made outside of the classroom are hindering, restraining, or conflicting with work in the classroom. To be sure, effective teachers are adept at bridging with those aspects of the larger school that facilitate their efforts to manage classrooms. Yet teachers are more sensitive to those school-level dynamics that hinder work in the classroom. Stated somewhat differently, individuals tend to become conscious of the air-conditioner when it fails to cool (negative), rather than when it is cooling properly (positive). Teachers vary in their ability to identify and assess school-level decisions that would hinder or facilitate work in the classroom. Teachers also vary in their ability to effectively buffer and bridge school-level influences.

Decisions and the Dual-Authority Control Structure

To describe schools as professional bureaucracies (an oxymoron) is to recognize the dual authority-control structure that defines them. Each regulates teacher behavior. As noted above, professional authority for teachers is the authority associated with the norms of the teaching profession. Regardless of one's school, there is an authority associated with the profession that guides professional judgments among teachers. This authority is independent of any school or district. For some teachers, professional authority is the most important source of authority.

Bureaucratic authority is the authority associated with hierarchical position in the school or district. It is authority based on position or line authority. Power flows from top to bottom. Bureaucratic authority does not hold across school or districts. A principal or superintendent of one school or district does not have authority over teachers in another. In this way, schools are similar to hospitals and decisional dilemmas doctors face: To what extent will my decision be influenced by the administrators in this particular hospital or the larger medical profession?

Educational leaders should make decisions in light of the defining tension created by these competing authority-control structures. Though not always possible, they should avoid making decisions that pit professional against bureaucratic authority. Certain decisions can put teachers in the uncomfortable position of reconciling the competing demands of these authority-control structures. A leader that asks teachers to place the athletic interests of a school over the academic interests is an example of such a decision. While a long tradition of winning encourages this in a school, the norms of the teaching encourage an academic emphasis.

Decisions and the Teacher Autonomy Norm

The organizational context in which decisions are made also suggests that principals make decisions with the teacher autonomy norm in view. Rooted in the flexibility needed to address the varying needs of students, this norm is deeply embedded in the teaching profession (Lortie, 1975; Moore-Johnson, 1990).

Teachers are vigilant in warding off classroom encroachments that would diminish this autonomy. Educational leaders are wise to consider the impact of decisions and their decision-making style on teacher autonomy. To what extent will this decision facilitate or threaten this professional norm? This is not to suggest that leaders be held captive to this norm, only that they are aware and craft decisions accordingly. Over time, consistent and excessive encroachments on autonomy will alienate teachers, weaken their morale, and undermine leader legitimacy.

Decisions and Client-Control Demands

Closely aligned with teacher autonomy is the client-control theme and the extent to which this contextual feature influences the decision making process. When making decisions, the educational leader must be sensitive to this defining feature. Will this decision exacerbate the efforts of teachers and other school personnel to control the flow and movement of students? Will it enhance or threaten teachers' ability to maintain classroom order? How will this decision affect such things? Decisions that reduce the ability of school personnel to create and maintain a functional level of student control will be resisted because they prevent teachers from doing the work required in the classroom. Even if imposed from above and initially successful, such decisions cannot be sustained over time.

Decisions and the Stimulus-Overload Working Environment of Teachers

The stimulus-overload work environment that defines human service organizations also has implications for how decisions made by educational leaders are received by teachers in schools. As noted above, navigating this environment in functional and efficient ways are ongoing challenges for teachers. Decisions made at the school level are assessed by them in the context of this environment. How will it affect me? Will it contribute to the stimulus overload I am experiencing?

Proposed changes to instruction and classroom routines are also assessed using these criteria. Will this decision ameliorate or exacerbate this hindrance level? Will it require more effort, paper work and noninstructional time of me? If, for example, English teachers in a school are called upon to collectively engage in an extensive revision and realignment of departmental course-offerings and release- or compensation-time is not allocated for it—that is, teachers are not released from other pressing responsibilities—the chances of realizing an authentic collaborative effort will be greatly diminished. Will this time represent an *added demand* on teachers or will provisions be made by the leader to reduce temporal demands on teachers in other areas? Will teachers be freed from other obligations to provide time for collaboration? Decisions that add to the stimulus-overload environment of teachers will not be accepted and sustained over time.

On Decisions that Increase the Environmental Vulnerability of Teachers

As noted above, the public vulnerability of school organizations creates special problems for educators. School personnel find themselves dealing with a number of functional and dysfunctional environmental influences. The public nature of the educational enterprise makes these influences inevitable. Of particular importance are those disruptive influences that threaten the ability of school personnel to perform. If teachers at the core of the organization are to be fully engaged, work in the classroom must be buffered from these disruptive environmental influences (Goldring & Rallis, 1993; Ogawa, 1996; Johnson & Fauske, 2000).

While it is naive to think that all environmental influences can be eliminated, their disruptive effects can be minimized. Decisions that *increase* environmental vulnerability will eventually encounter resistance from school personnel. Will a decision to fire the football coach in midseason increase the public vulnerability of the school? Will this decision threaten the integrity of mechanisms used by the leader to buffer teachers from environmental disruption? When faced with a decision, leaders should consider the potential effects of the decision on teachers. An effort should be made to buffer personnel from disruptive influences.

QUESTIONS FOR REFLECTION AND DISCUSSION

- What was the stated purpose of this chapter and why was it included in this volume?
- What is meant by the "context" of a decision? Define and describe this context. Consider a recent decision made by a leader in your school or district. Describe the context of this decision. How did this context influence the decision process?
- What are "human service organizations?" What distinguishes them from the other?
- What is meant by the "organizational context" of a decision?
- Define and describe the distinguishing features of schools as human service organizations. As an educator, do these features resonate with your experience? Discuss.

- What does it mean to describe schooling and school organizations as "institutions?" What are some commonly held institutional myths associated with them? What role do these myths play in defining the decision-making context educational leaders face?
- In what ways are schools vulnerable to the public and environment? What are the implications of this vulnerability for the decisions the leader is called on to make? In what way are the decisions he or she is called on to make like a stage performance?
- What issues must the educational leader consider when dealing with decisions that focus on teachers, classrooms, or instruction?

CHAPTER FOUR

The Political Context of Decision Making in Educational Leadership

As noted in previous chapters, the decisions educational leaders are called on to make are not made in a vacuum; they are made in a *context*. Decisions both emerge and are defined by a context. A simple though familiar example from life in schools can be used to illustrate this.

The science faculty at Woods Cross High approaches the principal with a request for funds to further equip the new lab in the school. Highly supportive of the department and the success its students have enjoyed at the annual science fair, Darlia is torn. A shrinking tax-base has resulted in lean, conservative budgets throughout the district. Principals have been instructed to maintain the essentials while trimming the proverbial fat. Over the years, however, Darlia has stashed away a small cache of discretionary funds. From time to time, she has drawn from these funds to support successful and promising projects. The science faculty has developed a strong reputation for excellence in teaching through the years. They are among her most loyal supporters. The recent budget crisis, however, has decreased the flexibility once available to her. The money in the account is far short of the amount requested. Yet there is enough to get things rolling. Funding the department's request would not only diminish the funds in her account, but that would significantly reduce her flexibility to act in similar ways in the future. It could also create resentment from other departments. Nevertheless, she wants to find some way to reward their success. She is faced with a decision. What should she do?

This scenario provides an example of a typical decision faced by an educational leader. The decision subject is rather straightforward: *to fund or not to fund?* Making the decision, however, is complicated by several contextual factors. The decision is intimately tied to context.

Decision context is an abstract, multidimensional concept. It consists of a variety of factors that facilitate, constrain, and channel the decision-making process. To speak of *decision context* is to speak of such things as *the setting* in which a decision emerges and is addressed, *the specific features* of that setting, and *how these features interact* to define and influence the decision-making process. A decision cannot be considered apart from its context.

Dimensions of the decision context include but are not limited to factors such as the following: the (1) *cultural* (values, norms, traditions, artifacts), (2) *social* (individuals, groups, institutions, and social patterns), (3) *community* (values, arrangements, demographic mix), (4) *organizational* (see chapter 3 of this volume), (5) *informational* (quality, quantity, and availability of decision data), (6) *resource* (abundance vs. scarcity), (7) *temporal* (time horizons and constraints), and (8) *risk* dimensions of a decision. Many of these contextual features occur as givens; others are dynamic and variable. Certain features of the context are open to human manipulation; others are not. The decision context both influences and is influenced by the decision maker. Effective decision making proceeds from an awareness of these influences.

While there are similarities among the many decisions educational leaders are called on to make, the specific *constellation* of factors that defines the context of each varies. In this sense, no two decisions are alike. The specific context in which a decision is made distinguishes it as unique. Decision context is an important variable that complicates the decision-making process. Attention to the information embedded in it is critical for effective decision making.

PURPOSE AND OVERVIEW

This chapter explores a prominent dimension of the larger decision context: *the political context*. Though recognized as important by experienced educators, its legitimacy as a topic of study awaits full acceptance in many preparation programs. At least three reasons account for this hesitancy. Failure to recognize the legitimacy of politics as a curricular focus is in part due to the ideological agenda promoted by progressives in the early twentieth century (Cuban, 1988; Tyack & Cuban, 1995; Wirt & Kirst, 1997; Spring, 2005). The *apolitical myth* touted by these reformers was motivated by a desire to insulate public education from the political scandals of the day. Embracing Taylor's principles of 'scientific management' as the defining rule of governance, this ideology left no room for politics and the political. Some remain idealistically enamored with this normative myth. Though fading, its influence persists in our thinking.

Closely aligned with this orientation are the negative connotations associated with politics. For many, politics remains a *four-letter* word. Excessive preoccupation with the negative aspects of political behavior blinds many to the functional aspects of politics. Yet politics are not always negative. Furthermore, politics are ubiquitous. Where there are people, there are politics. Many refuse to accept these dual realities.

Finally, while the reality of politics has been acknowledged in the larger educational sector, the political nature and dynamics within schools has received less attention. In the words of Viteritti (1986), the politics *of* schools has co-opted attention away from the politics that occur *in* schools. Though a change has occurred in the literature, there remains hesitancy among some leaders to acknowledge and discuss *overtly* the political realities of decision making. This hesitancy is perhaps rooted in the negative connotations associated with politics. For others, such an attitude springs from a need to conceal the advantages gleaned from engagement in *real politik*, that is, to avoid the loss of legitimacy that potentially comes from overtly revealing one's political motives (while all the while remaining politically attentive and engaged).

In spite of these and other objections, our intent in this chapter is to explore the political dimensions and dynamics of the decision context and how these inform the decision-making process. Drawing from multiple literatures, we provide a working definition of politics. This is followed by an exploration of the origins and emergence of politics in social collectives and the play of power. We examine how decision-making is *the* focal referent for political behavior and provide three frameworks for mapping the multiple audiences and agendas that define decisions. The chapter concludes by identifying several political realities for educational decision makers.

POLITICS/MICROPOLITICS: WORKING DEFINITIONS

Numerous definitions of politics can by found in the social science literature (Johnson, 1999). Many represent variants of those offered by Lasswell (1958) and Easton (1965; 1979). Both define politics in the context of the authoritative allocation scarce yet valued resources. Politics is that set of human activities surrounding these allocative decisions. As such, politics reflect the efforts of mobilized interests to realize partisan values in decision outcomes (Gamson, 1968; 1990). These efforts are typically conflict-ridden. As Schattschneider (1975) observes, politics is the *socialization of conflict*. Individuals and groups coalesce, mobilize, contest, and negotiate *quid pro quo*—all in an attempt to influence decision outcomes (Cobb & Elder, 1983; Lindblom, 1993; Dahl, 1991; Kingdon, 1995). Based on this working definition, decision-making is the focal point of political behavior.

While traditional definitions of politics focus on individual and group activities in government, the literature on micropolitics describes similar activities *within* organizations, for example, business, educational, human service organizations and other types of human collectives (Baldridge, 1971; Mintzberg, 1983; Morgan, 1986; Ball, 1987; Blase, 1991; Pfeffer, 1981, 1992). Micropolitics refers to those activities and strategies used by organizational participants to influence decisions that allocate scarce but valued resources within the organization. It consists of overt and covert processes through which individuals and groups acquire and exercise power to protect, promote and realize vested interests (Ball, 1987). These interests are closely aligned with the technical, managerial and institutional levels which define most organizations (Thompson, 1967; Elmore & McLaughlin, 1988).

OBSERVATIONS ON THE ESSENCE
AND CHARACTER OF POLITICS

The political science, organizational theory, and social science literatures provide a context for analyzing the political dimensions of decision making. A number of observations follow from our working definition of politics. We offer these as narrative summaries. First, *politics is not a phenomenon confined to the halls of government.* It can be found in any social collective. For the purposes of this chapter, political activity can be observed at various levels of the education sector from state house to school house, from Congress to the classroom, and from organized interests to loosely-organized student groups.

Second, *the gravitating focus of most, if not all, political activity is decision.* Decisions provide *the* focal point of political activity. Political contests are animated by decision making. As a consequence, most if not all political activity centers on those specific locations and roles in the collective where important decisions are made. Political activities coalesce around these loci. Given the leader's role as decision maker, there is a political element associated with many of the decisions educational leaders are called on to make. The contests and struggles that *antedate* and *post*date these decisions are inherently political.

Third, *the point(s) in the collective at which decisions are made constitutes a decision-making arena.* This arena is typically a populated place animated by competing interests. It consists of a collection of individuals and shifting coalitions with varying agendas and timetables (Firestone, 1989; Malen, 1995). Issues that emerge and reach the decision agenda are the result of multiple inputs and events, some strategic, others fortuitous. At stake are value-laden decisions regarding the allocation of costs and benefits.

Whether granted *formally* (via appointment or election) or *informally* (through, for example, skilled political maneuvering), certain participants have been authorized to make decisions for the collective in this arena. At the school and district levels, board members, superintendents and building-level administrators serve as designated *authorities* (Gamson, 1968, 1990). There are also those who lack direct decision authority. Though lacking this authority, *partisans* (Gamson, 1968, 1990,) have a vested interest in the decisions made in the collective.

For a given decision it cannot be assumed that the interests of authorities and partisans are congruent. Neither can it be assumed that all partisans share the same interests. Efforts to reconcile competing interests are undertaken in a series of discrete yet interrelated transactions. The political processes that take place between authorities and partisans during the decision process are personified in a number of *public* and *private* transactions. *Public* transactions occur in the formal decision arena; *private* transactions take place behind the scenes, outside the formal arena among key decision participants and through informal, unofficial channels.

Furthermore, *conflict rooted in human diversity is the source of all political behavior.* Diversity along a number dimensions exists as a fact of life. The goals of individuals and groups vary; diverse interests have diverse interests. For any given decision, decision preferences likewise vary. As a result, the probability of perpetual agreement on all decisions within a social collective is *nil.* Where diversity exists, the potential for conflict is present. Conflicts of interest are an animating force in political behavior. Although the level of political intensity varies across decisions, partisans mobilize to influence in a manner consistent with and designed to realize these preferences in decision outcomes.

While the overt conflict that springs from diversity can be suppressed by the centralization of power (Morgan, 1986; Pfeffer, 1992), politics provides a means for addressing and resolving conflict. Politics—like diversity and conflict—is a fact of life to be anticipated and addressed in social collectives. Though there are times when politics reflect dysfunction, political activity should not always be seen as aberrant organizational behavior. Politics arise out of conflict. Conflict is rooted in diversity. All three are important facts of social life.

Fifth, *the content of decision—that which is being allocated—may be material or nonmaterial.* Many erroneously reduce the focus of politics to the allocation of valued *material* resources (e.g., benefits, property, programs, and money). However, politics is also concerned with the allocation of *nonmaterial* resources. Intense political struggles often ensue around the allocation of such nontangibles as values, symbols, world views, interpretation, preferred meanings (Foucault, 1969; Habermas, 1971; Ricoeur, 1974). Decisions regarding the allocation of nonmaterial, ideological phenomenon provide the backdrop for understanding material allocations. Both types of resources are the focus of political activity.

Finally, as implied in the definitions of politics and micropolitics, *exchange* describes social interaction in the political sphere. Multiple actors driven by diverse agendas interact in numerous ways to produce decision outcomes. Yet decision outcomes rarely reflect the full agendas of all competing interests. Compromise through *negotiated exchange* is the typical order of the day.

Social exchange is used by sociologists to describe human interaction (Homans, 1950; Blau, 1964; Cook & Emerson, 1984). Using concepts from microeconomics to describe interactive behavior, theorists argue that humans— as rationally driven entities—seek to maximize the benefits (material or nonmaterial) derived from exchanges with others. This logic can be used to describe political interactions. The idea of exchange is implied in Easton's (1965, 1979) classic theory of political systems. Human interaction in the political sphere involves negotiation and exchange among authorities and partisans in and around the decision-making arena.

Viewing politics as exchange facilitates our understanding of the decision context in two fundamental ways. First, it provides insight on how social collectives represent systems of negotiated order (Cyert & March, 1963). While such collectives vary in the extent the structure is formalized; organizations consist of individuals bound together by a series of exchange relationships. Second, an exchange perspective allows for the identification of individual entrepreneurs—formal authorities or resource brokers, or both—within social collectives. The political entrepreneur is that hypothetical individual who exploits opportunities to create, amass and exchange resources in the realization of an agenda (Deutsch, 1963; Salisbury, 1969; Moe, 1980; Kingdon, 1995). In exchanging resources with others, the entrepreneur provides others with incentives for sustained interaction.

These observations define in part the political context of decisions for educational leaders. Each is rearticulated as a bullet statement below:

- Political behavior occurs in all social collectives, not just governmental organizations.
- The focal point of most, if not all, political activity is the decision.
- Conflict rooted in human diversity is the source of political behavior.
- The point(s) in the social collective when decisions are made constitutes a *decision-making arena.*
- The content of decision—*that being allocated*—may be a material or non-material resource.
- Human interaction in the political sphere involves negotiation and exchange among authorities and partisans in and around decision-making arenas.

THE CENTRALITY AND NUANCED CHARACTER OF POWER IN POLITICAL BEHAVIOR

Absent from the discussion above are explicit references to the role played by power in the political process. The exercise of power is a cardinal assumption in politics. Politics is concerned with the overt and covert processes used by actors in and around the collective to acquire and exercise power. This power is directed at the realization of parochial interests in decision outcomes (Mintzberg, 1983; Morgan, 1986; Ball, 1987; Blase, 1991). Viewed in this manner, power is the *currency* of politics. To appreciate how the exercise of power defines the decision context, two brief digressions into the meaning and nuances of power are in order.

NOTED DEFINITIONS OF POWER

Power and its companion terms—control, influence and authority—are defining yet primitive concepts in the social sciences (Reynolds, 1971; Bacharach & Lawler, 1980). The literature focusing on these concepts is vast and transcends disciplines. Definitions and theories of power dot the conceptual landscape.

Of interest here are definitions of power offered by two notable theorists. Both provide insight into the acquisition and exercise of power in decision arenas.

Max Weber (1947) defined power in the context of three interrelated ideas: *decision preferences, resistance*, and *ability*. As a social phenomenon, power is something that occurs between two or more parties. It is *the capacity of an individual or group to realize desired ends in spite of resistance offered by others.* This ability becomes apparent in the context of resistance. Power exists only as potential until threatened or actual resistance is offered. Only then—and, as importantly, subject to the *willingness* of the one possessing the power—is the potency of this capacity revealed. Conceived in this manner, *power* and *the ability to resist this power* are two sides of the same conceptual coin. Likewise, both are variable. In a given social arena, the ability to offer and overcome resistance vary across actors. Some in the collective are more powerful than others; some in the collective can offer more resistance than others

Weber's emphasis on capacity begs the larger question as to its source: *What is the source of this ability? Where does this ability originate?* Beyond the threat or use of brute, illegitimate force, Weber argues that legitimate power—or *authority*—is rooted in one of three sources: *tradition, law*, or *charisma*.

Traditional authority is anchored in the established institutions, customs, and beliefs of the collective. For the sake of these traditions, obedience is owed to those whose power is rooted in this authority. This authority is exemplified in the following statement: "I have power over others because of my association with the Catholic Church."

Legal authority is based on enacted rules and laws established through legiti-mated procedures. The powerful are those to whom the law gives power. Legal authority is exemplified in the following claim: "As the individual appointed by the board to lead this district, I have legitimate power over those so designated by the law." Legal authority provides the ideological justification for bureaucracy. *Charismatic authority*, and the power that ensues from it, is authority granted to an individual based on the extraordinary personal qualities attributed to him or her by others. Those who possess charismatic authority possess power.

Weber's influence and conceptualization of power *as capacity* is seen throughout the social science literature. In the context of decision making, one's power in the decision arena is enhanced if seen by others as rooted in one or more of these bases of authority. Regardless of the source of one's power, it should be remembered that possessing power cannot be equated with the willingness to exercise this power.

Emerson (1962) provides a definition of power that remains influential in the social sciences. Building on Weber's definition of power as capacity, Emer-son raises a more fundamental issue by identifying the important social pivot on which capacity turns: *asymmetrical social relationships.* Whereas *preferences, resistance*, and *ability* provide the conceptual anchors for Weber's definition, Emerson defined power in terms of *relationship, desired object, exchange*, and *dependence.* According to Emerson, the primary root of power is not capacity but the *asymmetrical social relationship* that exists when one party in the relationship possesses something needed by the other (material or nonmaterial object) to realize its preferences. When this state of affairs exists, a relationship of *dependence* exists. When one possesses something on which others depend, a *power relationship* exists. For Emerson, power is rooted in and defined by dependence.

A rather straightforward example can be used to illustrate Emerson's definition. A party of three, yourself and two others (i.e., Sharon and Keith), gets lost at sea. If after several days, Sharon and your personal food supplies are depleted, your survival will then depend on Keith—the one individual in the party who anticipated this crisis by bringing an eight-month supply of food. This dependence creates an *asymmetrical* social relationship between you, Sharon, and Keith. Potentially, this is a *power* relationship. If so inclined, Keith could exploit this dependence to his advantage. In so doing, he would be exercising power over you and Sharon.

The social dynamic that follows from this asymmetrical relationship is what Emerson defines as *power.* Depending on what is at stake and valued by participants, an unequal distribution of power defines most decision arenas. The politics that follow from this unequal distribution of power can be explained by identifying (1) what scarce resources are being contested (*the what*), (2) which actor(s) possesses and monopolizes the distribution of these resources (*the who*), and (3) which actors are dependent on these resources and why (*the critical dependencies*). Several compelling lines of inquiry have emerged from Emerson's definition of power. The resource-dependence literature in organization theory provides an example of this (Crozier, 1964; Thompson, 1967; Pfeffer & Salancik, 1978; Johnson, 1998).

This review of competing definitions of power in a chapter on the politics of decision making naturally leads to questions regarding the utility of juxtaposing the ideas of Weber and Emerson. We suggest that both definitions highlight distinct yet related dynamics of the decision context. Awareness of each facilitates one's ability to map and navigate the decision terrain.

Weber reminds us that power is the ability to overcome and dominate others in social relationship. Beyond the use of brute force, this power is rooted in one of three sources: tradition, law, and charisma. On the other hand, Emerson reminds us that power is rooted in critical dependencies. A power relationship exists if one has *something* on which others depend. Power comes to those who amass and monopolize this something.

What is the relative distribution of power in a given arena? What are the bases of power? What is valued and being sought? What are the scarce resources? Who possesses and distributes these resources? What are the critical dependencies and asymmetrical power relationships created by the unequal distribution of resources? Who are the key actors? These questions follow from Weber and

Emerson's definitions of power and as such sensitize leaders to the political context of decision. Attention to them can lead to an informed decision response.

THE NUANCES OR FACES OF POWER

A handful of educational leaders remain unaware of the political context that defines the decisions they make. For those who are aware, some choose to look past the dynamics created by this context. Combining a commitment to rational planning with an appeal to the nonpartisan aspects of education, their hope is that all political elements of the process will be driven out and overcome. Such a perspective, we suggest, is hopelessly naive. Politics is endemic to all social collectives. We err to think otherwise.

We are likewise prone to err if, while examining the context of decisions, we are unduly occupied with *overt* manifestations of power. The exercise of power can assume multiple forms, from the subtle and hidden to the obvious. These underscore the nuanced, elusive and at times hidden quality of power. Though the literature supporting them is uneven, at least three forms of power can be identified (Lukes, 1974; Gaventa, 1980; Johnson, 2004; Malen, 1995).

The *pluralist* view of power draws attention to the *overt manifestations of power* in decision arenas. As the traditional focus of much of the political science literature (Dahl, 1991; Lindblom, 1993), this exercise of power is witnessed in efforts to *overtly* influence decisions deemed important to the collective. An example of this is seen in a superintendent's decision to deny the request of students to protest as district representatives the policies adopted by the city to not hire undocumented workers. As the formal authority in the district, the superintendent acts on the basis of this power by saying "no." The mobilization of parental support to protest the superintendent's decision at the upcoming board meeting represents a second example. With these examples, pluralist power is displayed in the form of maintenance and adversarial politics.

In contrast to the pluralist perspective, the *elitist view* draws attention to covert displays of power. It is seen in the efforts to exert power in less visible yet strategic ways. These include but are not limited to the following: defining and structuring decision agendas *and* the governance system to perpetuate advantage; suppressing dissent and suffocating demands in subtle, covert ways, and; rhetorically manipulating data, meanings and the positions of others to promote the agenda of ruling elites (Bacharach & Baratz, 1970; Majone, 1989; Johnson, 1999). As implied its name, elite expressions of power are associated with those who advocate and critique elite theories of governance (Mills, 1956; Michels, 1962; Bacharach & Baratz, 1970; Freire, 1973; Pareto, 1984). The decision of the superintendent to leave students' request *off* the meeting agenda or to place it at the *end* of the agenda (knowing that time will expire before it is discussed) are examples of the covert yet calculated use of power. A decision to add an item to this same agenda after the deadline for new items has passed exemplifies a similar use of power.

The third face of power is less conscious and visible than the two described above. Consistent with its Marxian roots, the *radical* exercise of power focuses on how class, ethnic, and gender interests shape attitudes and aspirations through the subtle processes of socialization and indoctrination (Foucault, 1969; Lukes, 1974; Gaventa, 1980). These processes occur in ways that are subconscious and elusive. As a result, they often go unchallenged.

The potency of this face of power lies in its ability to control those processes, institutions, and ideas that define reality for others. Of special interest are the ways that dominant interests impose reified meanings that perpetuate advantage thus co-opting the meanings that arise from marginalized subcultures *and* potential resistance. Radical power defines what is to be taken as legitimate. It defines aspirations and expectations in taken-for-granted yet potent ways.

Because of the powerlessness they experience in the collective, marginalized populations (those silenced, denied voice and/or disadvantaged by current processes and structures) tend to have a heightened sensitivity to radical power. Once awakened to its essence, marginalized voices use the oppression these arrangements impose as a rallying cry for emancipation.

In describing politics as the contests which emerge in decision arenas, radical power justifies the distinction made earlier between the material and nonmaterial allocations that result from these decisions. A concern with radical power motivates us to look beyond material allocations to those nonmaterial yet consequential values, world views, ideologies, definitions and assumptions also being allocated (Foucault, 1969; Habermas, 1971; Ricoeur, 1974; McIntyre, 1989). Whose interests are served by these allocations? Whose interests are *not* being served? Who is advantaged and disadvantaged by these allocations?

This examination of the nuances power underscores the need for leaders to be attuned to the obvious and less obvious faces of power in decision arenas. In addition to the easily recognizable pluralist face, there are the less obvious elitist and radical faces of power. Discerning theses requires knowledge, skill and experience. Successfully addressing them calls for an ethically-guided response sensitive to those individuals or groups at the margins of power.

CONCEPTUALIZING DECISION STAKES AND STAKEHOLDERS

Seeking to decide what items to trim from her budget for the upcoming year, a superintendent in a large district once observed to the board that behind every line item stood an identifiable set of interests. For each item, there were individuals and groups who benefitted from its inclusion. Reducing or removing the item from the budget would result in the reduction or removal of benefit. Loss of benefit could in turn invite political mobilization, opposition and a challenge to leader legitimacy. This observation by the superintendent reflects her sensitivity to the political context which defines the budgeting process.

In a similar fashion, there is an identifiable set of interests associated with many of the decisions educational leaders are called to make. For these decisions, there are those individuals and groups who stand to gain and those who stand to lose; those who will be advantaged by the decision and those who will be disadvantaged. This allocation of advantage-disadvantage, gain-loss has been described by Schattschneider (1975) as the *mobilization of bias*. Many decisions educational leaders make are *biased* in the sense that they advantage certain individuals and/or groups over others. These same decisions *mobilize* this bias by allocating resources toward advantaged groups and away from others.

Viewing decisions in this manner defines the decision-making process as a moral and political endeavor. Knowing that decisions regarding the allocation of resources will have a profound affect on lives of students—society's most valuable yet vulnerable population—underscores the moral context of decision making. Knowing that these same decisions may be challenged by others vested in the system highlights the *political realities* of the decision-making process. These realities call for an additional skill: the ability to discern decision stakes and stakeholders. Just as it is wise for educational leaders to assess the distribution and sources of power in the decision arena, it is imperative that educational leaders identify the stakeholders and stakes embedded in a specific decision. The two go hand-in-hand.

Several conceptual and heuristic devices can be employed to facilitate the conceptualization of decision stakeholders. We offer three for consideration. The first provides a means for conceptualizing competing interests at the *individual level*, the second at the *group level* and the third at the *environmental level*. These frameworks are purposely pitched at levels of abstraction divorced from specific decision content and arenas in order to facilitate their use across decision contexts. Our intent is not to be exhaustive. Rather it is to provide examples of conceptual tools that can assist in identifying decisions stakes and stakeholders at various levels.

Individual interests in the decision arena—A logical place to begin thinking about the decision stakes and stakeholders is with the interests the individual brings to the decision arena. The ideas of Morgan (1986) and Ball (1987) provide insight into thinking about these interests. Whereas Morgan offers a typology for conceptualizing the interests of individuals in *any* organization, Ball's typology focuses on the interests of individual teachers within educational organizations. Synthesizing the ideas of these theorists to create a hybrid typology, it is reasonable to suggest that the interests of individual organizational participants are defined by three interconnected domains: *task-vested*, *self-career*, and *extramural* interests. These are captured in the Venn diagram labeled Figure 4.1.

Task or *vested interests* are those interests connected with the specific task or role in the organization the individual is asked to perform. When assessing decisions made by others in the organization, this set of interests leads individuals to

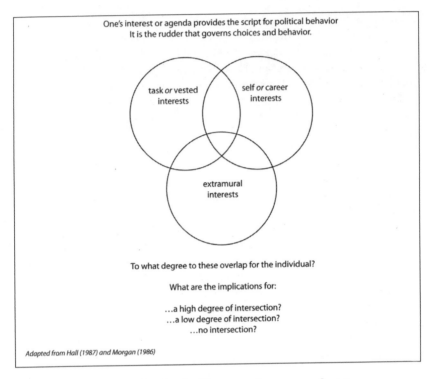

One's interest or agenda provides the script for political behavior
It is the rudder that governs choices and behavior.

task *or* vested
interests

self *or* career
interests

extramural
interests

To what degree to these overlap for the individual?

What are the implications for:

...a high degree of intersection?
...a low degree of intersection?
...no intersection?

Adapted from Hall (1987) and Morgan (1986)

FIGURE 4.1. Typology of Individual Interests: Interests as Script

ask: How will this decision facilitate or hinder my ability to successfully perform this task? To what extent will this decision expand or diminish the autonomy I enjoy? Will this decision reduce or increase critical resource dependencies for me? Most people are inclined to support decisions that facilitate task success, expand autonomy and reduce critical dependencies. Tasks interests are a matter of contention between individuals, especially when resources are scarce and promotion prospects limited.

Beyond one's task in the organization, *self* or *career interests* are defined by the aspirations the individual has for his or her career. The temporal horizon of career interests is longer than the more immediate task interests. Task interests may or may not be compatible with one's career interests. Career interests lead the individual to assess organizational decisions along the following lines: Is this decision consistent or inconsistent with my career goals? Will this decision facilitate or hinder me in realizing these goals? Individuals are more inclined to support organizational decisions that are consistent with and facilitate the achieving of career goals.

Most people are also driven by interests that lie outside task and career domains. These interests provide an additional script for individual behavior. Morgan identifies such interests as *extramural*. Extramural interests arise from one's commitments, relationships, endeavors and associations outside of work. For some, these interests are more important than task and career interests. When weighing an organizational decision, extramural interests will lead the individual to ask questions such as the following: Will this decision hinder or facilitate the pursuit of my extramural interests? What will this decision require me to relinquish? What will free me to do? To what extent is it consistent with these interests?

Though not exhaustive in what they claim to capture, Morgan (1986) and Ball (1987) provide a useful guide for conceptualizing decision interests at the individual level. Several qualifications to this model are worth noting. First, while there appears to be an identifiable center of gravity that defines each interest-domain as unique, these domains should not be taken as mutually exclusive. The boundaries between them can at times be quite vague. Second, it is the influence of these domains *in combination* that provides the animating script for interest definition. To be sure, the relative strength of each domain in defining one's interest varies across individuals, yet it is these domains that define one's interests. The mix of interests that defines the individual provides the political script from which decisions are made and assessed.

Furthermore, the extent to which these interest-domains intersect varies across individuals. It is rare that one finds an individual for whom these domains share no points of intersection (the divided and conflicted individual); it is equally rare to find one for whom these domains are congruent (the one-person organization and owner perhaps). It is reasonable to suggest a positive relationship between the degree of intersection between interest and domain experienced by an individual and his or her willingness to voice these interests as a stakeholder in the decision-making arena.

Finally, much like the interests of identifiable *groups* in the organization, the interests of *individuals* in the organization vary. It is reasonable to suggest that the level of interest-domain intersection experienced by an individual and his or her willingness to voice these interests as a stakeholder in the decision-making arena are positively related.

GROUP INTERESTS IN THE DECISION ARENA

Not only do interests vary across organizational groups, Ball and Morgan's ideas suggest that there are variations of interest to be found across individuals within these groups. The second analytic tool we offer for is rooted in the ideas of Parsons (1960), Thompson (1967), and Elmore and McLaughlin (1988). Its focus on multilevels within the organization draws attention to *group interests*. The multilevels of the organization and the interests which define each are presented in Figure 4.2.

Note: Work in the organization can be divided into three distinct hierarchical levels. Each is defined by its own set of purses and tasks. Motivating incentives vary across levels.

Institutional Level

The institutional level functions *to generate legitimacy and support* from the organization's internal and external environments. Individuals working at this level seek to garner the "right" from the environment to command resources and to determine how to shape the demands of competing constituencies into an agenda that builds *political support*.

Managerial Level

Workers at the managerial level work to *service, control and administer the technical level* by: 1) mediating between the technical level and the environment, and; 2) procuring the resources necessary for carrying out the organization's core task.

Technical Level

Workers at the technical level of an organization actually *perform of the organization's core task*. Since the concern at this level is efficiency, preoccupation with creating an environment of certainty is of foremost concern. In educational organizations, teachers work at this level.

FIGURE 4.2. Three Hierarchical Levels of the Organization and Defining Interests

According to Parsons (1967), work in the organization can be divided into three hierarchical, interdependent levels: the *technical, managerial,* and *institutional*. There are qualitative breaks in the continuity of line-authority between levels. These breaks are a function of defining tasks and purposes. As a basis for distinguishing one organizational level from another, these tasks or purposes play a significant role in defining the agendas, interests and working incentives of each group. Just as the tasks or purposes of these groups vary, the agenda and interests of these groups vary. These agenda and interests inform the working political scripts of each level. These scripts define in part the stakes held by these stakeholders in the decision arena.

The *technical level* of an organization is oriented to the performance of the organization's core task. The core task is that task in the organization that defines its identity. In educational organizations, the core task is teaching. Those who work at the technical level in schools are teachers. This work is done primarily in classrooms. Since the concern at this level is efficiency, creating an environment of teaching certainty and autonomy are foremost concerns.

It is these concerns that define the primary working incentives and political scripts of teachers. As noted in the previous chapter, teachers' collective interest in decisions made by those at other levels are defined by concerns for teaching efficiency, classroom autonomy and material interests (supplies, salaries and benefits). Generally speaking, teachers will support decisions that increase material resources in the classroom, facilitate teaching efficiencies, and protect teacher autonomy. They are likely to oppose decisions that do not.

The *managerial level* of the organization leads, administers, controls and services the technical level by (1) mediating between the technical level and its environment, and (2) procuring the resources necessary for carrying out these technical functions (Thompson, 1967). District and school administrators populate the managerial level in educational organizations. Organizational maintenance and development are the defining challenges. According to Elmore and McLaughlin (1988), animating incentives at the managerial level are partly professional, bureaucratic, and political. Success means turning conflicting demands into concrete organizational fixes that create stability for teachers at the technical core. This comes by juggling the competing demands of those in the environment with those in the organization and professional practice. Generally speaking, those at the managerial level approach and support decisions that contribute to this definition of success.

The *institutional level* functions to generate legitimacy and support from the organization's environment. Individuals at this level seek to garner the "right" from the environment to command of various resources to do the work of the organization. The primary challenge for institutional personnel is to determine how to shape competing environmental and organizational demands into an agenda that builds political support (e.g. visibility, popularity, and reelection) Those working at this level are driven by the need to establish, maintain, and expand legitimacy with various publics. The goal is the creation of political legitimacy and capital.

Board members and superintendents occupy roles at the institutional level. For these individuals, success comes through shaping the demands of competing constituencies into an agenda that builds one's political legitimacy and capital. Decisions that support these goals are supported by institutional-level personnel. Decisions that hinder these goals are not.

Parson's framework provides one means for conceptualizing decision stakes and stakeholders. Though the line separating them is ambiguous (particularly the managerial and institutional), these levels can be discerned in most educational organizations. As importantly, these levels provide the working political scripts (bases) for three distinct interest groups in the organization. For any given decision, representatives of these competing interests are likely to be found the decision arena.

Using a similar logic, there are other divisions in educational organizations that lend themselves to the emergence of common interests. These include but are not limited to structural and cultural divisions such as the following: department or academic discipline, grade-level, line vs. staff authority, cosmopolitans vs. locals, union vs. nonunion, racial distinctions, gender distinctions, younger vs. older, faculty vs. students, and competing student subcultures.

Environmental Interests in the Decision Arena

A third framework for thinking about decision stakes and stakeholders focuses on those interests found in the *environment* of the school organization. As noted in chapter 3, all organizations exist in an environment. Organizations such as schools influence and are influenced by this larger environment.

To speak of environmental constituents in monolithic, homogenous terms is to mask the diverse and competing demands that exist among them. In education, there is not one public, but a number of publics to which educational leaders must attend. The stakes and level of involvement in the decision arena vary within and across these publics. With the intent of providing the reader with a straightforward and manageable means for conceptualizing these publics, it is reasonable to classify them into four broad yet overlapping categories.

Geographic Publics

The most obvious publics in and around the decision arena are those geographical publics and patrons in the immediate environs of the school. These include but are not limited to the larger community, district, and attendance area served by the school. Included within these geographic areas are numerous neighborhoods, households, parents, and businesses. All vary along a number of important social and cultural dimensions. The homogeneity-heterogeneity of these publics varies across districts and schools.

Of these geographic entities, parents of students served by the school or district are primary. Relationships between professional educators and parents revolve around two key issues (Malen, 1995): (1) the demand for parental voice, and (2) the demand for the "adequate and appropriate" distribution of educational services. As a whole, educators adhere to the deeply-held belief that professionals should make school policy and parents should follow (Davis, 1980; 1987; Moles, 1987). While parents generally accept this governing assumption as normative, it does not go unchallenged by the public. For those decisions perceived to exceed the ambiguously defined zone of tolerance (Barnard, 1938; Simon, 1976, 1991; Hoy & Tarter, 2004;), parents vociferously reassert their demands and challenge this premise. Parental demands can threaten the stability and legitimacy of both leader and school. Tensions regarding parental involvement, concerns about excessive intrusion by outsiders, conflicts over the appropriate distribution of educational resources and nagging uncertainties about the school's ability to withstand sustained public scrutiny are political realities that define the decision context for educational leaders.

These realities can neither be ignored nor fully controlled. To some extent, however, they can be managed. Effective management begins with an awareness of parental stakes and tensions that define the professional-patron relationship in education. Not all parents are willing to voice demands. Not all are political active. Of those parents who are willing and active, not all are equally effective in making these demands known. All draw attention to the leader's ability as decision-maker to discern within the parental public the politically active from the inactive, the politically effective from the ineffective and the powerful from the less powerful.

Economic Publics

The *economic public* is that part of the public that finances education. For any given decision, the primary (not sole) demand of taxpayers is efficiency. Broadly defined, efficiency refers to the act of minimizing inputs while maximizing outputs or of minimizing costs while maximizing gains, or both. Stewardship, accountability, responsibility and thrift are defining metavalues for the economic public. In addition to issues concerning tax burdens and revenue distribution, the demands of this public in the decision arena focus on defining *what* educational leaders will be held accountable for and *how* this accountability will be assessed.

Governmental Publics

In addition, there exists in the environment of schools the *governmental public*. For districts this public consists of federal, state and local authorities within and outside of the education sector. For schools this public consists of these entities *and* the district office. Generally speaking, these governments are interested in seeing that mandates, program guidelines, civil rights, special court orders (e.g., discrimination, equitable funding, specific programs), and other items of interest are adequately addressed. The demands made on local educational leaders by this public are an important part of the decision-making context. They combine to create a "web of policies" within which schools are situated. These demands circumscribe the decisions educational leaders are called on to make.

MARGINALIZED PUBLICS

Though often unrepresented and lacking the access to voice demands, the *marginalized public* exists in the decision environment of schools. This public consists of a variety of groups who, for various reasons, stand at the margins of power (e.g., identifiable class, ethnic, gender, racial, and religious groups) many of whom represent minority populations. This public is bound together by a commitment to social and distributive justice: the moral and political effort to order human relationships in accord with that which is deemed moral, right, or fair. Though unified in their claims for social justice at an abstract level, the specific demand foci of subgroups within this larger public can vary widely. The hidden faces of power that deny these groups full participation in the decision arena perpetuate restricted access. Beyond mere rhetorical nods and recognition, educational leaders should morally commit themselves to an awareness of the silenced demands of these groups. This commitment should further lead to the identification and elimination of those elements in the decision arena that restrict access *and* to the championing of these marginalized voices.

IDEOLOGICAL PUBLICS

Ideology refers to that relatively coherent system of ideas or values held by members of an identifiable social class or group (Mannheim, 1936; Kristol, 1995; Lowi, 1995). These ideas and values provide the justification for the group's identity and play a central role in defining its political interest. Though framed and historically contested in a variety of ways (e.g., communism vs. capitalism, federal vs. state rights, etc.), ideology has found its most recent expression in the familiar terms liberalism and conservatism.

As implied by the Latin roots, liberalism and conservatism are concepts used to describe one's attitude toward change (*liberalis*–"free, freedom"; *com* + *servare*–"to keep, guard or preserve"). In and of themselves, the referent of change for these concepts is unstated. In the context of ideology, these concepts have come to define two ends of an ideological continuum that permeate much of the political discourse in the West. Two referents can be used to bring these contrasting ideologies into relief. Public debates regarding the legislation of *markets* and *morality* exemplify ideologies that currently dominate the American political landscape (Kristol, 1995; Lowi, 1995).

When used in reference to markets, conservatives seek to "protect" freedom in the marketplace. This sense of protectionism translates into an attitude that seeks to "guard" the market from excessive government intervention. Conservatives resist change that challenges this freedom and those advantaged by it. On

the other hand, liberals advocate market change. Concerned with the dispari-
ties perpetuated by market arrangements, liberals seek greater governmental
involvement to ensure social justice through the reduction of social inequities.
Regarding morality, conservatives seek to "guard" or "protect" traditional morality (as defined primarily by the Judeo-Christian ethic); liberals, on the other
hand, seek freedom from traditional moral constraints. While other change
referents could be used to exemplify the competing ideologies currently found
in the public square, markets and morality are primary referents for much of
this discourse. Educational issues rooted in both referents provide the basis for
the mobilization of various ideological interest groups.

A measure of ideology defines the agenda and political activities of most
interest groups. The extent to which ideology serves as the defining incentive
for interest group formation and maintenance, however, varies considerably from
group to group. At one extreme in the education sector is the *Eagle Forum*, an
ideologically defined organization concerned with the decline of morality in
public education. At the other extreme is the local teachers union, which is
less concerned about ideological issues and more concerned about promoting
the status and material interests of its teachers.

Ideology exerts both a positive and negative influence on interest group
behavior. On the positive side, it provides the initial impetus for organizing,
unifying, and animating an interest group toward action. It breeds a sense of mission, ties the individual to the group, generates an *esprit de corps*, discourages exit,
quells voice (Hirschman, 1970), and in sum, provides a powerful mechanism
for mobilization and unification (Mintzberg, 1983). However, much like the
leading character in a Greek tragedy, these strengths are potentially its greatest
weakness. Just as ideology animates and promotes group unity, it can likewise
animate and promote disunity. The existence of conflicting ideologies within a
group functions to divide. Debates on issues in education such as vouchers, sex
education, evolution-creationism, and prayer in schools are ideologically driven.
These issues—and the presence of competing interests contesting them—create
the potential for an emotionally-driven, highly-charged decision context.

While the analytic tools outlined above are useful for discerning decision stakes and stakeholders, they are not to be taken as exhaustive. They
are offered as exemplars. Other strategies for framing these interests are possible. Given the specific decision, subject, and context, certain tools may be
of greater benefit to the decision maker than others. Regardless of how one
chooses to identify decision stakes and stakeholders, it is wise to think in terms
of multiple levels. We have described a set of analytic tools for conceptualizing interests at three levels: the individual, group (intraorganizational), and
environmental level. In many decisions faced by the educational leader, the
probability of having multiple stakeholders at multiple levels is high. These

stakeholders vary in the levels of power and access they enjoy with authorities in the decision-making arena.

POLITICAL REALITIES FOR EDUCATIONAL LEADERS AS DECISION MAKERS

This chapter has explored the political character and dynamics of the decision context and how these affect the decision-making process. Drawing from multiple literatures, we began by providing a working definition of politics. *Politics* refers to those activities and strategies used by organizational constituents to influence decisions through which scarce, but valued resources are allocated, or to influence values in the larger collective. Several observations regarding politics were offered. Foremost is the realization that the focal point of most if not all political activity is the decision. The location(s) in the organization where primary decisions (Barnard, 1938; Simon, 1976, 1991) are made is known as a decision arena.

We have likewise explored the central role power plays in political behavior. The acquisition and exercise of power are cardinal assumptions in politics. Yet we err if we become unduly occupied with overt manifestations of power. There is a multifaceted, nuanced quality to power that often goes unrecognized. The exercise of power can be obvious or subtle and quiescent. Distinctions between the pluralist, elitist, and radical faces of power underscore the elusive, hidden quality that power can assume.

We have also argued that there is an identifiable set of interests associated with many of the decisions educational leaders are called on to make. For most decisions, there is a *mobilization of bias*: those who stand to gain and are advantaged by the decision and those who stand to lose. As means for identifying decision interests, three frameworks for identifying stakes and stakeholders were outlined. Each focuses on a different level of analysis: the individual, organizational group, and environmental level.

While other aspects of the decision-making process could be examined, the features outlined here are rudimentary and sufficient for providing one with a feel for the political character of decision making. Considered together, they draw attention to the influence of this context on the decision-making process. We conclude by highlighting several political realities that face the educational leader as decision maker: the fundamental political character of educational organizations, political variables at play in the decision context, and the necessity of developing political skill.

FUNDAMENTAL POLITICAL CHARACTER OF EDUCATIONAL ORGANIZATIONS

To begin with, the fundamental *political character* of educational organizations should be recognized. Educational organizations are mini polities, nested in multilevel governmental structures. These organizations are charged with providing a variety of public services and are dependent on diverse taxpaying constituencies. Confronted with contested ends, uncertain means, competing demands, perennial resource shortages, uncertain supports, and value-laden issues, schools face difficult, and at times controversial allocative choices.

While these defining features do not mean that conflict is inevitable, they do suggest that conflict is an endemic feature of educational organizations. Given that politics is evoked by conflict, politics as a phenomenon is something that is a reality in schools. The focal point of much if not all of this activity is the decision. Common political flashpoints in educational organizations include decisions regarding the ends, means, and the distribution of valued services.

POLITICAL VARIABLES AT PLAY IN THE DECISION CONTEXT

Regarding the political context of decision, several aspects of the decision-making process are worth noting. First, most decisions made by leaders are consequential for others. Although the number of individuals or groups affected varies by decision, there are stakes and stakeholders associated with most decisions the educational leader is called on to make. Decisions vary in the extent to which they affect and are consequential for others. Some decisions affect many people and publics, others do not.

Second, the level of political intensity varies across decisions. Decisions vary in the extent to which they are politically charged, generate political activity, and/or animate political action and response. This intensity is a function of several factors, some of which include the following: (1) the number of individuals or groups affected by the decision; (2) the extent to which the decision is ideologically laden and/or pits one deeply-held value against another; (3) the redistributive character of the decision, that is, the extent to which it involves taking something from one population and giving it to another (e.g., from the haves to the have-nots); and (4) the extent to which the decision requires a change in historically rooted and sustained behavioral patterns.

Regardless of the level of interests being considered—individual, group or environmental interests—decision stakeholders also vary along a number of important dimensions. For example, stakeholders vary in the extent to which they are conscious and aware of the political dynamics of the decision context. Some are quite attuned to political dynamics, while others exhibit sensitivities that border on naïveté. Groups vary to the extent that they recognize or are conscious of what is at stake for them in a given decision.

For those who are aware, stakeholders vary along the following dimensions: (1) the specific interests and demands made on decision makers; (2) the access they enjoy to decision authorities; (3) the relative power they enjoy in the decision arena; (4) the willingness to act on these demands; and (5) the ability to act on these interests and demands (that is the ability

to organize, mobilize, and voice decision interests and demands). The distribution, acquisition, and exercise of power between and among actors is an
important part of the political reality of schools. For any given decision, the
unequal distribution of power among stakeholders in the decision arena(s)
is the norm, not the exception. This power can assume multiple forms and
range from the obvious to the subtle.

REALITIES FOR THE EDUCATIONAL LEADER AS DECISION MAKER

In light of these givens, it is incumbent upon leaders to acknowledge the political
realities of decision making. For those who ignore them, politics remains the
proverbial "elephant in the room," a critical decision component of profound
interests that goes "officially" unrecognized. Yet politics and the political
processes of decision constitute legitimate topics of discussion for educational
leaders. There is a need to address the political realities of the decision context
head-on. This means acknowledging and attending to these political dynamics
as needed while remaining true to one's core beliefs as an educational professional. Seasoned practitioners recognize and accept these realities.

There are also important political skills that should be developed by educational leaders. Political skill in decision making means having the ability to
identify, navigate, and mediate the competing agendas of multiple interests.
Principals vary in the political skill they possess. Key components of this skill
include but are not limited to the following, having the ability to:

- *recognize* the diversity-conflict-politics dynamic and decisions likely to
  animate it;
- *define* and *map* decision stakes and stakeholders in and around the organization;
- *identify* the sources and distribution of power in the decision arena;
- *identify* those marginalized interests who lack the resources, power and
  access to act but whose educational needs are nonetheless legitimate and
  compelling;
- *identify* the common ground across competing interests that can lead to a
  workable solution;
- *know when* to give and take, when to engage in maintenance as opposed to
  adversarial politics, when to avert, contain or expand conflict with others;
  and
- *stand by* one's professional principles.

To the extent that they possess these component skills, educational leaders
vary in their ability to successfully map and navigate the political aspects of
the decision-making process.

It is likewise prudent for educational leaders to recognize their *role* as decision makers in the organization and the *perspective* they bring to decisions. On
the one hand, educational leaders are in positions to define and control the

decision agendas for themselves and others. The formal authority they possess allow for this. On the other hand, leaders are often frustrated in the decision process. Held hostage by various publics, they are frequently caught in the cross fire of the following multiple, conflicting demands: legislative mandates, union contracts, competing expectations, the learning needs of students, and personal conviction (Malen, 1995). Given their position, formal leaders are inclined to protect managerial prerogatives by controlling the agenda content, information flow, and interactions with others in the decision process (Gronn, 1984; Ball, 1987). This is done by recruiting supporters to important positions, forming coalitions with trusted allies, and blocking unwanted decisions through selective nonimplementation. As gatekeepers, educational leaders can filter demands and affect decisions in potent ways.

Beyond the politics associated with the substantive outcome of any single decision, there is an additional politics that should be noted here. It is the politics of personal legitimacy associated with the leader as decision maker. As noted in the previous chapter on organizational context, public vulnerability and the continual search for environmental legitimacy are defining features of human service organizations. These dual realities lend a life-on-the-stage quality to the leader's role. The vulnerability created by this glass-bowl existence provokes an ongoing need for the leader to attend to his or her legitimacy with others. The zone of public confidence is not without limits. It is something that leaders must vigilantly nurture and manage. Critical to the leader's stage performance is the ability to nurture and bank legitimacy capital with various audiences. When making decisions, this means attending to others' perceptions of one's competence. Legitimacy comes with perceived competence. Personal management also means attending to public perceptions regarding the boundaries of one's decision authority. Educational leaders interact with the publics they serve within a *zone of tolerance* (Barnard, 1938; Simon, 1976; Hoy & Tarter, 2004). Though the width of this zone varies across people, publics, and time, leaders who exceed this zone risk the loss of legitimacy. For the educational leader, personal and professional legitimacy are at stake in the decisions he or she makes.

CAVEATS ON ANALYZING THE POLITICAL CONTEXT OF DECISION

The political realities of decision making in school organizations underscore the need for educational leaders to be politically savvy. As one seeks to develop his or her skills in this area, however, there are three important factors to consider. We offer these as concluding caveats to our discussion.

First, it is important to understand that many aspects of the decision-making process—particularly the political element—are difficult if not impossible to control. Although there are times when these factors can be controlled, they are typically beyond the *complete* control of the decision maker. Given this, we suggest that the leader avoid the misguided delusion of decision omnipotence. The political element is not necessarily something to be controlled, but managed. From a practical standpoint, this means channeling the political dynamics of decision toward functional ends when possible. Understanding these dynamics and having the ability to map the political terrain contribute to the successful management of the decision process. This knowledge and skill place the leader in a proactive decision stance.

Second, hypersensitivity to the political context can have a debilitating effect on the leader as decision maker and the larger decision process. It is all too easy to read motives into actions that completely subvert the meanings and intentions of actors and stakeholders (Ball, 1987). It is wise to remember that not all organizational actions are motivated by political intent. Further, not all individuals are politically aware and engaged. Excessive sensitivity to the political framework can lead one to erroneously impute political intent where none exists (Morgan, 1986). Conversely, excessive preoccupation with the political lens as the way of framing invites increased politicization within the collective. When one understands social organizations as political systems, one is more likely to behave politically. As with other aspects of decision making, one can hyper-analyze the political context of decision making to the point of paralysis.

Finally, it is important to remember that the political context of a decision is but one of several dimensions that define the decision context. Decisions are not made in a vacuum; they are made in a context. These dimensions must be viewed holistically and handled with skill and artistry. To unduly attend to one dimension at the expense of others is to overlook the organic interrelatedness of the larger decision context.

QUESTIONS FOR REFLECTION AND DISCUSSION

- What connotations come to mind when you hear the word "politics" and why?
- Provide your own working definition of "politics." Compare and contrast it with ours.
- Discuss the differences and similarities between the politics in governments and organizations.
- To what extent are politics of decision making recognized as a legitimate area of study in your preparation program? To what extent are political decision skills addressed in it?
- What does it mean to say that the focal point of most if not all political activity is decision?
- What are the origins of politics and political behavior? What animates these activities?
- Define the concept *decision arena*. How is it used in reference to the decision context?

- Provide examples of specific *material* and *nonmaterial* resource allocations that have been recently allocated in your school or district, department, or university.
- How can political behavior be conceptualized as social exchange? What is being exchanged?
- Provide your own definition of power. Compare you definition with our definitions.
- Distinguish the three faces of power discussed in this chapter. Provide specific examples from your experience of each. How do these nuances of power affect decision making?
- Consider a decision recently made in your organization of which you have considerable knowledge. Using the three analytic frameworks for mapping decision stakes and stakeholders, construct a working list of these decision stakeholders and their stake in the decision.
- What role do you play in attending to the needs of marginalized publics? Provide two examples of decisions in which the needs were attended to *and* ignored. Discuss the moral or ethical implications of these decisions. What could be done differently?
- How can one overattend to decision politics? Provide an example in which this occurred. How can one attend to political dynamics without exacerbating the decision process?

PART III

The Decision Maker:
Logic, Intuition, Data Use, and Skill

CHAPTER FIVE

The Logic of Decision Making: Problematizing Decision Assumptions and Examining Inferential Leaps

If decision making lies at *the heart* of the administrative endeavor, then information or data is *the lifeblood* of the decision-making process. Regardless of the form, amount, validity, or means by which these data are collected, decisions are made using data. Yet much recent attention has been given to the need for *data-driven* decisions. In the educational sector, leaders have been called on to act and improve their skills as *data-driven* decision makers (Johnson, 2002).

In one sense this call is misleading. It suggests that decisions made by educational leaders in the past have somehow been devoid of data and that the time has now come to incorporate data into the decision-making process. It also suggests that decisions made by educational leaders have been driven by something other than data: whim, caprice, or perhaps a random cosmic force. Though bordering on the absurd, conclusions such as these follow from a misunderstanding of the descriptor *data-driven*. Apart from the arbitrary choices one might make, data drives the decision-making process. To say that decisions are *data-driven* is thus a descriptive redundancy. When used to describe the decision-making process, we need a more adequate definition or alternative set of descriptors.

In another sense, the call for more *data-driven* decisions means something quite different when placed in the context of the accountability movement that currently defines American education. An expression of this movement is found in legislation enacted by Congress at the behest of President George W. Bush. *The No Child Left Behind Act of 2001* (NCLB) represents a significant (though not uncontested) policy statement of educational accountability in the United States. Among other things, it calls on states to (1) set measurable learning goals for all students in public education; (2) allocate resources toward the achievement of these goals; (3) regularly assess student and school progress toward goal realization; and (4) hold schools and districts accountable for the learning and achievement of all students.

The demands placed on states, districts, and schools by this landmark legislation provide the context for understanding in part what is meant by the phrase *data-driven decision maker*. Not only does *NCLB* define the most important decisions to be made by educational leaders, it provides a framework for how these decisions are to be made. The most important decisions in schools are decisions regarding student achievement: not just any student, but *all* students.

The *No Child Left Behind Act of 2001* also defines the specific kind of data and logic to be used in addressing these decisions. According to *NCLB*, evidence of teacher and school effectiveness in helping students achieve is to be found in a *very specific kind* of data. This data consists of standardized achievement scores aggregated and disaggregated in various ways, for example, by classroom grade-level, subject matter, school, and other notable demographic variables. The power of *NCLB* rests in the way it defines and specifies these and other educational essentials for the states.

At the risk of oversimplifying both the decision-making process and *NCLB*, current calls for more *data-driven* decisions by educational leaders can be understood accordingly. When placed in this context, *data-driven* decisions are decisions directed toward specific goals *and* informed by data aligned with the realization of these goals. Stated more accurately, data-driven decisions are *goal-oriented, data-rooted, and data-aligned*. This description implies a *logic* that seeks to maximize the alignment between decision ends and means Also implied is *skill in the use of this logic* by decisions makers. In general, this would include the ability to identify and operationalize decision goals, the ability to collect and analyze data that inform strategies leading to goal achievement, and the ability to construct and implement valid program assessments.

The call for more *data-driven* decisions is thus a call to increase the logical alignment between decision ends, means, and decision data. As such, it is a new name for an old idea, a reincarnated variant of the rationality expressed in classic decision theory (Simon, 1976; March, 1988, 1994). This rationality personifies the ongoing institutional cult of efficiency that defines American public education (Callahan, 1962; Tyack & Cuban, 1995).

As noted in other chapters of this book (chapters 1, 2, 3, 6, 7), the explanation of decision making offered by classic decision theory is highly normative. It describes how decisions *should* be made and personifies the perspective of the omniscient decision maker making optimal choices under optimal conditions (Simon, 1976; March, 1988). Behind the call for data-driven decisions lies the assumption that complete information exists regarding the decision topic, decision preferences, the ranking of preferences, alternative solutions, and the cost-benefit analysis of decision alternatives.

While the decisions faced by educational leaders are rarely defined by these conditions, there is a place for this type of theorizing in our thinking. The utility of classic decision theory is found in the emphasis it places on two key elements of the decision-making process: (1) the logic that guides decision making, and (2) the decision maker's use of data to inform this logic.

The emphasis given to logic and data availability in traditional decision theory is certainly overstated. In spite of this, there remains an identifiable logic common to most human decisions (Simon, 1981; March, 1988). This logic is also reflected in many descriptive theories of the decision-making process. Descriptive theorists seek to explain how decisions are *actually* made. The logic of the decision-making process portrayed in both normative and descriptive theories is remarkably similar yet distinct. Both are driven by a desire to maximize utility. Whereas normative theorists see no obstacles to maximization, descriptive theorists see many. For the normative theorist, maximizing means *optimizing*; for the descriptive theorist maximizing, means *satisficing*, or making a workable decision in light of various and multiple decision constraints. Both call for the decision maker to define decision preferences, articulate and prioritize decision means, collect and make use of valid data, and to draw inferences from these data. Whereas normative theorists view these as rather straightforward exercises in rational calculus, descriptive theorists see them as circuitous and elusive. For the descriptive theorist, there are internal and external limits to human reason.

What distinguishes normative from descriptive theories is not the fundamental logic of the decision process but the amount and character of information available to the decision maker when engaged in this logic. In contrast to the normative perspective, descriptive theorists assume that the information available for decision is limited, incomplete, and at times, confounding. This assumption validates the presence of uncertainties that often define the decision context. Information is the lifeblood of decision making. Information uncertainties limit the decision maker. While these uncertainties should not prevent one from approaching decisions in a logical and systematic fashion, uncertainties set boundaries on the effectiveness of this logic in predicting and controlling decision outcomes. As Simon (1976) notes, information uncertainties and the cognitive limitations of the decision maker do not completely negate but severely limit and bound optimizing logic in the decision-making process.

PURPOSE OF CHAPTER

Within the context of these larger issues, the purpose of this chapter is to explore two underexamined elements of the decision-making process. Both focus on the logic of this process and the uncertainties presented by the limited, incomplete, and equivocal data that often surround it. The specific aspects of the decision process examined here are the following: (1) the working causal assumptions the educational leader brings to a decision, and (2) the inferences and inferential leaps made by the educational leader as he or she iterates between data and decision.

The working causal assumptions the decision maker brings to a decision constitute an important data source in the decision process. These assumptions often assume a tacit quality in decision making. The first section of this chapter seeks to increase our awareness of these causal assumptions. The validity of our working assumptions often goes unexamined. We suggest that it is incumbent upon the decision maker to explicate and problematize these assumptions.

Likewise, it is prudent to look before you leap when making decisions. The second part of this chapter examines the logic of the inference process in decision making and the potential errors associated with what we refer to as *the inferential leap*. For any given decision, multiple inferences are made. Building on the data available for making a decision, these inferences and the logic that guides them often go unexamined.

The centrality of decision making to life makes these logic-elements of the decision-making process experientially familiar. We constantly assume and infer. At the same time, we unconsciously assume and infer. Excessive familiarity often means unfamiliarity. The more routinized our approach to decisions becomes, the less critical we are tempted to be. Our intent is to raise the reader's consciousness of the potential errors associated with these decision elements. We argue that both are underaddressed in the leadership literature. This oversight provides a justification for the thoughts that follow.

ON THE WORKING CAUSAL ASSUMPTIONS WE BRING TO DECISIONS

The causal assumptions an educational leader brings to a decision represent an important source of data in the decision-making process. These working assumptions not only frame the way one approaches decisions but often assume a tacit, taken-for-granted quality. Although a discussion of origins is beyond the scope of this chapter, these assumptions are informed by such things as one's world view, ideological commitments, life and professional experiences, formal training, the society and organization(s) of which one is a part, and one's patterned and preferred ways of thinking. Unless consciously recalled, the nature and validity of these assumptions and the influence they exert on the decision-making process often go unexamined.

Philosophical discussions of the meaning of cause, causation, and causality have a long history. This is due in part to the realization that behind the conscious activities of most humans lies a working concept of causation. As Pedhazur and Schmelkin (1991, p. 696) note, "The notion of causation is so ingrained in our thoughts . . . that attempts to understand myriad phenomena or to communicate about them without resorting to causation are practically inconceivable."

It is not difficult to understand why causation is central to our thinking. As we attempt to understand the social and physical world, we naturally seek reasons for the events we perceive and experiences we encounter. The causes of these events are often more interesting than the events themselves. Not only do we expend effort in identifying causes, we also seek to understand the nature of causation. Causation remains a controversial topic in philosophy and science. Philosophers such as Aristotle, Hume, Kant, Mill, and Popper have traversed this philosophical labyrinth with unequal success. Because of its controversial nature, some philosophers have refused to define causation. Yet many definitions of it exist. Based on this literature (Popper, 1974; Hume, 2000), we offer this working definition of cause or causation: *a cause is a change in one variable that produces a change in another variable.*

The terms cause and effect are key concepts in causal logic. An example of a working causal assumption familiar to most is reflected in the following statement: *If one applies enough heat to a kettle of water over a sustained period of time, the water in the kettle will boil.*

There are two primary variables in this simple example: heat and water. As the heat (X) applied to the kettle of water increases, the water in the kettle comes to a boil (Y). This variable relationship is captured visually below as Figure 5.1a. It should be noted that the logic of the movement is from left to right. The posited cause or independent variable is depicted on the left and the effect or dependent variable on the right.

Several important ideas follow from this example. First, the dependent variable on the right is so named because the change that comes to it depends on the change of the independent variable. In addition, the causal relationship shared between X and Y is conveyed using a one-way arrow that moves from left to right: *increased heat causes* H_2O *to boil.* Further, the relationship depicted in this example is *delimited.* One could map relationships that lead to or follow from this abstracted causal relationship in either direction. For example, the heat on the stove increased because Ben turned on the heating element (AV_3), which in turn caused the heat to increase. Further, he turned on the heating element because he wanted have a cup of hot tea (AV_2). He wanted a cup of hot tea because it was cold (AV_1). Figure 5.1b depicts the relationship mapped with these *ante* and *postcedent* variables.

In addition, at least two variables have been excluded from this delimited relationship: the specific altitude at which one is seeking to boil water and the purity of the water. As depicted in Figure 5.1c, these variables influence the relationship between heat and boiling water and are thus designated *mediating* variables. At sea level, sustained heat will cause water to boil at 212° F. However, water will not boil at this temperature at elevations above or below

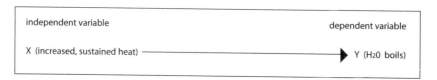

FIGURE 5.1A. Simple Causal Relationship: Heat and Water

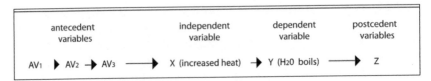

FIGURE 5.1B. Simple Causal Relationship with Ante- and Postcedent Variables

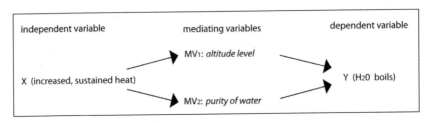

FIGURE 5.1C. Simple Causal Relationship: Heat and Water with Mediating Variables

sea level. Likewise, impurities in the water have an effect on the temperature at which it will boil.

Both variables are significant in that they qualify or mediate the heat-water relationship. In so doing, they increase our understanding of the nature of this relationship and the conditions under which it is valid. Ignoring these *mediating* variables provides an example of the tendency decision makers have to simplify or gloss over the working causal assumptions we hold.

Finally, social life tends to be more complex than this rather straightforward example from the physical sciences. The relationship between two or more variables may be more difficult to determine. For example, two variables may share a reciprocal relationship. We may be unable to determine with certainty which variable is the cause and which is the effect. Consider the relationship shared between a principal's overt praise of teachers in her school and the teaching effectiveness of teachers. Is it the principal's praise that leads to teacher effectiveness *or* the teacher's effectiveness that evokes praise from the principal? Which action causes which result? Such questions highlight the classic chicken-and-egg causal dilemma.

Additional challenges arise when a given effect can be attributed to multiple interacting causes. Returning to the principal praise—teacher effectiveness example above, is this effectiveness due to several factors:

1. the extensive praise the principal showers on her teachers, *or*
2. the fact that the average years of teaching experience in this school is higher than any other in the district, *or*

3. the fact that there are more teachers with advanced degrees in this school than any other in the district, *or*
4. that this school serves students from the wealthiest section of the district, *or*
5. a specific combination of these and other variables?

A review of the literature (Shulman, 1986, 1987; Darling-Hammond, 2000) suggests that these and other variables have an effect on instructional effectiveness.

In our efforts to make sense of and navigate the complexities of life as efficiently as possible, much of our thinking tends to be reductionist and simplistic. This also characterizes the working causal assumptions we embrace. It is these assumptions that guide the decision-making process. Not only is there a tendency to gloss over the complex, multivariate nature of these assumptions, there is a tendency to let the validity of these assumptions go unquestioned.

To speak of the validity of a causal relationship is to question its accuracy in describing the relationship. For example, if we decide to jump out the window of our third floor office to the sidewalk below, the chances are high that we will suffer painful consequences. In this case, we can say with confidence that X (our jump) will lead to Y (a broken bone—arm, leg, ankle, rib). There is a high level of validity associated with this causal relationship. This validity contrasts sharply with that implied in my claim that an increase in teacher morale is attributable to my decision to adopt a new reading program. The validity of this causal assumption can easily be called into question. How can one be sure that this increase in morale is not attributable to factors such as (1) my leadership style; (2) the recent 8% raise teachers received from the district; (3) the advent of spring; or (4) other reasonable explanations that make use of these and other variables? The confidence with which some educational leaders approach decisions is indicative of the simplistic causal assumptions they hold. It likewise suggests that little thought has been given to the larger issue of causal validity.

CAUSAL PREREQUISITES

The challenges associated with identifying and assessing the validity of our working causal assumptions beg the larger question of how causal relationships are established. Babbie (2004) and Asher (1976) identify three conditions that must be met in order to infer a causal relationship, summarized in Figure 5.2. One must first establish temporal precedence. It must be demonstrated that the proposed cause occurred *before* the identified effect. Returning to our decision as principal to adopt a new reading program, an improvement in teacher morale (Y) occurred after the adoption of the reading program (X). The working assumption driving our decision meets the first causal prerequisite. It should be noted

C1:	**Temporal precedence**—Independent variable X must precede dependent variable Y in time.
C2:	**Co-variation**—Independent variable X must co-vary with dependent variable Y. As a change is witnessed in one, a subsequent change is witnessed in the other.
C3:	**Negation of rival explanations**—Rival independent variables and explanations for the dependent variable X have been conclusively addressed and ruled out.

FIGURE 5.2. Conditions for Establishing a Causal Relationship Between Two Variables

that the ease with which temporal precedence is established varies with the relationship in question. At times it is easy to determine temporal precedence, although it can be quite challenging in the social sciences.

Does temporal precedence allow us to conclude that the relationship shared between two variables is a causal relationship? No, by itself it does not. In order to identify with confidence a causal relationship, one must also establish that two variables X and Y covary. That is to say as a change is witnessed in variable X a *subsequent* change is witnessed in variable Y. This second causal prerequisite is known as *correlation* or *covariation*.

Though needed to establish a causal relationship, in and of itself, correlation is insufficient for establishing this relationship. Drawing again from the reading program—teacher morale example above, there is a correlation between the adoption of the program and the rise in teacher morale. However, can we say with confidence that this is a *causal* relationship? No, as the third causal prerequisite examined below will reveal, we cannot. While the correlation between these variables suggests a causal relationship, it must be remembered that correlation is not the same as causation.

A familiar example of this faulty line of reasoning is exemplified in the high positive correlation found to exist between ice cream consumption and the homicide rate in a large city. Can we conclude that eating ice cream causes in individual to commit murder? Conversely, can we conclude that committing a homicide causes one to eat more ice cream? No, one cannot equate correlation with causation. The spurious correlation between these variables suggests the presence of an antecedent variable to which both are related. Much like the criterion of temporal precedence, correlation is a necessary but insufficient condition for establishing a causal relationship. In the context of decision making, it is not unusual for educational leaders to equate correlation with causation. Explicating and critiquing one's causal assumptions greatly reduce the chances of succumbing to this reasoning *faux pax*.

The third condition for making valid inferences regarding causal relationships focuses on ruling out rival or competing explanations of the effect in question. Are there factors other than the proposed independent variable that explain the dependent variable? If so, can these rival explanations be ruled out with a reasonable level of certainty? Adequately addressing these questions presents the reflective decision maker with a formidable task. Whereas experimental designs *may* allow researchers to address these questions with a reasonable level of certainty, these designs are imperfect at best. The controls called for by these designs are difficult to achieve in the social sciences.

Returning again to our example above, how can I be sure that the low morale expressed by teachers in my school was due to the *old* reading program? How can I be sure that this decline was not attributable to such variables as, (1) the death of a beloved teacher in the school; (2) the failure of the board to increase teacher salaries for the second straight year; (3) the scarcity of teaching and classroom supplies; (4) the harshness of the winter; or (5) a combination of these and other independent variables?

CRITIQUING CAUSAL ASSUMPTIONS

To show how these conditions for establishing a causal relationship can be used to critique and clarify the working causal assumptions we bring to our decisions, consider this set of assumptions held by the principal at Robertsville Middle School on a variety of topics and issues. As you read each statement, seek to, (1) identify the key variables and working causal relationship(s) embedded in each, and (2) visually map this relationship. How valid are these assumptions? What other factors might explain the dependent variable(s) in question? Use the ideas offered above as the basis for your critique.

- *Professional development*—Requiring teachers to attend professional development workshops provided by the district will increase the quality of teaching found in the school. I will thus require my teachers to do this.
- *Students who are academically successful*—Students who excel academically in this school come from relatively stable homes where parents are supportive of their educational endeavors. These students will find much success in life. Those students who come from homes that are less stable and supportive will, on the whole, find less success. I will thus pursue policies that encourage this parental support.
- *My leadership style*—If I, as a principal, assume a transformational leadership style, my legitimacy with teachers will increase. This legitimacy will free me to do many things.
- *Decision acceptance*—To ensure acceptance of this decision by the community, I must solicit feedback from the parents served by my school. The most reliable way to solicit and receive this feedback is to send a survey

home with students and require that they return it to the school after their parents have completed it.

- *The effects of increased funding for education*—If funding at the state and district levels were increased, teachers in my school would be happier and the achievement scores would increase. The community in turn would be much more supportive of me. I will therefore make it a point to remind leaders at both levels to increase educational funding.
- *Involving teachers in decisions*—Involving teachers in this decision will lead them to buy in to the proposed change. Thus, I have decided to involve them. Their involvement will ensure decision acceptance and increase my leadership legitimacy.

These are six causal assumptions held by the principal at Robertsville Middle School on a variety of topics. Unexamined working assumptions such as these are not atypical of those held by many educational leaders. While there is an intuitive validity associated with each, closer examination reveals a simplicity that leads the reflective practitioner to question this validity. In the context decision making, we suggest that it is incumbent upon the educational leader, when possible, to explicate and problematize the working assumptions he or she brings to a decision. In so doing the tacit, taken-for-granted quality of these assumptions, and the potential causal errors inherent in them, can be used to inform the decision-making process.

This same logic is also useful for critiquing and predicting the relative success of proposed educational reforms. We suggest that any given reform is rooted in a working set of causal assumptions. Though pitched at a high level of abstraction, Figure 5.3 offers a working causal map assumed by many school-improvement policies. It suggests that student learning is a function of three global variables: (1) the vision and strategies pursued by the site leader; (2) the policies and procedures enacted by the governing body; and (3) the structural configuration to pursue this end.

The direction and nature of the arrows connecting these four variables should not go unnoticed. Neither should the validity of the causal links and logic in the model go unchallenged. Causal assumptions underlie most if not all policy decisions in education. Consider for example what appear to be the working assumptions driving *NCLB*:

- The public education system in the United States is underperforming.
- This less than desirable performance is due to the fact that educators and the educational system have not been held accountable for student learning and achievement.
- Holding teachers, leaders, schools, districts, and states accountable for this performance will improve the quality of education as measured by standardized achievement scores.

We suggest that neither these nor the assumptions of other decisions be reified and accepted as givens. It behooves us as leaders to problematize and

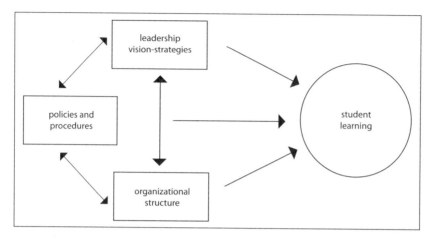

FIGURE 5.3. Causal Assumptions Regarding School Improvement

assess the validity of these working assumptions. Faulty decisions often rest on faulty unexamined causal assumptions.

ON DECISION INFERENCES AND THE INFERENTIAL PROCESS

Additional elements of the decision-making process that often go unexamined are the inferences and inferential leaps made as the decision maker moves from data to decision. An *inference* is a working cognitive conclusion driven by data. It is an inductive summary whereby one seeks to bring coherence to decision data. In seeking to determine the meaning of data, the decision maker is required to go beyond or *infer* conclusions from this data.

The ongoing classroom adjustments made by the seasoned educator provide an example of the inference process. Based on the facial expressions and body language of students, the competent teacher is adept at inferring the extent to which a given teaching method is having the desired effect. Puzzled looks from students, off-task behavior, boredom, and incorrect responses to strategic questions provide the raw data from which this inference is made.

Regardless of the validity of one's data, *inferential logic* is the logic that characterizes the cognitive movement from the data we perceive and the conclusions we reach. This process is a defining mental activity. We are constantly inferring, constantly engaged in moving beyond the data and information given. As Mill (1850, p. 27) notes, "There is a daily, hourly, and momentary need to ascertain facts. . . . The judge, general, navigator, physician and farmer are preoccupied with judging and acting on evidence. The mind never ceases to engage in inferring."

Drawing inferences is also a defining cognitive activity in decision making. For any given decision, multiple inferences are made. Building on the data available for decision, these inferences, and the logic that guides them, play a key role in the success or failure of a given decision. Figure 5.4 provides a means for conceptualizing this important mental activity. The inference process is portrayed as a triangle resting on its base. Three observations are worth noting about this process. First, an inference is the product of a series of *cognitive processes*. It is in essence a rationally driven conclusion. This conclusion is typically reached following a series of trial-and-error thought experiments using the data at hand. These thought-experiments consist of the interrelated cognitive processes of analysis and synthesis.

Second, an inference is *data driven*. To infer is to derive by reasoning using data. In the context of decision making, data is information about something. These data assume a variety of forms, facts, perceptions, assumptions, research findings, guesses, words, numbers, past experiences, and can be collected in a variety of ways, both systematically and unsystematically. These data also vary in quality. All things being equal, the reflective decision maker seeks to base his or her decisions on the most valid and reliable information possible. Without data inferential thinking cannot occur.

Third, the defining logic associated with the inference process is *induction*: the move from particulars to the abstract. This movement is rooted in data particulars and finds its terminus in the inference abstracted from this data. The upward-pointing arrow depicted on the left-hand side of the triangle in Figure 5.4 captures this process. It is in this sense that an inference is an inductive conclusion abstracted from data.

THE INVITATION: AN EXAMPLE OF INFERENCE

A humorous example can be used to illustrate the extent and quality of the inferences we make when encountering new situations. Carefully consider

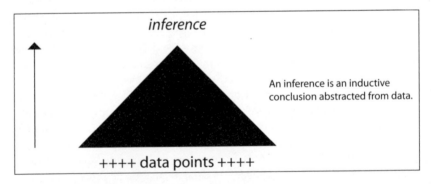

FIGURE 5.4. The Logic of the Inference Process

the scenario below. Information about it is strategically revealed in a series of ten statements. As you read each statement, pause, and consciously attend to the inferences you are making. Likewise, attend to the story line that emerges as you infer beyond the data given.

S_1: I receive an invitation to a party.
S_2: I am invited to a black-tie affair honoring the President.
S_3: I have a dog. His name is Amos.
S_4: I decide to accept the invitation and thus respond to the RSVP in a timely manner.
S_5: I go dressed in Levis, a western shirt, a pair of cowboy boots, and a black hat.
S_6: I also go with my guitar case and amplifier in hand.
· S_7: My name is Willie.
S_8: I drive a Ford pick-up truck.
S_9: Upon my arrival at the party, the Secret Service immediately asked me to leave.
S_{10}: I am convinced that the Pittsburgh Steelers will win the Super Bowl next year.

Now that you have worked through these statements, reflect on how the data gleaned from each contributed to or distracted from the scenario that emerged in your mind. Consider the back-and-forth nature of your thinking as you iterated through the statements to construct an identifiable and reasonably coherent story line. The multiple conclusions drawn from these data are examples of inferences and the inferential process.

To further sensitize us to the nature of the inferential process, consider the following questions about this story line and the cognitive processes that led you to it. As you answer these questions, feel free to return to the data contained in the ten statements and to reformulate your story line as needed. Carefully attend to our use of the following adverbs to describe the inference process: *conclusive, reasonable yet inconclusive,* and *unreasonable.*

Q_1: What can be *conclusively* inferred from this incident?
Q_2: What can be *reasonably, but inconclusively* inferred from this incident?
Q_3: What *cannot be reasonably inferred* from this incident?
Q_4: What data *coheres* across the ten statements? Why?
Q_5: What data is *irrelevant or inconsistent* with the many inferences you have drawn?

While space prevents us from providing an exhaustive response to each of the questions posed above, compare your answers with the ones we offer below.

Conclusive inferences—These inferences follow *conclusively* from the data above: "I received an invitation to a party; the requested dress at the party was black-tie (formal dress); a president is being honored at the event; I have a dog whose name is Amos . . ."

Note how these inferences are firmly rooted in the data given. They are recapitulations of the data presented in the scenario. The close proximity of these inferences to the data justify our labeling them as *conclusive*.

Inconclusive yet reasonable inferences—Inferences such as the following *reasonably* yet *inconclusively* cohere from the data given: "The request of my presence at the event suggests that I am in someway valued by those requesting it; the affair is for the President of the United States; my dress suggests that I have misread or have blatantly disregarded the formal nature of the affair; I have been invited to be the music entertainment at the affair; I am a country singer; my name is Willie Nelson; security personnel failed to understand who I am and what I have been invited to do, and so forth."

Note how this set of inferences is based on the data. The *reasonableness* of these inferences lies in the coherence they provide to the emerging story line. The inconclusive nature of these same inferences rests on the fact that we have gone beyond the data given. Without further data, we cannot determine the full validity of these inferences. They are *reasonable* yet *inconclusive*.

Unreasonable, inconclusive inferences—Examining once again the ten statements above, several *unreasonable* and *inconclusive* inferences can be made: "A large black limousine escorted me to the party; my dog, Amos, is a Beagle that has competed in many dog shows; I was asked to leave the party because my favorite color is green, and so forth."

The distinguishing feature of this set of inferences is that they go far beyond the scenario data offered above in a way that is *unreasonable*. For example, what data in this scenario allow us to make inferences about the subject's favorite color? What data lead us to infer that Amos is a show dog?

Irrelevant or inconsistent data—There are likewise four data points from this scenario that do not seem to cohere with the emerging story line: "I have a dog. His name is Amos; I drive a Ford pick-up truck; and the confidence I express in the Pittsburgh Steelers." It should be noted that these data were identified as irrelevant *after* iterative rounds of analysis and synthesis. Engaging in these cognitive processes, we sifted, distilled, and recombined bits and pieces of data in our search for a coherent story line (Dewey, 1933, 1938). These data do not appear to fit with the other data from which the story line was abstracted.

The distinguishing feature of these inferences and the emergent classification scheme is their *distance from the data*. Figure 5.5 captures this idea. Whereas conclusive inferences are firmly rooted in the data at hand, unreasonable, inconclusive inferences go far beyond these data.

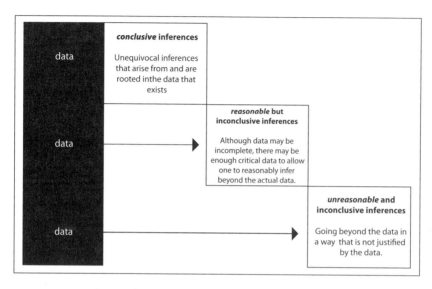

FIGURE 5.5. Inferential Conclusiveness: Assessing Data Distance

Iterative Nature of The Inference Process

Comparing your answers with ours draws attention to the roles of perception and cognition in the inferential process. When faced with a decision, the inferences we make depend not only on the data we see, but on our ability to connect the dots presented by this data in our search for a reasonably coherent story line.

Decision makers vary in their ability to see, discern, discard, and connect data while inferring. Weick (1978) attributes this variation to what he labels requisite mental complexity and argues that one's cognitive complexity is a function of the variety and richness of one's past cognitive experiences. The more varied and rich one's past experiences, the greater one's ability to discern, discard, and connect the data encountered in decision making.

This variability is again evident when one compares the novice and experienced teacher. When determining the effectiveness of new unit, the seasoned educator is more attuned to what student data is needed to make this assessment. While there is an overwhelming amount of data embedded in the context, not all data is relevant for this purpose. Schools are data rich but analysis poor. There is skill involved in discriminating relevant from irrelevant data. There is also skill involved in relating this data in a reasonably coherent manner. Seasoned teachers typically diagnose and identify learning difficulties much quicker than their first-year counterparts. In addition, the seasoned educator often proves more adept at gleaning the most from the data at hand. The successes and failures of the past reduce the probability of committing inferential errors in these types of decisions.

The examples offered above hint at some of the logical errors associated with the inference process. Together they beg the larger question as to the precise nature of these errors and where they are likely to occur. At the risk of simplifying the complex and iterative nature of this logic, Figure 5.6 offers a delimited description of its movement. The movement is from left to right. While the logic that animates this movement is somewhat linear in nature, that is to say, the movement is from data to inference, there is an iterative, cyclical quality to it. The logic is moving toward a destination, an inference; yet this movement may is iterative and at times circuitous.

Five specific stages of this process are identified in Figure 5.6. Step 1 consists of data. As the decision maker collects and attends to these data, a series of judgments is made regarding their relevance, relatedness and meaning. It is at this point that the decision maker discerns, discards, and connects data in his or her search for patterns of meaning (Weick, 1979, 1995). This involves analysis and synthesis: the pulling apart and reconnecting of data. These mental activities characterize the movement from step 1 to step 2.

Step 3 consists of a series of initial inferences made from these data. Not only are multiple inferences made from these data (step 3), but also judgments regarding the relationship and collective meaning of these inferences are likewise rendered (step 4). From this the decision maker moves to step 5 where a summary conclusion of data and the multiple inferences drawn from these data is reached. Step 5 may be thus described as a summative inference from one's prior inferences.

Much like the other efforts to model cognition (Dewey, 1933, 1938; Piaget, 1977; Kohlberg, 1984), Figure 5.6 masks the complexity that define the inferential process. To be sure, the demarcation between cognitive steps is more ambiguous than our model reveals. Nevertheless, we suggest it reflects

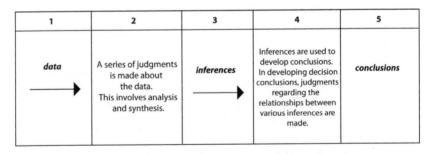

FIGURE 5.6. The Logic and Cognitive Movement of the Inference Process

a validity that not only assists in identifying common logical errors associated with the inference process, but also hints at the places where these errors are likely to occur. The inferential errors described below tend to occur in the movements between steps. These movements are depicted as unidirectional arrows in Figure 5.6.

COMMON INFERENTIAL ERRORS

With no intent of being exhaustive, we offer brief descriptions of five generic errors commonly exhibited by decision makers in the inference process. Several of these errors are subtle. If unattended they can easily undermine the quality of one's decisions and the larger decision-making process. Figure 5.7 offers a visual summary of five inferential errors.

The first potential error is to *overinfer from the data at hand*, to go beyond one's decision data in a way that cannot be justified. Three inferences from the scenario above exemplify this error: (1) Amos, the dog alluded to in S_3, is a beagle; (2) having descended from a champion bloodline, Amos has competed in many dog shows; and (3) Willie was asked to leave the party because his favorite color was green. A review of the ten statements that provide the foundation for our working scenario reveals that there is no data to support these inferences. Further, there are no hints that these inferences are remotely related to these data. They border on the absurd.

There are at least three reasons for committing this logical error. The temptation to overinfer is perhaps most acute when: insufficient time is available to

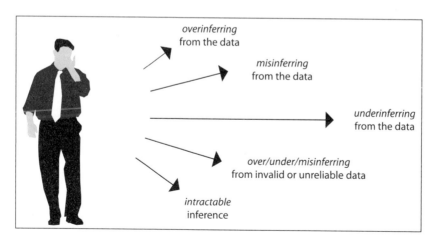

FIGURE 5.7. Potential Inferential Errors

attend to decision data; if after an initial analysis, no story line appears to be emerging from the data; or when one's predispositions lead him/her to impose patterns and meanings on the data that are otherwise unjustified. Regardless of the reason, the distinguishing feature of this error is its distance from the data. It represents an unreasonable inferential leap.

Closely related to this error, and perhaps a more inclusive variant of it, is the temptation *to misinfer from the data at hand*. While there are several ways to misinfer, only three types of misinference are reviewed here. All spring from faulty or forced logic.

The first type of misinference is attributable to the *non sequitur* error. As a concept indigenous to the fields of rhetoric and debate, *non sequitur* is Latin for "nonsequential" or "does not sequentially follow." Preparing for a legal defense, it is important for a lawyer to construct an argument in a logical fashion. The goal is to convince both judge and jury that (1) the argument made is *valid* to the data evidence in the case; and that (2) the conclusions reached by the lawyer *logically follow* from his or her argument. Success depends on the lawyer's ability to articulate this logical sequence. *Non sequitur* reasoning undermines the probability of success. It is *the* cardinal sin of rhetoric and debate. In a similar fashion, *non sequitur* reasoning can lead the decision maker to misinfer. The inferences reflected in a decision may not *logically* or *sequentially* follow from the data that surrounds that decision. It is in this sense that *overinferring* is *misinferring*. To infer that Willie was turned away at the party by the Secret Service because his favorite color was green is to over and misinfer from data givens. This inference is rooted in *non sequitur* reasoning.

Yet one does not have to overinfer to misinfer. There are other ways to misinfer. One can misinfer from *red herring* or *dead-end* data. In the context of data analysis, red herring data are extraneous data that distract or divert attention from the emerging story line contained in the data. Such data are typically identified *ex post facto*. One does not know the red herring quality of data until *after* comparative judgments have been made about these data in the larger decision context. These judgments typically occur after multiple passes through the data.

Identifying red herring data is analogous to the logic used by young children to solve picture puzzles. Five pictures are presented on a page. The child is asked to identify the one that does not fit: *ear, foot, nose, elbow*, and *boat*. To solve the puzzle and identify the red herring, the child must review and compare data points. As this is done, a story line that brings coherence to the data points emerges (ear, foot, nose, and elbow are all parts of the human body) and the red herring is identified (a boat is not an anatomical part). This logic is similar to that experienced as we worked through the ten scenario statements above. As we read and reread these statements, data patterns were inferred and a reasonable story line emerged. Working iteratively through this process, red herring data came into bold relief: *I have a dog whose name is Amos*; and, *the Steelers will win the Super Bowl next year.*

These data were identified as irrelevant after the fact. Certain types of misinferences are rooted in the unreasonable pursuit of red herring, dead-end data.

A third type of misinference can be attributed to the faulty heuristics one brings to a decision. Heuristics are simple rules-of-thumb that allow us to meet and manage the complexities of life more efficiently. Decision heuristics are the mental algorithms we develop to simplify and guide the decision-making process. Controlling the center of the board is well-known heuristic in chess. Taking a hit on 16 and sticking on 17 is a familiar decision heuristic in the game of blackjack. A district's policy to suspend students after three truancy violations is an example of a formalized heuristic. As such, it is intended to facilitate the discipline decisions faced by leaders in the district. Under ideal conditions, these working scripts facilitate the decision-making process by helping decision makers avoid the paralyzing effects of uncertainty. Though well-intentioned, however, heuristics such as these are not infallible.

As educational leaders, each of us brings our own set of working heuristics to the decisions we face. If used judiciously, these heuristics can serve as powerful aids to the decision-making process. They can be used to frame the decisions we face and guide our data collection and analysis efforts. However, much like the working causal assumptions we bring to decisions, there is a taken-for-granted, reified quality imposed on these heuristics. This reification prevents us from attending to the potential errors and pitfalls associated with their use. There is therefore a need to periodically articulate, problematize and evaluate the utility of these heuristics as cognitive aids. Faulty decision heuristics can lead to faulty decision inferences.

A line of research in cognitive and social psychology explores the reliability of these heuristics as guides to decision making (Tversky & Kahneman, 1973, 1974, 1981; Abelson & Levi, 1985; McClintock, 1987; Simon, 1991, 1993; Smith & Kida, 1991; Wilson, et al., 1996). This work is helpful in conceptualizing decision heuristics and the errors associated with them. Nisbett and Ross (1980) in particular identify three categories of heuristics that can be used to facilitate our thinking on these issues: *knowledge, judgment,* and *weighting heuristics.*

Knowledge heuristics arise out of the working knowledge one brings to a decision. This knowledge is rooted in our life experiences: the working theories, scripts, beliefs, and values that are products of our interactions with others. Past experiences serve as guides to present action. Our working theories provide a framework with which to define and frame the meaning of decisions we face. The working scripts developed over the years serve as interpretive grids for our experiences. In addition, our values serve as filters through which we frame decisions, attend to decision data, and entertain solution alternatives. Persona-based scripts inform our perceptions of how people act. These perceptions are rooted in our past interactions with others.

The selective nature of memory coupled with the interactive manner in which these events are experienced undermine the reliability of these heuristics as fool-proof inference guides. If for example a student is sent to the assistant principal's office, past experience leads us to conclude that a discipline problem exists. Though reasonable, this inference is not always valid. Students are sent to the office for other reasons.

The second group of cognitive aids consists of *judgment heuristics.* Judgment is a critical skill in the decision-making process. It is an inference reached after decision data and one's assumptions about these data have been analyzed and tested. To *prejudge* is to judge before the available data or evidence is fully considered. Dewey's (1933, p. 126) thoughts on the centrality of judgment in thinking support this observation, "thinking is a continual . . . judging of both data and ideas. Unless the pertinence and force of each seemingly evidential fact and seemingly explanatory idea inferred from these facts are judged, the mind goes on a wild-goose chase."

Nisbett and Ross (1980) define judgment heuristics as those shortcuts developed to aid in this inference process. Two factors play a role in informing the inferential judgments we make: *representativeness* and *memory availability.* Representative heuristics are rooted in the bank of experiences that defines one's life. In powerful yet subtle ways, these experiences mold, shape, and define who we are and what we are becoming. These experiences likewise inform the way we frame new situations. In the context of decision making, the human tendency is to frame new decisions in ways that are consistent with past experiences. This tendency is known as *representativeness.*

Representativeness facilitates decision making by economizing the thought processes associated with it. Building on past experiences, the decision maker has no need to reinvent the proverbial wheel with every decision. It is in this sense that representativeness qualifies as a potent though not infallible guide to decision making. While representativeness enables one to recognize and attribute common data patterns across decisions, it can also prevent one from recognizing the unique, idiosyncratic qualities of a particular decision. As an experienced leader who has dealt with the debilitating effects of poor instruction in four schools, there are things learned from these experiences that can assist me in addressing similar issues in my new assignment. The commonalities I have witnessed across schools will illuminate this new context. At the same time, these commonalities can prevent me from discerning the uniqueness of the decision context. The inferential enactments of my past can empower *or* imprison the future inferences I make.

The utility of memory-availability heuristics parallels that of representativeness. Availability refers to the extent to which memory is retrievable. While advances in the development of electronic storage media have increased our collective ability to store and retrieve data at the point of decision (Simon, 1981, 1991, 1993), the memories of individual decision makers are fallible and their ability to retrieve these on demand memories is unreliable and variable. This fallibility and variability function to undermine the utility of memory as a decision heuristic. The effectiveness of memory-availability heuristics is further threatened by *what* one chooses (or does not choose) to remember.

The conscious, subconscious, and otherwise fickled aspects of memory retention led Nisbett and Ross (1980) to identify a third set of decision aids: *weighting heuristics*. These heuristics focus on incoming stimuli and how much weight is given to these stimuli in our thinking. What is it that we store in our memories and why? When faced with a decision, what is likely to be recalled most readily? What data exerts the greatest influence on the inferences we make? Answers to these questions provide the focal point of research on weighting heuristics.

In attending to data, there is a tendency to weigh information in proportion to its *vividness* (Smith & Kida, 1991). Several factors enhance the vividness of otherwise mundane data (Nisbett & Ross, 1980; Abelson & Levi, 1985): (1) the emotional appeal of the data; (2) the concreteness of the data; (3) the credibility of the data; and (4) the sensory (the five senses), temporal (the most recent), and spatial (physical closeness) proximity of the data. Stated differently, as decision makers we tend to remember and weigh more heavily data that are emotionally appealing, concrete, credible, and closest to us in sense, space and time.

A useful example of how this weighting can influence and undermine the decision process is seen in a recent decision of a friend to buy a car. Ginny was determined to get the biggest "bang-for-the-buck." Toward this end, she expended considerable time and energy collecting data from various sources on the repair histories and reliability of several high-end sedans. After several weeks, a decision was reached. Careful analysis led her to conclude that the Lexus ES-400 was *the* car for her.

Excited about the prospects of her new purchase, an appointment was made with the local dealership. On the eve of her appointment, however, she had an experience that changed her mind. Ginny was invited to a dinner party to honor a colleague who had recently retired. While there, she ran into a long-lost friend from college. She shared with her the news and excitement of her upcoming purchase over a glass of wine. The reaction of her friend was unexpected, "A Lexus!" She exclaimed. "You've got to be kidding! I purchased a Lexus from that dealer three years ago and it has been one big headache! Not only has the car been unreliable, the dealership has given me nothing but trouble!"

The animated response of Ginny's friend caught her off guard. Yet it had an effect. Early the next morning, and contrary to the excellent repair records and positive data on the dealer's reputation, she cancelled her appointment. The following week she was seen driving a Cadillac.

The vividness of her friend's reaction made an indelible impression on Ginny. It led her to weigh the anecdotal data gleaned from it more heavily than the reliable and valid repair data she had spent weeks collecting. This tendency and subsequent misinference we suggest is not uncommon. Vivid information is more likely to be remembered and exert a disproportionate amount of influence on the decision process than more reliable, ho-hum data.

Each of the decision heuristics reviewed above is useful in the decision-making process. Collectively they represent a means for dealing with the absence, incompleteness, and low quality of data that often define the decision context. Yet we should be aware of the subtle and not so subtle errors inherent in each. These errors revolve around our tendency as decision makers to *look for* the wrong data, *see* the wrong data, *retain* the wrong data, *weigh* the data improperly, and as a result, to *misinfer* from these data.

A third common error associated with the inference process is the tendency *to underinfer from the data at hand.* This tendency is analogous to a gold or silver vein that is undermined. While there is a bonanza to be had, it is of little value to the owner unless it is mined. The full potential of the mother lode remains unrealized. The young and those new to a role are particularly susceptible to this error. For the young, the cognitive complexity needed to identify and discriminate relevant from irrelevant data is lacking. The skills inherent in this process develop with time as they explore, discover, and experience the world around them. As Weick (1978) reminds us, a requisite level of cognitive complexity is needed to recognize the complexity in one's outer environment.

For those new to a role, the sources of this error can lie in the absence of requisite cognitive complexity. More often than not, however, the tendency to underinfer is rooted in a lack of familiarity with the role and the specific knowledge and information needed to perform this role. Contrasting abilities between new and experienced teachers in knowing what student data to attend when managing the class exemplify this phenomenon. Although there is a wealth of data from which to infer, the neophyte teacher cannot see it. His classroom is data rich, yet his analysis is poor. As a result, he underinfers from the data. Experience and socialization into the teaching role opens ever-widening data vistas to him.

A fourth error common to the inference process focuses less on the process and more on the quality of data on which inferences rest. This error profoundly affects the inferences that are made. It is the temptation to infer from biased, invalid, and otherwise "bad" data. When used to describe data, validity is the extent to which data is an accurate indicator of the phenomenon of interest. A student who is crying is a valid indicator of emotional distress; laughing is not.

The ability to discriminate valid from invalid data as well as the ability to collect these data varies across decision makers. Among other things, this ability (or inability) is a function of the cognitive and perceptual grids one brings to the inference process. Our cognitive predispositions determine what data we attend to and what data we choose to ignore. Much like the knowledge and judgment heuristics we use to sense-make our experiences, these serve as filters through which data is processed. While it is naive to deny the influence of these filters on our thinking, it is wise to reflect on how these filters affect what we see and the biases they introduce. The decision inferences we make are only as valid as the data on which they rest. Insufficient, biased or low quality data suggest a cautious, conservative approach to decision making. It likewise suggests that the inferences that are made should be based on those parts of the data where an acceptable level of validity exists. Sensitivity to the issue of data validity is critical to sound decision making.

Closely related to the four errors is the tendency to be intractable with the inferences one draws in the face of incomplete, conflicting, and/or countervailing data. While there are times when this intractableness may be justified, it reflects a cognitive or volitional stubbornness that may go against the data at hand. This orientation can be rooted in a number of related factors: the politics of the decision context, historical or social precedence, the faulty causal assumptions one brings to a decision, or the cognitive limitations of the decision maker (i.e., one's inability to see). Each of these alone or in combination can contribute to an *unwillingness* to see.

Weick (2001) provides some insight into tensions created by inordinate adherence to past theoretical enactments and the temptation to tenaciously adhere to questionable inferences in the decision process. Noting that growth comes as one both embraces and doubts past enactments, he finds value in the precedent and progress of the past. However, Weick argues that we should avoid becoming prisoners of these enactments. We should remain open to new and heretofore unseen data and the logical inferences that would follow from these data. This mind-set of accepting and doubting creates an adaptability that is conducive to progress. Yet this mind-set is paradoxical, ambiguous, and at times tension-inducing in that past enactments must be embraced and doubted, accepted, and rejected. One must be willing to live with such dissonance. In the context of decision making and the incomplete information that defines most decision contexts, one must be open to the possibility that competing inferences are possible from the data at hand. These factors work against a rigid, intractable adherence to decision inferences.

SUMMARY AND CONCLUSION

Within the context of recent calls for more *data-driven* decisions, this chapter has explored two underexamined elements of the decision-making process: (1) the working causal assumptions the educational leader brings to a decision; and (2) the inferences and inferential leaps made by the educational leader as he or she moves from data to decision. Both elements focus on the logic of the decision-making process and the uncertainties presented by limited, incomplete, and equivocal decision data. The demand for more data defines most of decisions. Both likewise speak to the cognitive limitations of humans as decision makers. We cannot always know, control, or predict the multiple factors which surround the decisions we face.

The centrality of decision making to life makes these logic-elements of the decision process experientially familiar. We constantly assume and infer. At the same time, we *unconsciously* assume and infer. Excessive familiarity often means unfamiliarity. Our intent has been to raise the reader's consciousness of the potential errors associated with these elements. We argue that both have been underaddressed in the leadership literature.

The working causal assumptions the educational leader brings to a decision constitute an important source of data in the decision process. These assumptions often assume a tacit, taken-for-granted quality. In our efforts to efficiently sense-make and navigate the complexities of life, much of our thinking tends to be simplistic and reductionist. This also characterizes the working causal assumptions we embrace. It is these assumptions that guide the decision-making process. Not only is there a tendency to gloss over the complex, multivariate nature of these assumptions, there is a tendency to let the validity of these assumptions go unquestioned and to ignore the fundamental prerequisites for establishing causal relationships.

There is a need to increase our collective awareness of these causal assumptions and how they frame our approach to decisions. In the context decision making, we suggest that it is incumbent upon the educational leader, when possible, to explicate and problemize the working assumptions he or she brings to a decision. In so doing, the tacit, taken-for-granted quality of these assumptions, and the potential causal errors inherent in them, can be used to inform the decision process. Faulty decisions often rest on faulty, unexamined causal assumptions.

When making decisions it is also wise to periodically look before you leap. The second part of this chapter has examined the logic of the inference process in decision making and the potential errors associated with making what we refer to as *the inferential leap*. An inference is a working cognitive conclusion driven by data. It is an inductive summary whereby one seeks to bring coherence to decision data. Inferential logic is the logic that characterizes the cognitive movement from the data we perceive and the conclusions we reach. We are constantly inferring, constantly engaged in moving beyond the data. In seeking to determine the meaning of data, the decision maker is required to go beyond or *infer* conclusions from this data.

For any given decision, multiple inferences are made. The inferences we make depend not only on the data we see, but on our ability to connect the dots presented by this data in our search for a coherent story line. Decision makers vary in their ability to see, discern, discard and connect data while inferring. In making these inferences, decision makers are also vulnerable to a number of logical errors. Five of these have been explored here: over inferring; underinferring; misinferring; over / under / and misinferring from bad data; and intractably adhering to the inferences one draws in light of equivocal data.

Building on the data available for decision, these inferences, and the common errors associated with them, often go unexamined.

To be sure, the exploration of these issues complicates our thinking about the decision-making process. The confidence assumed by some decision makers reflects not only a hyper-simplistic and reductionist view of the world, but an inadequate grasp of the importance these issues. There is much involved here, almost too much to attend to at once. Using the language and logic of experimental research designs, we live in a multivariate, interactive, second and third order effects world (Cook & Campbell, 1979; Gall, Gall & Borg, 2006) that at times challenges the assumptions we bring to decisions and the inferences we draw while making them. Decision makers should be aware of this.

At the same time, however, awareness of these issues should not lead the educational leader to decision paralysis, that is the paralysis that comes from hyper-attentiveness and sensitivity to the analysis of decision context (the proverbial *paralysis of analysis*). There is an organic, holistic quality to the decision-making process that binds these multiple elements in a way that makes decision making manageable. Excessive preoccupation with any single aspect of the decision process at the expense of the others and the whole can paralyze the decision process. Much like learning to drive a car, there is much to remember and integrate in one's thinking while driving. Excessive attention to any specific aspect of the process will distract from one's ability to think holistically about the larger driving process. Whereas hypersensitivity to the individual components by the new driver makes our ride with him an uncomfortable adventure, the experienced driver approaches the task more holistically.

Our purpose here has been to highlight the potential errors introduced into the decision making process by faulty causal assumptions and erroneous inferential logic. We are tempted to impose causal maps and assumptions on decisions that cannot be supported by the data at hand. We are likewise tempted to draw inferences on decisions that, upon closer examination, the data cannot and will not support. We encourage educational leaders to engage in a healthy second-guessing of themselves on these issues as they engage in the decision-making process and seek to further develop their decision skills. It is in this spirit that we offer these thoughts.

QUESTIONS FOR REFLECTION AND DISCUSSION

- What were the purposes of this chapter? What justifies the inclusion of this chapter?
- What does it mean to say that data or information is the *lifeblood* of decision making?
- What is meant by *data-driven decision*? How do the authors define this particular type of decision? In what ways is *data-driven* a redundant descriptor for decision making?

- What is meant by *cause or causation* and *one's working causal assumptions?*
- To what extent are the working causal assumptions we bring to the decisions explicitly known to us? What can be done to increase our awareness of these?
- How does one go about articulating and then assessing the validity of one's working causal assumptions regarding a specific decision?
- Select an educational policy that is being debated by your legislature or local district. What is or are the causal logic and assumptions on which it rests? Are they valid?
- What are the prerequisites needed to establish a causal relationship? What are the challenges and difficulties associated with addressing these prerequisites?
- To what extent do policy-makers in general and you as a leader reflect on the causal assumptions which drive your educational decisions?
- In the context of decisions, what is an inference and what is the inferential process?
- What aspects of the inferential process are susceptible to logical error?
- Cite examples from your decision experiences of the inferential errors identified above.
- What practical steps can be taken to check the validity of the inferences one is called on to make in the decision-making process?
- How can one remain sensitive to and aware of the logical errors examined in this chapter when making decisions without falling victim to the paralyzing effects of hyper analysis?

CHAPTER SIX

The Intuitive Decision Maker in the Information Age

The decisions we make shape our lives. Whether we make our decisions consciously or unconsciously, with careful consideration or impulsive haste, our decisions direct our journey through life. Some decisions come easily. Red or white sauce on my pasta? An action thriller or romantic comedy for a Friday night video rental? What book to take on the airplane? Others are more agonizing. Buy a new car or shoulder the cost of repairs for my current vehicle? Take the new position or stay in my current role for another year? Invest additional time and effort in professional study? Obvious decisions, those that come without much effort, tend to have minimal consequences. We make hundreds of these kinds of decisions each day. At best, our decision has the potential to brighten our day. At worst, we do not enjoy our lunch.

Better viewed as choices, these simple decisions ask us to select between several straightforward and clear options. While we might wish to make the best choice possible at any given time, the lack of serious consequences allows us to rapidly consider the choices we have, make a decision and move forward. Serious decisions, on the other hand, require us to pass judgment, reach a conclusion and take action. The important decisions we make in life are complex. They often affect others, with potential impact for our families, coworkers and, in schools, our students. Frequently, they have far reaching consequences. They are hard to reverse and have the potential to cause us great embarrassment or earn us great praise. As we discussed in our chapter on tough decisions, important decisions are often made under stressful circumstances. We regularly lack the data and time we would like to optimize our decision making.

Yet we reach our decision. At times that decision is the result of sleepless nights, careful planning, and agonizing internal debate. However, other times, we simply *know* the best course of action to take. Our "gut" tells us which way to turn. There is a small voice at the back of our head that leads us to our choice. Our palms might be sweaty, our breath may quicken, or a sense of calm may wash over us as we become aware of the prompts that stimulate our intuitive instincts. Rarely are we able to articulate why and how we know what we do but we believe it as strongly as if the data was squarely in front of us. In seeking to describe these insights, some call them a hunch, others claim they have an innate sense for "reading" a situation, and still others claim they reflexively form accurate first impressions. Dependent on who makes the characterization, these inspirations might also be described as snap judgments, blind faith, following one's heart or just plain reckless behavior. Either way, our immediate impressions help to form our decisions as readily as does our data. Commonly, we think of these influences as intuition—the power to apply our insight and experience to the decision-making process.

Whether we openly claim to be influenced by our intuition or not, considerable research suggests that we all use our intuition in the decision-making process (Simon, 1987, 1993; Khatri & Ng, 2000; Hogarth, 2001; Klein, 2003; Sayegh, et al., 2004). Regardless of whether you personally embrace your intuition or choose to be less forthcoming about your flashes of brilliance, understanding how insight functions in the decision-making process is quite beneficial as we seek to understand the decision-making process. Furthermore, as the sheer amount of information and our access to a variety of information sources have exploded in the past decades, we may find ourselves in situations in which there is too much information to rationally consider. When faced with an overwhelming amount of information and high uncertainty regarding our course of action intuition, our sense of just knowing, often kicks in and helps us to optimize our choices.

Building upon other chapters in the text we seek to explore the ways in which intuition serves us in the decision-making process. First, we develop a definition for the construct of intuition and describe the ways in which intuition can be identified and utilized. Second, we offer a word of caution concerning intuition in the decision-making process. Finally, we offer examples of using your intuition to enhance your decision-making skills.

THE MEANING AND ROLE OF INTUITION

One of the our most basic assumptions about decision making is that systematic and careful analysis yield better results than those coming from less rational processes. We hold tight to our belief in the scientific method, strategic planning, and other organized forms of goal attainment (Cohen, et al., 1972; Simon, 1976; March, 1988, 1994; Willower & Licata, 1997). Yet, our faith in rational forms of decision making is more mythological than realistic. Experience tells us that it is the rare decision that follows the straightforward path. For example, many research efforts have a story that is not part of the official published record. The experimental sciences are replete with stories about serendipitously discovered substances, products, and inventions. Post-it Notes, Velcro, and penicillin are examples of familiar substances that were discovered unexpectedly. Stories about the creation of these products often revolve around a similar theme—while in the pursuit of another substance, an accident occurs and the new substance is identified by chance. The accident might be a glue that does not hold permanently (Post-its), a walk through a field of clingy cocklebur (Velcro), or a human tear in a Petri dish (penicillin). In each of these examples the common thread is that the scientist intuitively noticed the usefulness of the new material and goes on to refine their nascent ideas into something significant (Roberts, 1989).

In the experimental sciences persons who are graced by the windfall of intuition are not reluctant to admit their good fortune. Rather than being defensive about the role intuition played in their discoveries, they are often eager to describe it and these tales become part of the cultural mythology of invention, discovery, and innovation. Intuition does not diminish the prior efforts and knowledge that allowed them to be in the right place at the right time nor does it lessen the credit due to them for making the discovery.

Similarly, the presence of intuition is well documented in the business literature. From Bob Lutz at Chrysler to Donald Trump, successful CEOs often claim their business acumen to be based in part on their good instincts. Bob Lutz was president of Chrysler in the 1990s when the auto maker was in trouble. Out for a Sunday drive, he noted the joy he was experiencing driving his vintage Ford Cobra. The power and performance of the vehicle reminded him why he had decided to become an executive in the automotive industry. He reflected that currently Chrysler had no cars on the line that could provide the driver with the kind of driving experience he enjoyed behind the wheel of his beloved Cobra. Chrysler did, however, have several high-powered engines designed for their new series of pick-up trucks. He wondered if Chrysler might benefit from placing one of those engines in a luxury car. Lutz came home that afternoon with the broad outline of the Dodge Viper. The Viper went on to become an amazing success. A well-designed strategic plan? Hardly. However, Lutz claims that he intuitively knew there was a market for a distinctive powerful automobile.

Likewise, regular viewers of *The Apprentice*, Donald Trump's talent search and reality show are often reminded by "The Donald" of the importance of trusting their instincts in business settings. Weekly, Trump extols the virtues of intuition in his own decision-making practice, stating that he knew when certain ventures would prove successful or others would tank. Indeed, his practice of firing an apprentice each week is based as much on their performance as it is on his sense of how well the contestant will fit into his organization. Entertaining? Certainly. A moneymaker and image enhancer for Trump? Absolutely. A rational manner to hire top executives? Never.

We do not want to argue that rational analysis is a pointless exercise. As we argue elsewhere in this text, rational analysis is an essential tool in decision making. In agreement with Simon (1987), our viewpoint is that one needs to consider both rational and intuitive decision-making processes when forming a theory of strategic decision making. Our contention is that if we combine our sense of *just knowing* with our sense of reason we can respond far better to the problems at hand.

So what is intuition? For most people, intuition is a type or source of knowledge (Hogarth, 2001; Klein, 2003; Miller & Ireland, 2005). Based on sources of information outside of traditional explicit forms of knowledge, intuition is formed through a *process of rapid cognition* that lacks deliberate and evident logic or effort. Unlike the kinds of things we know because we learned them through courses of study such as statistics and French or directly orchestrated experiences such as driver's education or sewing class, intuition encompasses those things we have learned through relevant experience and expertise. For example, if you grew up in a house where the preparation of dinner was a familial activity, as an adult you may intuitively know when a sauce needs salt, pepper, lemon, or spice. If you learned these tastes and preparation cues on your mother, father, or grandparent's knee, the process of correcting the seasoning in a dish is second nature. You may not be able to say why you know that a hint of lemon is needed to brighten the sauce you just know it will contribute the necessary freshness.

Additionally, intuition is immediate and quick. It is based less in specific processes of retrieval such as deliberative or logical thinking and more in rapid and instinctual processes of response. *Instinct* is the word we choose when we are seeking to describe the things we know without awareness that we know them. We also claim our actions are instinctual when we are unable to provide a detailed description of the reasoning or process we used to make a decision. It is best thought of as our ability to comprehensively draw on our accumulated experiences, in or with a body of knowledge, and produce original or innovative responses to events, stimuli or situations.

Before we go further, we want to make clear that intuition is not the opposite of reason or rationality. It is not a process in which we wish our way to success. Nor is it a random process of guessing. Furthermore, we do not believe that intuition is an untapped source of knowledge that can be accessed by getting in touch with our feelings. Our contention is that intuition is a logical *form of reason*, where our accumulated knowledge and skill culled from years of life and professional experience come together to allow us to make decisions subconsciously, quickly, and with conviction. For us to begin to understand how this happens, let us turn to a discussion of how individuals and organizations store and use knowledge.

EXPLICIT AND TACIT KNOWLEDGE

Within the last decade, researchers have developed a growing interest in formalizing and increasing the accessibility of individual and organizational knowledge (Leithwood & Steinbach, 1994; Olivera, 2000; Miller & Ireland, 2005). In both corporate and academic circles, much of this interest has been channeled into knowledge management strategies and research. Within the corporate knowledge management literature, much has been written about different theories of organizational and personal knowledge, strategies for managing knowledge, and knowledge management's impact on organizational success (Argote, et al., 2000; Olivera, 2000; Kuvaas & Selart, 2004). While much of the focus has been placed on the technological information systems that support the cataloging and storage of knowledge, increasing attention is being paid to the social and organizational conditions that support knowledge creation and sharing between individuals (Cross & Baird, 2000).

When organizations create information systems to support knowledge use, the organizational challenge is one of data input and accessibility (Simon, 1976, 1981; March, 1988). Intellectual energy is focused on the development of structures that allow personnel to input data, often from a variety of unrelated sites and projects, into a shared structure from which still other employees can access the data. This view of data storage and access is the basis of traditional organizational knowledge and decision-making structures (Simon, 1987; Karsten, 1999; Weick, 2001). The theory holds that organizations retain information that has been stored as data pieces and the problem is then to locate and retrieve the essential information needed for a particular project (Weick, 2001). The data is then analyzed and categorized by employees who then present findings, implications, and solutions as needed (Stovall, et al., 2004).

Knowledge conceived of in structures such as these is wholly explicit. Explicit knowledge is a formal and tangible form of knowledge that is easily shared among personnel. Explicit knowledge is formal, systematic, and is easily categorized into words and numbers (Easterby-Smith, et al., 2000; Cross & Baird, 2000). This form of knowledge is often found in organizational publications, official documents, and operating procedures. It is decontextualized and static, separate from the contexts in which it was generated, previously useful and understood. Certainly, such structures are necessary for an organization to run smoothly and efficiently. However, they are not sufficient for growth nor can they be nimble or adaptive in responding to quickly shifting environments (Simon, 1987, 1993; Leithwood & Steinbach, 1994). Furthermore, in environments where attention has been solely focused on the development of structures to support explicit knowledge, it is common for administrators to be blindsided when a new organizational challenge transpires.

To illustrate this point, consider the plight of a large urban school district that, in response to a pressing disciplinary situation, drafts a new discipline policy. However, when a similar situation surfaces, the policy lacks the necessary robustness to be generalized to this new, slightly different, situation. Upper administration is then forced to redraft and recirculate new policy with each permutation of student behavior. The knowledge that was generated in the memo is explicit as it correctly suggests actions one should take in response to a given disciplinary situation. However, as student behavior changes, the policy and the explicit knowledge contained within it lacks usefulness as a problem solving tool and utility for principals attempting to resolve the current difficulty.

In contrast, nimble and adaptive responses rely almost exclusively on *tacit knowledge* (Schon, 1983, 1987; Simon, 1987; Browne & Pitts, 2004; Welter &

Egmon, 2006). Tacit knowledge can be thought of as the knowledge individuals develop over time and experience. It is a highly personal form of knowing, hard to formalize and, therefore, difficult to communicate to others. Tacit knowledge consists of both technical and cognitive skills. It is the know-how one needs to get the job done and the experience-based skill set to know what is and what ought to be. Additionally, it is action-centered, learned when one interacts with their environment over increasingly longer periods of time and distinctive experiences. It can be thought of as housed in the memories of individual experiences rather than in the memory of paper and policy.

Furthermore, individuals most often exclusively hold tacit knowledge. It defies easy structural categorization and data-set configuration. Consider the example of telephone support services in industry. Many of us have had the opportunity to call for technical support concerning our computers or other electronic devices. Sometimes the problem is easily assessed and repaired. However, time and again, these calls can be outright frustrating. Either the problem cannot be fixed or the repair that is suggested does not really address our situation. Many times, several calls need to be placed until the problem is fully addressed. In either case, from our vantage point, we want quick, effective service.

From the call center personnel's viewpoint, they want to provide efficient and successful service. However, as questions come into the call center, agents are faced with a wide variety of customer questions and unique situations occurring in rapid fashion. When a problem first surfaces, an agent may need to spend several hours or engage in multiple customer contacts concerning the problem until (hopefully) a solution is located. The troubleshooting effort uses the explicit materials included in support manuals; however, agents must also employ their knowledge from prior similar experiences. Call center operators draw on the wide range of solutions that have worked with similar problems on similar machines in the past. The troubleshooting decision-making process is one part technical assistance and one part detective work. By pairing the explicit technical knowledge with their tacit knowledge of how similar problems have been solved, expert call center operators can develop high quality customer service skills. However, tacit knowledge is rarely shared across call center personnel. Unfortunately, this is why it often takes multiple calls to multiple service agents before your unique problem can be addressed.

Our ability to employ our intuition relies on our ability to draw on tacit knowledge and apply it in decision-making situations. The difficultly is that our tacit knowledge lies just below the surface of our conscience. It commands very little of our attention and we are rarely aware when we are forming tacit understandings. Yet, tacit understandings become part of who we are and how we approach our daily lives. Developed as we interact with the environment our tacit understandings allow us to develop shortcuts within our daily thinking, routines, and structures.

Consider, for example, your reactions when driving. You constantly make small adjustments with little conscious attention to the process. Yet, when you first learned to drive all those adjustments took a great deal of effort, you had to deliberately remember to check your blind spot, use your mirrors and hold the wheel steady when you glanced left or right. As you gained expertise, those actions become more automatic. They become rooted in your tacit knowledge system. Now, imagine yourself driving down a crowded freeway. Suddenly a car shifts into your lane. All at once you hit the brakes and the horn, check your rear- and side-view mirrors and safely switch lanes. Almost second nature, these defensive driving tactics, honed over years behind the wheel occurred with even a second thought. Your tacit knowledge system took over, drawing on your years of driving expertise and skills. Once safely in your new lane of traffic, you might turn to your passenger and say, "I just knew he was not paying attention."

Intuitions are outputs of our tacit system of understanding. They allow us to work through our daily lives without explicitly needing to deliberate over each of our actions. By working automatically, tacit understandings allow us to act and react without conscious awareness. They accelerate our reactions in life-threatening circumstances and guide our response in daily professional situations. Now let us turn to thinking about how we acquire tacit knowledge in professional settings.

DEVELOPING PROFESSIONAL INTUITION

Where does our professional intuition come from? In part, it comes from our ability to recognize the patterns that are present in our daily activity (Weick, 1979, 1995, 2001). As we participate in activities and events that repeat themselves, we build up a set of experiences with the potential to inform future action (Simon, 1987; Klein, 2003; Miller & Ireland, 2005). Thus, our sense of knowing something seemingly without awareness is based on our ability to unconsciously catalogue these small slices of information. Gladwell (2005), based on the work of others (Ambady & Rosenthal, 1992), popularized the notion of *thin slicing*, our ability to find patterns based on very narrow slices of information.

Think for a minute about the last time you had an appointment with a parent of a student in your school. For purposes of this example, let us assume that as you enter into the meeting you have very little information about what the parent is seeking. You do know that the child is a good student, has not experienced any recent trouble (that you know of), and is in the band. As the parent enters the room you begin searching for cues concerning their demeanor so that you might know if the meeting will be a pleasant encounter. Based on your own thin-slicing ability, rank the following cues on a scale of either potentially positive or potentially negative signals concerning the meeting. The parent is . . .

Potentially Positive   *Potentially Negative*

.... Smiling ....

.... Alone ....

.... Casually dressed ....

.... Carrying a briefcase ....

.... Extends a hand to shake yours ....

.... Female ....

.... Male ....

.... Makes no eye contact ....

.... Is ten minutes late ....

.... Has a small child with them ....

.... Appears nervous ....

As a seasoned educator, you were probably able to make easy associations with several of the prompts above. In general, smiling, handshaking, causally dressed parents, do not walk into your office with difficult situations. On the other hand, a briefcase carrying, nervous parent who fails to make immediate eye contact may spell trouble. In your experience, a female parent may be less threatening than a male parent or than a couple who arrives to discuss an issue. What we are seeking when we thin slice is a recognizable pattern. Try to thin slice the information presented below. In this case, imagine you are trying to assess the quality of a teacher's classroom practice.

High Quality   *Low Quality*

.... Student desks are neatly aligned in rows ....

.... Chalkboards are clean ....

.... A classroom library appears ....
to hold over 100 books

.... A calendar marks the number of ....
days to the next holiday break

.... Homework assignments for the week ....
are posted on the side wall

.... The teacher is female ....

.... The teacher is male ....

.... The classroom pet is a python named Monty ....

.... The teacher lectures from the back of the room ....

.... The students are listening quietly ....

.... The teacher uses a *PowerPoint* presentation ....

This scenario should have proven more difficult as the information provided is less easily grouped and identified. Identification of the cues may be more difficult because you lack a context in which to place them. Furthermore, the construct of quality teaching is harder to define. Counting the days to the next break might be indicative of a teacher who cannot wait until they get time off or a teacher working to help students establish number sense. The use of a *PowerPoint* presentation might be seen as incorporating technology into the classroom or as inappropriate because it cannot be easily adjusted to meet student needs. The posted homework might be seen as an excellent organizational tool for student learning or an effort to be sure all the material in the textbook is covered by the end of the school year. Absent a more complete scenario, it is much harder to thin slice the data and locate the pattern. Without the appropriate *environmental definitions and cues* it is harder to make an accurate prediction of what might happen (see chapter 5 within this text for related ideas and theory).

Our ability to find patterns in environmental cues allows us to make effective decisions without conducting a deliberative analysis. As we enter any situation, we begin to scan the environment for cues that let us understand what might happen and how it might occur. Our *learned expertise* (Simon, 1987) tells us what cues to attend to and which cues we can ignore. A veteran educator can walk into a school or classroom and sense whether the climate is inviting or unpleasant. Similarly, physicians and mechanics can often make rapid diagnoses. By comparing the presenting symptoms they can quickly scan their prior knowledge set and suggest that the problem is strep or a malfunctioning carburetor. Experts have amassed a large body of knowledge that is both deeply rooted and automatically retrievable once stimulated by appropriate cues. Simply put, when you compare experts to novices it is clear that the experts know more. As such, learned expertise establishes the foundation for tacit knowledge (Schon, 1983, 1987; Simon, 1987; Welter & Egmon, 2006).

Proceeding from these ideas, we can start thinking about how intuitive understandings become rooted within our decision-making repertoire. Crossan (1999) suggests that learning occurs as an individual moves from early intuiting, through midstage interpreting to ultimately integrating the learning into their schema of action. Not unlike other forms of knowledge acquisition (see chapters 5 and 7 for discussions on data use in schools), Crossan's stages of learning suggest that initial knowledge is strongly influenced by one's intuitive sense. Crossan contends that the very nature of what we choose to pay attention to and subsequently learn is influenced by our sense of need and familiarity with the stimuli. That is, we more readily accept and learn those ideas and skills that appear useful to us and fit within patterns we currently recognize and employ in our decision-making processes (Hansen & Helgeson, 1996; Ratner & Herbst, 2005). This can be both good and bad. Weick (1978, 1995) argues that important data clues that are not captured by us due to our established recognition patterns (i.e., cognitive routines and patterns that prevent us from recognizing this data) can work against and blind us to important decision data.

We are always seeking to find patterns in the world around us (Weick, 1978, 1995; March, 1988). As we locate patterns in the world around us our thinking becomes more efficient and effective (Simon, 1976, 1981). Ascetically, we seek patterns we find pleasing. One such pattern that is common in art, photography, and architecture is that of the rule of thirds. The *rule of thirds*, also known as the *golden ratio*, suggests that most designs can be made more interesting by visually dividing the space into thirds vertically and/or horizontally and placing our most important elements within those thirds. Although this pattern is taught as part of art curricula across the Western world, even amateurs will often place the elements of a photo automatically into relationships that follow the rule of thirds. The pattern is one that is both visually pleasing and familiar to the eye.

Similarly, we search for recognizable patterns in our social and intellectual interactions. Socially and academically, we are most comfortable in situations where patterns of behavior run similar to our own. Often known as *social skills*, our patterns of behavior are influenced by our home and national cultures. In recent years, the significant increase in numbers of international students on campuses in English-speaking countries has paralleled an overall trend towards globalization, and makes cross-cultural encounters an inevitable part of the educational and employment experiences of professionals. Intercultural social interactions can potentially enhance personal development and provide excellent opportunities for building global professional networks. Nevertheless, they can also impose significant challenges for international students from a linguistic and cultural background very different from that of the host country. Various cultural disadvantages in the students' experiences, including adaptations required in classroom deportment such as asking questions, participating in classroom discussions giving presentations, and understanding the norms and values underpinning classroom interactions can make intercultural study difficult. As the behavioral scripts and patterns vary across cultures, even the most basic interactions can become fraught with difficultly.

However, by locating familiar patterns of logic and behavior in the stimuli we encounter, we are better able to respond. Once we have mastered the rule of thirds to frame our pictures, fewer vacation photos are discarded. Students with one international experience are better able to handle a second. Decision making is no different. As we identify patterns in day-to-day situations, we become adept at triggering the appropriate actions more quickly and immediately. When this behavior becomes second nature, our intuition begins to aid our responses and we are able to develop responses without having to think through our actions. Our behavior becomes reinforced with each new situation, and in turn, becomes more deeply embedded in our unconscious.

Once we sense the situation in which we find ourselves, *intuition* is the way we translate our experiences into judgments and decisions. We seek to find a pattern in the events unfolding around us, and our intuition allows us to recognize what is going on within the situation, and to recognize a set of appropriate actions with which to react. Once experienced, intuitive decision makers identify the pattern, any decision they have to make is more apparent.

The cycle then becomes self-informing and our intuitive behavior becomes more deeply rooted in our practice and response to the stimuli and events that confront us. When our pattern matching becomes automatic, and we are often not sure how we arrived at our responses to the events and stimuli that confront us, we then say that our behavior was *intuitive*—we *just knew* what was going to happen and how to respond.

INSPIRATION, INSIGHT, INTUITION, AND UNCERTAINTY

One of the goals of leadership is to confront and overcome challenges. Leadership is also about—at least in big picture terms—anticipating, dealing with, and minimizing the negative effects of uncertainties for the organization. At times, we can easily see our way. On other occasions the answer is less clear, more puzzling, and demanding. When writing about tough decisions, we noted that difficult decisions often force a leader to dig down deep for inspiration, information, and ability. When we find ourselves digging down deep for inspiration we are calling on our reserve of intuition. As complimentary ideas, inspiration, and intuition both rely on *insight*; the ability to solve a problem by seeing it in a different way (Hogarth, 2001; Barals, 2003).

We have argued that intuition is the unconscious application of tacit knowledge developed over multiple experiences in similar situations and with comparable stimuli. Conversely, inspiration is thought of as being more creative in nature where suddenly we find ourselves motivated to produce new thinking and/or outcomes. We say we are inspired to act when our thoughts and creativity are suddenly illuminated in new ways. However, both inspiration and intuition depend on insight, which allows us to actively employ knowledge that we already possess to solve a problem. Insight differs from intuition in how we employ and articulate our knowledge. It requires us to make explicit the knowledge we are employing in the problem solving process, whereas intuition relies on unarticulated, tacit understandings. From our viewpoint, the subconscious nature of the process is what links inspiration, intuition, and insight. When we are inspired to act and can articulate what knowledge we are applying, we can credit our success to insight. When we are inspired to act and cannot articulate from where our knowledge has come, we credit our success to intuition. In each case, we call upon our deeply held prior knowledge and apply it in ways we had not previously considered.

Nowhere is this distinction and ability more valuable than when we are facing uncertainty (Hansen & Helgeson, 1996; Sayegh, et al., 2004). Consider the flood of decisions made every day in schools across the nation. Educational leaders face curricular, instructional, disciplinary, fiscal, and physical plant issues daily. It has become commonplace for educational leaders to make many quick decisions in the course of their daily activities. Some of these decisions are easy;

others involve more difficult circumstances where we are uncertain about one or more aspects of the conditions surrounding the decision.

Uncertain circumstances share several key characteristics. There may be high ambiguity, the event may be unusual or unfamiliar, rapid response may be required, and the consequences of the decision may result in major change for the school organization (Crossan, 1999; Sayegh, et al., 2004). An example of this is when the safety of students may be in jeopardy. A fight may break out during lunch or recess, a school bus may be involved in an accident, or a chemistry experiment may go awry. In all these cases, a quick decision must be made in a highly charged atmosphere typically characterized by conflicting interests, high emotion, and uncertain outcomes. When faced with these immediate challenges leaders simply act, calling upon their reserves of explicit knowledge and intuitive awareness to quell the situation.

What appears to occur is the melding of explicit education and training with tacit perceptions and interpretations of the event at hand (Khatri & Ng, 2000). The adaptive outcomes that follow the melding of explicit and intuitive knowledge enhance the decision-making process. We are at once, by employing our intuition and insights, able to be imaginative, responsive, and visionary.

A WORD OF CAUTION

In this chapter we have been encouraging of the use of intuition in the decision-making process. We have tried to highlight the ways in which intuition, through the use of tacit knowledge, professional judgment, and pattern recognition can strengthen decision-making skills. However, we believe it is important to note the potential unreliability of gut reaction. Just as our initial reactions to a situation may lead the way to greatness, they may be equally damning. Our initial judgments may not be accurate. Bias may distort our thinking (See chapter 5 for more on this point). The root of a great deal of prejudice and discrimination are snap judgments made on outward appearances and associations (Weick, 1978, 1979, 1995; West, 1994; Hogarth, 2001; Myers, 2005).

Studies show that discriminatory behavior based on gender and race is broadly present throughout the United States when it comes to hiring practices and retention in academic and corporate employment (Bem & Bem, 1973; Glick, 1991; Petersen & Saporta, 2004). Even NBA selection processes and *American Idol* voting are not immune (Burdekin, et al., 2002; Lee, 2006). Simply put, even subtle biases can result in discrimination.

In an effort to create welcoming environments, business owners often try to hire employees with whom customers might relate. Known as customer discrimination, consumers will frequent establishments in which people with whom they feel some affiliation are employed. In turn, research shows that the racial composition of an establishment's customers has sizable effects on the race of who gets hired, particularly in jobs that involve direct contact with customers

(Holzer & Ihlanfeldt, 1998). A similar finding is echoed in the voting patterns of the public for *American Idol* contestants. Chiefly among African American viewers, strong evidence exists for same-race preferences (Lee, 2006). Viewing patterns are affected as well; as the show features more African American contestants it attracts more African American households to tune in to watch the show. As more African American viewers tune in, an African American contestant is less likely to be voted off the show (Lee, 2006).

In the NBA customer discrimination is more subtle (Burdekin, et al., 2002). Research has found that based on player performance statistics, no evidence of discrimination is found at the league level. The best players appear to be playing in the league regardless of race. However, players categorized by race are not randomly distributed across teams. Teams located in areas with greater concentration of white population find it revenue enhancing to cater to customer demand for viewing teams that include white players. This effect appears to be more pronounced for teams located in cities with larger white populations (Burdekin, et al., 2002).

Disheartening as the research may be, there are ways in which we can improve our sensitivity to bias and prejudice. We can find ways to develop accuracy in our judgments. Accuracy, it turns out, is based on four complimentary factors: relevance, availability, detection, and use (Hogarth, 2001; Klein, 2003). To better understand how these factors work, let us consider the attribute of responsiveness.

Responsiveness is a trait that is seemingly is short supply. Let us say you wanted a quote on painting your house. You place four calls to painters listed in the local telephone directory. Within hours, two painters return your call. You schedule appointments for quotes. However, you really wanted several more quotes to compare prices and be sure you were getting the best deal. Several days go by and another painter returns your call. You receive two quotes but a third painter fails to come at the appointed time. The estimates are hundreds of dollars apart. You grow impatient. You are not willing to simply hire the lowest bidder nor are you willing to over pay for the work. The deadline for when you wanted the work completed is approaching. Absent responsiveness, your ability to determine whom to hire is impaired. Although you wanted more choice in which painter to hire, feeling pressed for time, you book any painter.

In judging responsiveness, there are behaviors that are *relevant* to the behavior of responsiveness (Were your calls returned in a timely fashion? Were the painters able to schedule an estimate at a time that was convenient for you?). Second, what cues are *available* for observation (Did they come at the appointed time for the estimate? Were they careful in considering the complexity of the job at hand? Were factors such as the size and age of your house taken into consideration? Did they offer references?) Third, could you *detect* other indicators of their behaviors (When calls were returned did the painters seem rushed? Were they willing to discuss color choices with you? Did they offer to extend their discount on supplies required for the job?). Finally, could you actually *use* the data you collected at the estimate (Did you spend more time discussing the local sports team than the work? Did the references speak directly to the quality of the painting work or did they talk about other less pertinent matters)?

Each of these factors has an effect on the accuracy of your judgment. Obviously, if you are able to detect and attend to the relevance of the information you are taking in and then use it in your decision-making process, your chances of being biased or prejudiced are lessened. We have stressed that speed is an important aspect of intuitive thought. One of the wonderful things about the use of intuition in the decision-making process is that it can make the process faster. However, when speedy judgment reinforces bias and prejudice it serves us poorly.

SUCCESSFUL APPLICATIONS IN PRACTICE: QUALITIES OF SUCCESSFUL LEADERS

We build expertise as we build awareness of our own use of intuition in the decision-making process. No one begins anything as an expert. Even ball players, musicians, and artists considered having natural talent hone their craft in the minor leagues and on local stages before hitting the big time (Schon, 1983, 1987). They, and we, learn as we go, measuring our successes and failures against our ambitions and aspirations. What follows is some guidance for making better use of your intuition as you grow into a leader.

- *Be aware of what your intuition is telling you and then analyze it.* Pay attention to your first impressions. It is a long held truism that in testing, when students are unsure as to the correct answer in a set of choices, the first choice they make is most likely the correct one. When faced with a decision-making scenario, pay close attention to your gut reaction and then hold it up to scrutiny. Consider how your choice might play out. Examine your thinking for potential bias or prejudice. Then act.
- *Identify the conditions surrounding your choices.* As we have noted elsewhere in this text (chapters 3, 4, and 9), working to understand the context and conditions surrounding your decision can help you develop your intuitive skills. By paying attention to the conditions that surround you, you can better identify how this situation is like others in which you have acted in the past. Conversely, you may be able to identify why this new situation is unique and spare yourself the pain of misapplying an inappropriate script.
- *Do not confuse wishing with intuition.* Wanting something to happen is not the same thing as seeking patterns and trends in the situations that present themselves. We know people who repeatedly make the same mistakes, for example, dating the wrong person, running up charge cards with impulse purchases,

or overscheduling the workday. Intuition may tell them they are catching themselves in the same trap but they do it anyway. Why? They ignore the warning signs. More powerful influences are at work. Simply wanting things to be different rarely makes them so. On the other hand, intuition allows us the insight to see how things might be different this time around. We only need to pay attention.

• *Capitalize on uncertainly.* When faced with environmental instability use it to your advantage. Allow your mind to wander and see the possibilities. Brainstorming potential solutions and scenarios allows us to exploit the unknown. Take advantage of the opportunity to play, "what if?" It is in the spaces of our lives where we stop for a moment and consider the alternatives that often, our most inspired thinking occurs. View uncertainly as an opportunity for practicing using your intuition.

• *Know your limits.* At times we all need help. Even though you may be a great school leader you probably know less about the stock market than an experienced trader. Since intuition is based on the ability to unconsciously call upon experience and knowledge, know that seasoned experts can see subtle cues that neophytes might miss. However, once you have an expert you trust, be it for investing advice or addressing the school community, work with them. Ask them how they come to the decisions they make and try to plug into their intuitions in any given situation. In short, use their intuition to guide your decision-making process and work on learning from their knowledge and skill.

QUESTIONS FOR REFLECTION AND DISCUSSION

• Review and discuss the definition of intuition offered by the authors. How have they defined it? Reflect on how they have defined intuition both in terms of the actual working definition as well as what it is not.

• What is meant by *tacit knowledge* and what role or relationship does it share with intuition?

• Distinguish and discuss the relationship between the following concepts: *intuition, instinct, rationality,* and *insight.*

• How can understanding the characteristics and conditions of intuition and decision-making to help you to better understand decision making in context?

• To what extent do you use intuition in decision making? Can you identify a specific instance where intuition played a pivotal role in your experience?

• In what instances have you experienced the use of intuition to help frame, investigate, or resolve a problem in your school? What characteristics and conditions described in this chapter were present? In what ways did they support or hinder the decision process?

- When have you seen the use of intuition enhance decision making? In what ways has it helped focus attention on the tough questions of student learning?
- How do you view your intuitive skills? What are your strengths and limitations?
- What specific strategies might one engage in to increase one's intuitive abilities as a decision maker?

CHAPTER SEVEN

Data-Driven Decision Making for School Improvement

It has long been thought that school systems are under considerable pressure to progress but are often ill-equipped to measure their growth (Lashway, 2003a; Nitko, 2001; Short, Short, & Brinson, 1998). Yet as greater demands for accountability become required of school personnel, the environment of schools might be characterized as data-rich and knowledge-poor. Today, schools have available to them tremendous amounts of raw data supplied by a variety of sources. External sources include state departments of education, the federal government, local townships, and county educational offices. Internal sources may include data that is generated by the school itself: attendance and discipline records, student performance and demographic data, free and reduced lunch applications, drop-out rates, and the like. In spite of the plethora and availability of data, schools and educators often lack the capacity to process, analyze and communicate what this data has to say about the students and schools they serve (Easton & Luppescu, 2004; McCroskey, 1999).

THE CALL FOR DATA-DRIVEN DECISION MAKING

Historically, school leaders have not been rewarded or compensated in meaningful ways for efforts associated with data collection and analysis, nor have they been commended for suggesting programmatic changes on the basis of such reflection and review (Ladd, 1996; Tuomi, 2000; Tyack, 1974). As a result, the capacity of most educators and the organizations they lead to strategically collect and analyze data to address critical school problems remains underdeveloped. Moreover, the spatial isolation of schools and school districts works against developing strong linkages that encourage joint exploration of pedagogy (Darling-Hammond, 2000). As educators labor alone in classrooms, daily schedules do not allow for extended periods for deep discussion in relation to data collection, analysis, and use of results (Huffman & Kalnin, 2003; Louis & Kruse, 1995). Instead such conversations take place in short fragmented meetings often tacked onto the already full teaching day. These limitations, so much a part of school cultures, hinder focused examination of data related to student learning.

This is not to say there are not small, focused teams of teachers who engage in classroom research or action research projects. The findings teachers generate in action research projects can provide valuable insights into classroom practice. However, a few small action research projects do not lend themselves to policy decisions (Carr & Kemmis, 1997; Whyte, 1991). While these findings provide teachers with information concerning a teaching process or curricular implementation with a particular population of students (Huffman & Kalnin, 2003), work such as this cannot easily be generalized to other levels within the school much less other school settings. While action research may help an individual teacher develop understanding into his or her own problems of practice, the generalizability of such work is not strong enough for large-scale policy making.

As educators work to study their own practice in isolation, other equally distressing phenomena may occur. Collegial challenge, where teachers and school leaders frankly and openly discuss data and the potential it has to inform classroom practice, is necessary to develop a sense of deep understanding concerning the potential of any instructional or curricular innovation (Hargreaves, 1988). Yet what occurs in most schools suggests that an internal *groupthink* often develops. Lacking significant trust and access to new ideas, teachers often fall prey to discussions that simply validate their preconceived notions concerning students, curriculum, or instructional technique (Kruse, 2001; Scribner, Cockrell, Cockrell, & Valentine, 1999). The resulting dialogue often lacks the necessary content and depth to produce problem-solving deliberations and significant school improvement.

Likewise, the focus of internal research is often to validate the efforts of dedicated and industrious teachers. Hard work should be validated. Yet when validation efforts are the sole purpose of the analysis, questions of a more critical nature are often ignored. Questions such as "What works? How do we know that?" and "What could have been done better?" are important to the ongoing understandings needed to foster authentic, meaningful change with the potential to affect student learning in schools.

Inherent in the accountability movement are several barriers to the thoughtful use of data. As local, state, and national politicians and media put pressure on schools to deliver results, a sense of urgency can overtake school officials (Rubenfeld & Newstrom, 1994). Short-term solutions are often sought as this urgency increases. When the pressure to provide answers to the pressing questions of student achievement rises, traditional forms of data collection and analysis are often ignored for methods that produce quick answers (Leithwood & Steinbach, 1994). Disappointingly, short-term answers are embraced in an effort to solve complex problems, and thoughtful or critical evaluation is often relegated to a project to be attempted at another time. Shorter timelines hinder thoughtful investigation. This unintended consequence of the accountability movement can lead to attempted quick and dirty solutions to complex problems.

   Instead, thoughtful data analysis leads to rich decision-making actions as thoughtful analysis rests on purposeful and well-planned data collection strategies. Just as data is collected for purposes of school improvement, analysis plans must be undertaken with those ends in mind. These purposes may include a deeper understanding of the instructional practices employed by teachers, the ways in which students respond to the work tasks provided for them, and the ways in which particular curriculum are experienced by groups of students. In any case, the heart of data collection and analysis must be guided by a focus on high-quality teaching and improved outcomes for student learning.

   Schools have never been organizations in which data has been taken as a serious source of knowledge, generating effective change. Prior to the No Child left Behind (NCLB) legislation, the data collected on schools most often reflected the inputs of the system (e.g., tax dollars invested, number of books in the library, teacher–student ratios). NCLB shifted the attention away from models that focused on the inputs of the system-to-system outputs (e.g., test scores, graduation and attendance rates, and teacher qualifications). When we focus solely on inputs into the educational system, we often fail to consider how we might affect systemic outputs.

   There are, however, several indicators on the horizon that suggest the current landscape is changing. Accountability initiatives have created a need for targeted and focused data collection and skilled analysis (Cromey, Van der Ploeg, & Blase, 2000; Leithwood, Steinbach, & Jantzi, 2002). The national trend for required statewide tests has led to a redefinition of success for schools. Statewide testing has led many district personnel to shift their attention to scores and subgroup analysis with the potential to foster an increased focus on the implications of data for student achievement. As administrators and teachers develop skill with managing test score data, important findings are uncovered, revealing deficiencies in curriculum and instructional planning (Lashway, 2003b). As statewide testing becomes routine, achievement scores publicized by the media create for educators a sense of urgency for more data and for the answers these data might yield. Increased attention to data can help school leaders focus attention on what matters in classrooms and the most effective avenues to achieve preestablished instructional goals. In short, school data *strategically collected* and *strategically used* can stimulate high-quality decisions regarding student learning and school improvement.

   The heart of data based decision-making lies in the school leader's ability to identify the issues of student learning and achievement important for student success, collect meaningful data concerning those issues and analyze those data in ways that offer new understandings for classroom practice, school policies, and procedures. Only when decisions related to teaching and learning are based on the collection and analysis of data can school leaders be certain in what ways classroom practice influences student learning. In turn, it is only then that school leaders can set focused directions for school improvement and change.

ORGANIZATIONAL SUPPORT STRUCTURES AND TOOLS

Technology has allowed school personnel to manage large data sets such as those generated by state testing data (Petrides & Zahra Guiney, 2002; Streifer & Schumann, 2005). The ability to run analysis on desktop computers has increased educators' abilities to understand test and other school data in ways unavailable to their counterparts of early years. Additionally, computing has increased access to data sets. Test score information is now regularly provided in computerized files accessed by Excel or other common spreadsheet programs. Advances in data management have not only increased the ease and sophistication of data analysis but have unleashed the creativity of many school personnel as well (Kruse, 2001).

With the availability of these potent resources, the potential for bringing timely and relevant data to the point of decision has increased for educators. Educational leaders in particular can benefit from gaining both the knowledge and skills necessary to access and use this information to inform many of decisions they are called on to make. Yet all data are not created equal; nor are all data types equally appropriate for the variety of decisions leaders are called on to make. In addition, not all educators are equally adept at identifying, collecting, and using these data to inform the decisions they make. As implied by the title, this chapter examines data-driven decisions by educational leaders aimed at school improvement. In pursuing this purpose, we will describe and explore the following: the most prevalent forms of data found in schools (quantitative and qualitative), the systematic collection and analysis of data in school settings, and the issues and challenges associated with using data to inform decisions aimed at school improvement.

SCHOOL DATA—KINDS, FORMS, AND USES

Schools are data rich. Everywhere we turn there are obvious sources of data to help us understand how well our students are learning. Student grades, attendance, and other records abound. So do less visible and tangible forms of data. We might, for example, seek to understand how students experience the school setting or if they enjoy a particular subject. Data on these topics could be collected in a variety of ways: a formal survey or set of interviews, a student focus group or through informal conversations or observations. What we as educational leaders should seek when we collect and analyze data are better understandings of our school settings and the programs, policies, and practices that engage us.

At a very general level, the data we collect comes to us in one of two forms: as numbers or as words. *Quantitative data* are those data, which can be numerically represented. Be they demographic information, test scores, attendance rates, disciplinary actions or parent satisfaction survey results, quantitative data can be measured, counted, calculated, and computed (Nitko, 2001; Tuomi, 2000). They provide "hard numbers" on which analysis can be based. *Qualitative data* are those data that are represented with words or images. They may include interview or focus group text, classroom observations, and examples of student work or activities. While it is possible to count items within qualitative data such as the number of times a student might raise their hand in a particular lesson or how many parents comment on the new homework policy, qualitative data seek to offer school leaders a more complex and rich snapshot of how students, parents, staff, and faculty experience their involvement with and participation in the school organization.

Quantitative Data

Two examples of numerical data can be found in demographic data and student achievement data. Demographic data includes data such as background information on students and staff such as gender and ethnicity, number of years in a school or district, attendance patterns, teacher certification, and school enrollment. Achievement data includes student results on state proficiency or achievement exams, district and teacher developed tests, grades, and national tests such as the SAT or ACT. Knowing what each test measures is important for decision making. State standards-based tests measure student learning in relation to the standards schools are required to teach. Norm-referenced tests compare students with other students be they from within the district, in another district, or in another state or nation. They may or may not be aligned with standards in any given state. An example of a norm-referenced test would be the ACT or SAT. Criterion-referenced tests measure student performance on local or state curriculum and are based on expected levels of performance to determine mastery (Gall, Borg, & Gall, 2006; Nitko, 2001). State proficiency exams are examples of criterion-referenced tests.

The use of quantitative data can provide meaningful information for school personnel in their efforts to improve the level and quality of student achievement. One such example can be found in states and districts where annual tests are administered. Data generated from these tests are used to assess and align instructional practice and to compare these results across time, schools, and districts. During this process, trends, successes, and opportunities for improvement are noted. Testing results are viewed as valuable data to aid the decision process. Yet test scores are not the only form of quantitative data to which schools and districts might attend. Educators attentive to the learning patterns of students may also generate numerical data to examine assessment patterns within classrooms and courses. They may, for example, compare student grades to their standardized scores or engage in an analysis of common assessment items across multiple classes in a given subject area.

Educational leaders who are proactive in the use of quantitative data also attend to the ways in which that data is displayed and shared with internal and external communities (Tufte, 2001, 2003). Data on student progress can often appear overwhelming. States rarely provide these data in user-friendly formats. Long lists of item scores or subscale reports can be difficult to comprehend. Schools that have successfully integrated the use of quantitative data into their decision-making practices endeavor to display the complexity of numerical information as clearly as possible. Graphs, charts, and tables allow school personnel to become familiar with the data; clarifying, rather than obscuring the significance. As Tufte (2001) notes, "Graphics reveal data." By communicating numerical information through the use of tables and graphs, large data sets can be made coherent, the substance of the message can be easily grasped, and nuanced details made more vivid.

For example, if we wanted to compare the overall reading scores of third graders across several years of school, we might display those results as indicated in Table 7.1.

TABLE 7.1. Overall Reading Scores, Third Grade

	2001	2002	2003	2004
Percentage of passing students	68.5%	72%	82.5%	75%
State required pass rate	Not met	Not met	Met	Met

The table indicates that the majority of students in 2003 and 2004 passed the reading section of the state test, but we know very little about the nature of their performance. Similarly, in 2001 and 2002 they failed, but again we know very little about their strengths and weaknesses concerning the subscales and subpopulations within the larger reading portion of the test. Now, examine the following table that takes the same test data and provides subscale reports.

This table displays the reading scores on four subtests in reading where constructing meaning refers to the student's ability to understand the overall meaning of what they read and extending meaning refers to the student's abilities to interpret what they read. Certainly these data provide us with more information than the prior table presented. Whereas Table 7.1 pinpoints few, if any, specifics regarding student performance, Table 7.2 reveals more about this performance over time. Several reasonable inferences can be drawn from Table 7.2. First, there appears to be steady progress toward improved student

TABLE 7.2. Third Grade Subscale Data Overall Reading Scores: Percentage of Students Passing

	2001	2002	2003	2004
Constructing meaning (Fiction)	72%	75%	87%	78%
Constructing meaning (Nonfiction)	67%	69%	80%	76%
Extending meaning (Fiction)	70%	73%	85%	72%
Extending meaning (Nonfiction)	65%	71%	78%	74%

achievement over the 4-year period. Second, comparatively speaking, reading gains for students are greatest in nonfictional passages. Third, in 2003 something appears to have happened that resulted in a significant rise in reading gains. However, these achievement levels were not sustained in 2004. Other conclusions might be drawn as well.

What the table does not tell us are which students and what specific types of test questions—for example, true or false, multiple choice, short answer, and extended response items—with which students are having success or difficulty. Aggregate scores and reports do not provide the needed details of an item analysis. Consider the item analysis provided below in Tables 7.3a and 7.3b.

These tables provide us an even greater understanding of student performance. As can be seen, students are performing reasonably well on multiple-choice items related to functional passages and somewhat less well on those related to nonfiction passages. Student performance on short-answer and extended-response items, however, contrasts sharply with this. From 2001 to 2004, students have done consistently poorly on these assessments for fiction and nonfiction reading passages. Furthermore, the gender and ethnicity report provides us a sense that no group of students is doing better or poorly than

TABLE 7.3A. Third Grade Student Performance by Item Type, Overall Reading Scores (Number correct/total test items)

	2001	2002	2003	2004
Multiple Choice (Fiction)	18/22	19/22	19/22	19/22
Multiple Choice (Nonfiction)	10/22	17/22	19/22	17/22
Short Answer (Fiction)	0/4	0/4	1/4	1/4
Short Answer (Nonfiction)	0/4	0/4	1/4	0/4
Extended Response (Fiction)	0/2	0/2	1/2	0/2
Extended Response (Nonfiction)	0/2	0/2	0/2	0/2

TABLE 7.3B. Third Grade Student Performance (Gender and Ethnicity Analysis: Percentages of passing students)

	African American	American, Indian, or Alaskan National	Asian or Pacific Islander	Hispanic	Multiracial	White	Female	Male
Reading	57.6	NC	69.7	53.8	72.6	77.7	69.2	67.0
Math	55.2	NC	66.7	57.7	73.3	76.8	63.7	69.1
Science	42.8	NC	64.5	54.2	71.2	75.4	67.2	64.5
Citizenship	61.8	NC	67.8	55.6	74.5	74.7	68.3	67.4

others; yet, all are achieving below what the state would consider excellent performance.

An examination of these findings could raise numerous questions: What is the nature of these items on the test? Do we provide students an opportunity in classroom assessments to respond to short-answer and extended-response items? If so, do they mirror the ways in which the test presents these questions? If not, why not? In 2003, did we provide students more opportunity to practice short-answer assessments or was the 2003 test simply easier?

The point we want to stress here is that by taking the quantitative data and displaying them in a variety of ways, we are able to develop better understandings of the data that we are provided in relation to student achievement. As we delve into the data we already possess, we can discover valuable insights into where our students are achieving and where they are not. In turn, the data can then help us to understand what kinds of decisions we might consider as we seek to improve student performance. Results are often analyzed using statistics with attention to the validity and reliability of those findings (Gall, et al., 2006).

Validity and Reliability

Broadly speaking there are two dimensions of *validity*. In the context of data interpretation, *validity* refers to the extent to which one's interpretations of the data accurately reflect or are grounded in these data. The validity ascribed to the conclusions drawn from a data set is valid only to the degree that the data logically support these conclusions (Gall, et al., 2006; Nitko, 2001; Tuomi, 2000). Thus, when considering the validity of a particular set of data, one must not only examine how these data are *collected* but also how these data are *interpreted*. For example, we cannot say a particular test is valid in all cases. A mathematics test may be valid in one district or setting because it aligns with student-learning outcomes of that particular school district's program objectives. This same test, however, may not match program objectives from a neighboring district. It lacks validity for the teaching and learning that is occurring in that district. Only if the test is aligned with the curriculum objectives of the district can it be considered valid. Subsequently, only if the *interpretation* of these scores is rooted in the data provided by the test can it be considered valid. Valid inferences regarding the level of reading proficiency in the district rest on the validity of the measure used to assess this proficiency.

An example is helpful to further develop these ideas. In a school district outside of a large metropolitan area, it was decided that the Very Good Reading Assessment (VGRA) would be administered to all incoming fourth graders. Principals across the district questioned why the VGRA was chosen. The response from the district curriculum director was that the VGRA is the same assessment that a neighboring school district uses, and therefore, it was believed that they should use the VGRA as well. Perhaps the VGRA is a valid assessment for the fourth grade students. Yet until an alignment between what the VGRA assesses and the district curriculum in reading is completed, it is impossible to know if the results obtained from administering the VGRA will be a *valid* way to measure students' reading achievement against the goals set by the district.

If the question were instead, "Will the VGRA provide *consistent* results?" the concern would be for *reliability*. Reliability is the extent to which a measure yields consistent results (Gall, et al., 2006; Nitko, 2001; Tuomi, 2000). If a consistent result cannot be obtained from the assessment instrument, the data is not a valid measure of student achievement. Data obtained from an unreliable testing instrument can never be valid. On the other hand, a measure can be reliable but not valid for the assessment purposes at hand. A noted standardized reading measure may be reliable but not valid for the reading curriculum in your district. If the measures we are using to collect student achievement data in our schools lack validity or reliability, the data generated from these measures provide an inadequate foundation for sound decisions. Yet, quantitative data can only provide some of the data necessary for school leaders to understand what is happening within their schools. The collection of qualitative data can help to create a fuller snapshot of what is occurring on a day-to-day basis within the school.

Qualitative Data

Qualitative data are those data that are associated with words and perceptions. These types of data may include data from interviews, focus groups, and written questionnaires. Qualitative data might also include instructional or curricular data. While these data might be aggregated so that percentage means, standard deviations, and the like might be computed, the qualitative forms of the data most often include quotes from interviews or other types of texts with the potential to enhance understanding beyond numerical representation and allow for the development of a variety of perspectives to be considered and provide opportunity for evolving and adaptable methodologies to be employed during the collection and analysis phases of inquiry (Clandinin & Connelley, 2000; Nitko, 2001).

Qualitative data can include information about the curriculum, classroom observation data, student task analysis, attempted interventions, and the like. Furthermore, these data include material derived from interviews and focus groups, surveys, and questionnaires related to the ideas people hold about the school and the activities that occur at school. In each case, these data provide the school leader a fuller picture concerning the multiple factors that influence student performance. By using qualitative data in concert with quantitative measures, school leaders can begin to unravel the subtle intricate ways in which student learning is affected.

In schools where classroom level data is systematically collected, staff and faculty pose questions about how students engage with classroom practice and how parents and other stakeholders perceive the school's effectiveness. Two forms of classroom-level data collection we find particularly useful are student work assessments and studies of school and classroom time use. Student work collection and analysis answer the research question, "What work is supplied to students to enhance their learning?" The student work audit process may be used for several purposes, all of which allow school personnel the ability to comprehensively analyze the type and quality of work given to students. Purposes may include (a) alignment of student work with general content standards, (b) alignment of student work with the cognitive level at which standards are written, and (c) alignment of student work with best practices in the field. While an initial study of student work can be completed with the assignment as provided to the student, an assessment of completed student work might be attempted as well. However, completed student work assessment answers a different question—that is, "How do students respond to the prompts as supplied?"

Time studies can provide similar, useful, and important information concerning how time is used in schools and most importantly in classrooms. Time studies can take on two complimentary foci: study of school calendar and study of classroom activity. School calendar studies can be completed by creating a master calendar for the school inclusive of all school breaks, testing dates, events such as assemblies or parent conferences, and other activities that take time away from instruction. Additionally, the calendar should reflect the reality of school life (i.e., notation of the afternoons prior to breaks, football and basketball games, assembly practice schedules, and the like). Once noninstructional time is accounted for, leaders will obtain a more realistic notion of the potential time on task for academic purposes. Classroom-based time studies take on a more direct focus. Classroom study provides data with the potential to inform decision making concerning the implementation of instructional practices and new structural innovations such as block scheduling and integrated team teaching formats.

Validity and Reliability in Qualitative Data

Concerns for validity and reliability exist for qualitative data as well. Unlike numerical data, qualitative data assumes a point of view. What one reports in an interview, observes in a classroom, or identifies within a student assignment are all, in part, open to interpretation. Because, these data lie within the social narrative of the school, interpretations of these data may not remain constant over time. A parent who claims in a fall interview that the school is not responsive to her child's learning disability may change her mind by spring responding with praise to follow-up interview questions. The classroom practice of a novice teacher may improve greatly over the course of a year's coaching and mentoring. What was viewed in 2003 as a wonderful project for students to complete may be considered frivolous by 2006 after an alignment of student work alignment with the academic standards is considered. All of these changes could be seen as positive growth toward school goals. However, to be considered valid and reliable they must be confirmed by more than simple logic. We must be sure we can trust our conclusions. To determine trustworthiness of our data we must consider three related ideas: persuasiveness, coherence, and pragmatic use (Riessman, 1993).

Persuasiveness. Persuasiveness suggests that a conclusion is both reasonable and convincing. Persuasiveness lies not in clear statistical measures but in the ability of the conclusion to withstand critique and reflection. It is a persuasive argument that a coaching and mentoring program is having a positive influence on classroom practice when novice teachers can more clearly articulate the reasons for their instructional choices over time. However, this argument becomes more persuasive when school members come together to discuss the findings and suggest other potential causes for these increased skills (Were these teachers simultaneously enrolled in a master's program? Did the district offer considerable professional development over the year of the study? Was the observed growth uniform across all members of the mentoring program or did only some members' exhibit increased reflective capacity?). When school leaders can answer questions such as these in ways they find satisfying, they can trust their conclusion that the mentoring program was, in fact, a contributing factor in teachers' development. The conclusion is persuasive.

Coherence. Similar to the notion of consistency introduced earlier in this chapter, coherence suggests that there must be some congruity across themes within the data. When the data collected from the teachers in the mentoring program is reviewed, do common ideas emerge in the interview text? Do participating teachers indicate similar understandings of their classroom practice? Are they able to articulate their instructional choices in ways that suggest implementation of the theory on which the mentoring program was based? Once the collected data appears to be coherent, an organizational narrative may be constructed that suggests that the mentoring program has the potential to help the school reach its goals. Conversely, if the data collected has no consistency, suggesting random organizational impacts, the program cannot be considered successful.

Pragmatic use. Lastly, when considering validity and reliability of qualitative data, the question of meaning must be addressed—that is, do the findings have any relevant applications for classroom practice and school improvement? Simply put, the conclusions reached must be useful within the school context to contribute to the understanding of how the school functions. While it may be exciting to discover that novice teachers enjoy talking with a mentor about their classroom practice, if the nature of their reports suggests that the program serves a largely social rather than intellectual purpose, it may not be pragmatic to continue.

Once the criteria of trustworthiness are established, qualitative data can offer the school leader a rich and unique window into the practices and experiences of school members. When collected in concert with quantitative data, qualitative data has the potential to fill in the gaps and answer the questions of practice that numerical data often leave under explored. Yet, for data to be useful in the decision-making process it must be shared and discussed among school members. The next section of this chapter offers insight into how this might be achieved.

DATA ANALYSIS AND DECISION MAKING

Once data is collected and aggregated, data can be shared with the committee and faculty. Aggregation may take on a variety of forms. We might wish to aggregate the findings by grade level or subject-area department, allowing for comparisons across the full school setting. On the other hand, we might wish to aggregate the data by semester or grading periods, allowing for comparisons between time periods within the academic year. Data can be aggregated by any number of groupings—enrollment and attendance patterns, gender, ethnicity, language proficiency, or years of service. By aggregating the data within these categories we can begin to answer questions such as, What programs and practices do students or parents like best? How and why do they reach these conclusions? Do all students experience the school in the same ways? If not, how do they differ? In what ways do teachers report using their classroom time? Are there patterns in time use? If so, what can those patterns begin to tell us about student learning?

No matter what kind of data you are working with, once the data are collected and aggregated the next step is to take seriously what the data say about how classroom practice reflects the vision of instruction, curriculum, and assessment within the school. Do the data suggest that teachers are implementing curriculum with fidelity? Or do data suggest that commitment to the adopted curriculum is sparse and inconsistent? Do the data hint any differences among student or parent groups with new practices or policies? Perhaps one segment of the school community finds the new curriculum more challenging than others. By answering questions such as these, school leaders can better understand the subtle nuances of how school practice and policy affects student learning. Further decision making might consider how professional development might support vision or how other forms of mentoring, peer coaching, and the like might enhance existing expectations for instruction.

Data must be linked to an overall school improvement strategy. Data collected must help members of the school community to make forward progress toward organizational goals. Student achievement can be improved in schools where a tightly linked process is in place for the collection and analysis of school data that is then utilized to inform practice in the classroom. In schools where data might be reviewed and then shelved for some future day, student performance toward goals often stagnates. It is not enough to collect and review data;

meaningful action in the form of instructional innovation, curricular reform, and assessment redesign must be employed for change to occur.

MEANINGFULNESS OF DATA IN
THE DECISION-MAKING PROCESS

For data-based decision making to become institutionalized in school organizations, the process must be meaningful for all those involved. However, meaning is a difficult construct. Meaning conveys intention, as in, "I mean to exercise today." Meaning suggests consequences such as when we say, "This means trouble." Meaning confers importance, as in, "That really means something," or value, for example, when someone says, "It means the world to me." Meaning differs across people, places, events, and time. Items, events, and memories that held great meaning often fade with age, new experiences, or understandings. For example, high school homecoming dances, proms, and even graduation become less meaningful as one ages.

Meaning is also linked to hope (Wallis, 1996, 2002). Hope, according to Wallis, "is a readiness to keep striving to advance a particular quest or strengthen a particular relationship in the face of discomfort or disappointment" (p. 67). As we hope for what might be, whether it concerns our own lives or the lives of students in our schools or classrooms, we create visions of what might be. Once articulated, our vision helps us to make meaning of the events around us and to make decisions about the future. As we search to make sense and meaning of what confronts us, we draw on hope to see us through. In turn, meaning relies on hope. The process of placing our hope in certain goals involves a commitment of self in the understanding and realization of these goals. In this way, hope and meaning are connected. Simply put, we invest our time in making meaningful those things we hope to obtain, understand, or influence.

Similarly, when we do not believe in something, we do not tend to invest much effort in it. Without hope, it is easy to decide data are meaningless and cannot provide the information needed to fuel our efforts. As such, school leaders first need to develop a sense of need, a clear vision, and focus for the work of the school organization. Without vision and direction, data cannot have meaning. Furthermore, data are contextual. As what is considered important shifts with individual interest, external politics, or media attention, the importance we place on collected data shifts as well.

DATA AND SCHOOL IMPROVEMENT

For example, as school and districts begin to take data collection and analysis sincerely, using each year's findings to inform classroom practice, the message that school improvement efforts are valued becomes institutionalized. Teachers and parents begin to invest deep meaning in their role as part of the school improvement team. Rather than viewing each year's test score result with trepidation and fear, the release of the data becomes a time for shared inquiry and focus. Rising or failing test scores may well provide the impetuous for a school improvement agenda, but by themselves they cannot be the agenda. Instead, school improvement as a shared educational agenda is an important construct because it centrally places the professional endeavors of educators—teaching and learning, curriculum and instruction—as the work of the school. As such, school improvement efforts can become meaningful when they embrace what is important to the members of the school organization. Meaningful data help to facilitate faculty and staff improvement efforts when data help organizational members to understand and reflect on information that holds significance for classroom practice, school policies, and programs.

So what data can be considered reflective of a school improvement agenda? As we have noted previously, schools are literally drowning in data. Potentially, data could include anything you might be able to count or record—student attendance; student grades; state and national testing results; attendance at parent–teacher conferences; sporting and arts events; staff, parent, and student survey responses; demographic profiles of the school and surrounding community; retention rates for students and faculty; student–teacher ratios; interview or focus group responses with teachers, students, parents, or community members; classroom observations, lesson plan analysis—the list could be endless. Dependent on the school's focus, any of these data types might be meaningful. On the other hand, school improvement efforts often stall when too much data or data that is not central to the issues are collected. The technique thriving school leaders employ when posing thoughtful questions about student learning and school success is to target three to five complimentary data sources with the potential to provide insight into the issue at hand. By utilizing multiple data sources, subsequent decision making is based on accurate interpretations of data across several data points.

Multiple Data Sources

Multiple data sources allow leaders to better understand his or her data by triangulation, the process in which data and subsequent findings are supported by more than one source. Accurate findings increase a leader's ability to make good decisions. However, in the context of discernment, multiple data sources serve several related purposes. The first creates opportunity for members within the organization to base resultant understandings in sources they find credible. The second addresses the variety of values organizational members may hold as they consider potential futures of and for their schools. When shared understandings are paired with clearly understood future visions for the school, improvement efforts can become more focused and meaningful to organizational members because they can both see and understand their role in the process.

Data that school members find credible can be considered to fall along a continuum ranging from the informal to the formal. Informal data are in high supply in school settings. Informal data include data that teachers intuitively collect on a day-to-day basis (Clandinin & Connelley, 2000; Gall, et al., 2006). These data might suggest to the teacher which students are "getting it" and which are not, who comes to school prepared and ready to learn and who does not, as well as cultural cues concerning what types of learning experiences are valued within the school and, conversely, which are not. Informal data is meaningful because it is generated in highly personal settings and experiences.

Formal data are readily available in schools. These data include test scores and assessments, attendance records, and the like (Gall, et al., 2006; Northcutt & McCoy, 2004). Formal data are considered meaningful when it meets the statistical tests of validity and reliability. Formal data also becomes meaningful as others appropriate it for political or other purposes. For some school organization members, informal data might be considered more relevant and meaningful than formal data; for others, the reverse may be true. For the school leader, the challenge is to synthesize and triangulate the two, thus creating meaning concerning school-based data, events, and trends.

Organizational values, including those resulting from national, regional, and local initiatives, are one determining factor in assigning meaning to data. Values establish the parameter of what an individual or organization stands for and determines if they will commit to a course of action (Schein, 1985). Shared values provide a sense of organizational identity and common course that directs the school entity forward (Louis & Kruse, 1995; Peterson & Deal, 2003). As school members work together, values are nurtured and developed by deliberation over real problems of practice. A school faculty that considers data in the context of their values unavoidably finds meaning that reinforces their ideals and strengthens their overall organization.

An example serves well here. Faculty at Falls Middle School was concerned about student testing results. Far too many students appeared to be failing the state assessments in reading. Informal data suggested that student absences were to blame. Teachers reasoned that if students were not in class, they could not be learning the material. A small subcommittee was formed to create incentives to entice students to attend school more regularly. An attendance reward program was designed and presented to the faculty.

At the meeting where the plan to increase student attendance was presented, a teacher posed the question, "Have we looked at the attendance data? My kids seem to be in class most days." Dismissively, the planning team asserted they did not need to look at the data, their experience suggested otherwise. Additionally, they contended that trying to increase attendance could not possibly have a negative affect. A second questioning teacher pressed the issue asking for "the numbers." His retort was, "If we're wrong, we're another year behind." Seemingly, the group was at a stalemate. Finally, a guidance counselor offered to "pull the numbers" and look and see if the kids who had not passed did, in fact, have a high absence rate.

Within the month, the group convened again, this time with more formal data. The counselor's data supported the experience of the reluctant teacher—students who failed the reading tests were not absent at higher rates than other students, and, in fact, student absence in general was fairly low. She allowed that the school had a handful of chronic offenders and noted that the planning committee teachers did have several of those students in their classes.

The result of these efforts was that both the planning committee teachers and the questioning teachers had data they could find meaningful. By synthesizing informal and formal data, these teachers could each embrace data they found credible and could support the resulting decision. Furthermore, the values of the group were honored. Student success was at the heart of the discussion, as was decision making for the benefit of the school organization.

As this case illustrates, meaningfulness is strongly linked to experiences, factors, and values outside of the actual statistics on the page. It is also connected to numerical and statistical measures. As leaders strive to create policy and practice based securely in data, the issue of meaning must be considered. One must remember that meaning is constructed within the context of the school, the member's experiences within the school and the surrounding community, and in relation to the values and beliefs held by those members.

COMPLEXITY AND CHANGE IN
RELATION TO DATA-BASED FINDINGS

Organizations are complex social entities. Daily operations must be managed. Goals and foci change, and new policies and procedures must be developed to address increasingly complex dilemmas. Schools are no exception to this rule. The detail of daily operations—ordering lunches, pupil attendance, scheduling, planning meetings and assemblies, monitoring instruction and curriculum implementation, and so on—can be all consuming for school leaders. Yet, as we have argued elsewhere in this volume (see chapters 2 and 3), decisions related to the details of daily operation are relatively straightforward. Known as detail complexity (Heifetz, 1994; March, 1991), the decisions that comprise the day-to-day operations of the school organization are relatively clear. Policy and practice can be developed, implemented, and monitored. Although time-consuming, attending to detail complexity requires little creative action on the part of school leaders.

Less easily addressed are issues of dynamic complexity (Heifetz, 1994; March, 1991). Dynamic complexity addresses the results of decisions that have subtle and less obvious outcomes. Decisions related to data collection and analyses often have dynamic complexity. Decisions related to change always produce dynamic complexity. When teachers and school leaders collect and study trends in test scores or survey responses, it is all too easy to suggest that simply changing X (a teaching practice) will result in Y (student learning). Generally, teaching is a profession that gives credibility to explanations that suggest causality. Yet, as we all know, X does not always predict Y. Decisions made on the presumption of causality appear, at first glance, to hold great promise. Yet, they often fail due to the dynamic complexity of schools. Understanding the relationship of data to information and knowledge can help us better understand the nuances of dynamic complexity.

THE DATA-INFORMATION-KNOWLEDGE CYCLE

The knowledge–management literature suggests a difference between data, information, and knowledge (Leithwood & Steinbach, 1994; Streifer & Schumann, 2005). In this literature, data are most often seen as simple, factual statements or records. Thus, as test scores are reported, survey responses tallied, or interview text quoted, these raw data lack meaning. Only when collected data are placed into meaningful organizational structures do they become information. For example, an increase or decrease in reading scores is only data. Only when placed within the larger structure of a school's achievement goals does this fact become meaningful information for the decision-making process. In turn, these data become knowledge when they are put into context. Within this model, data without interpretation lacks meaning, and comprehensive meaning is only derived when information is endowed with relevance and purpose within a particular setting. Once endowed with meaning and within context, data becomes predictable, and intelligent choices about its use(s) may be explored by members of the organization.

Promising practices for the creation of knowledge from data within schools include the provision of time for teachers to meet and talk about findings (Hargreaves, 1988; Leithwood & Steinbach, 1994; Louis & Kruse, 1995). By pairing data with focused dialogue school personnel can begin to interpret their own work in new ways. Supported by the shared opportunity to articulate, verbalize, and structure information, faculty and staff can develop interpretations of information generated at the school site. These interpretations lead to the development of innovations based on student need rather than guesswork. Knowledge about student learning as derived from the data collection and analysis process emerges through interpersonal validation of shared experiences and understandings.

However, to suggest that the process of knowledge development is linear misses the mark. In practice, it appears that data-management and decision-making processes are essentially recursive social systems, where the data collection and analysis support the processing of knowledge and decision making related to change and innovation (Streifer & Schumann, 2000). An important implication of this idea is that as educators design structures to enhance activities of members of the school organization, attention to the communal social structures that underlie meaning processing is necessary. As such, data use cannot be understood as a stand-alone process; instead, successful implementation of innovations must combine daily procedural detail with more complex social and cooperative processes.

SUCCESSFUL APPLICATIONS IN PRACTICE: QUALITIES OF SUCCESSFUL LEADERS

Successful leaders utilize a variety of overlapping strategies and skills with the potential to enhance their use and understanding of data in their school setting. First, data is collected in a strategic and sustained manner focusing on data with the best potential to address meaningful inquiry. Second, data is analyzed with an eye toward action planning and progress toward student-learning goals. Finally, data is used as a means for and of developing professional efficacy and community among teachers.

Ongoing data collection. Data collection is the foundation of quality-data-based decisions. In fact, high-quality decisions can only come from valid, reliable, and triangulated data. So what do exceptional school leaders need to do to develop data collection skills? We recommend the following action steps to increase a leader's ability to use data collection to increase decision-making success:

- *Develop general questions to guide your inquiry.* When considering data collection, it is important to start with the end in view. There are a multitude of potentially rich data sources in any school setting. The first job of a leader engaged in data-based decision making is to determine the questions that you wish to answer. Knowing that at any given time there are numerous questions that might be posed and studied, it is important to assess which questions seem the most pressing and address those before others. These questions might be posed locally or influenced by state or national issues. Perhaps faculty and staff have noted a disparity between the performance of students based on gender, socioeconomic status, race, ethnicity, or more mobile families. Possibly parents have questioned the safety and security of the school. You may potentially be interested in determining if a new text or program adoption has made any impact on student learning. In any of these cases, a clearly worded question is needed to guide your inquiry. By beginning with focused questions, you are less likely to stray during the data collection phase and more likely to achieve the answers you desire. For example, your overall guiding question might relate to the kinds of assessments on which students appear to struggle. You might ask the following question, guided by the focus on student assessment. What kinds of information can your data tell you about your students' ability to respond to a wide range of assessment items?

- *Determine the data that is needed.* Once you have clarified the question(s) you wish to address, you must determine the data required to best address your focus area(s). This data may be in numerical or verbal form or a combination of both. Useful sources of student data include direct measures of student learning such as state and local criteria, and norm-referenced exams, and indirect measures such as grade point, graduation rates, and postsecondary placement rates. Additionally, you may wish to collect measures related to demographic indicators such as attendance, discipline, and school violence rates or measures of students' characteristics such as ethnicity, gender, and socioeconomic or disability status. Finally, there may be context variables for which you wish to collect information. Context variables may include data related to school and class size, teacher training and experience, parent–school partnerships, or perceptions of school climate. Questions that may help you to focus on the kinds of data required for your inquiry might include the following:

  - Where is data present or lacking?
  - What other kinds of data will you need to answer questions about those goals and how will you go about getting it?
  - Are there particular innovations or changes (curriculum, instruction, assessment policies, practices, and programs) in your district or school that have the potential to account for your findings?
    - How will you test the hypothesis?
    - What data should be collected to test it?
  - Are there particular groups of students who score better or less well than others?
    - What innovations or changes might be needed to address these issues?
    - How would you collect data on those efforts?
  - How are teachers using formative and summative assessment to guide instructional and curricular decisions?
    - How often are formative and summative assessments discussed? What students are discussed most often?
    - What kinds of data might you wish to obtain concerning student progress in relation to district achievement goals?

- *Locate multiple measures and different sources for complementary data.* By including multiple data points and measures in your data-collection plan, the validity of inferences drawn from these data in the decision-making process is potentially enhanced. Any single measure or data point has limited meaning. By incorporating multiple data measures *and* measures across time, the potential for drawing valid inferences and making sound decisions from these data are increased. Across multiple measures, the same strengths and weaknesses may occur. Gaps and overlaps in curriculum may become clear, and contextual data may illuminate information that is otherwise vague or equivocal.

- *Craft organization plans and methodologies.* Organize the data with appropriate student-learning questions in mind. These questions might derive from state-level testing data, or they may be more internally driven. In either case, focused, data-based decision making results from clarity when collecting and organizing data. Try to group your data as efficiently as possible. Grouping data helps organizational members determine the relationships among the data. For example, data related to student achievement should be collected by subject area and grade level, as appropriate. Additionally, consider your audience when developing your groupings. More sophisticated audiences may appreciate more complex analysis and less experienced audiences might require a more straightforward approach. In either case, craft organization plans that have the potential to foster, rather than complicate data interpretation.
- *Consider data display.* Data should be displayed in a manner that is simple, relevant, useable, and readily understood. Choose your presentation format wisely, you may want to use bar graphs to show rankings, information for multiple groups, and trends across time; line graphs to show trends across time and compare trends for different groups; scatter grams to show relationships between two sets of scores; and pie charts to show parts to a whole or percentages of a whole. Consider using tables for the easy display of large amounts of comparative data. Finally, be careful to limit the amount of data in any single chart or table to the significant facts, ideas, and trends as guided by your school improvement plan.
- *Develop ongoing data collection practices.* Most important for the data-driven educational leader is the need to develop an ongoing set of data collection practices. The goal is to develop an organizational culture that thrives on data. As opposed to decisions based on myth, opinion, or conjecture, data-driven decisions require an uncompromising focus on information, facts, figures, and records that inform current and desired school practice. The ongoing collection of baseline data identified as relevant by school improvement goals is critical to the development of a data-driven culture within the school or district.

DATA ANALYSIS SKILLS

Once collected, data must be analyzed to determine what it is reveals about the school, students, faculty, and community of which it is a part. Data analysis must be guided by an analysis plan that takes into account your area of interest and comparisons directly related to your questions. For example, using our assessment type example, we can see that a variety of data might be collected on the topic. Collected data might include assessment items from state testing data, items from homework and other classroom generated sources, as well as surveys from parents and students concerning how they believe students learn. As we suggested before, data collection can only influence student achievement results if it is used to inform decisions related to teaching and learning. Analysis of the data is the first step toward its use in school improvement efforts.

- *Determine what you wish to compare.* Comparisons can be drawn across a wide range of fields using a number of variables. Results can be compared to expectations and to baseline data collected in prior years. Current test score data can be contrasted to previous test score data. This year's students can be judged against other groups of students as well as within and among subgroups of students (e.g., SES, gender, and ethnicity). The important issue is to determine your *interests* and *priorities* for examining the data. Certainly, there are a number of ways to aggregate, disaggregate, and compare the data you collect. Data analysis is less a contest about who can create the most charts and graphs from the assembled material than it is strategically determining *what* is of value then focusing your analysis in those areas.
- *Locate the patterns within the data.* We analyze data to determine students' most significant strengths and weaknesses, student and community perceptions of school culture and climate, as well as changes of these measures over time. Data analysis is most productive when it is focused on the identification of patterns within the data. The search for patterns within the data may reveal that students are not achieving as well in areas of the curriculum that require higher level analysis or that participation in school-sponsored tutoring programs has decreased over time. Once identified, data patterns should provoke thought as to *why* these phenomena are occurring. These patterns should likewise inform subsequent strategies and decisions to address them.
- *Look for confirmation across data.* Each data point can provide only a small segment of the complete story. Confirmation by triangulation across types and sources of data adds power to the conclusions drawn and the resultant decisions. When data contradicts itself, school leaders should ask *why* and seek additional clarification, explanation, and description. Students often do well on teacher-made assessments yet poorly on standardized, state-level assessment items. These would appear to be contradictory data points. Yet, further examination reveals that teacher-created assessments may not have asked students to explain their thinking *or* that state-level assessments included content material not addressed by the teacher. By triangulating data, examining data discrepancies, and seeking to determine

what reasonable inferences can be drawn from these data, decisions aimed at school improvement and student learning are enhanced.

• *Develop interpretations of what the data mean.* As examined in chapter 5 of this volume, causality can be difficult to determine. It may be difficult to pinpoint the exact reason for rising or falling standardized test scores in a school. Did scores rise as a result of the new curriculum adopted? Can recent gains be attributed to the strategically based professional development workshops held earlier in the school year? New issues may emerge in response to events across the nation or globe. School leaders need to develop careful interpretations of their data yet always hold these interpretations up for further consideration. New programs may suggest promising practices, but further data should be collected to determine if gains hold over time and across groups of students. Increased parent communication may be proving effective; however, follow-up work might still need to be completed. Teachers may report strong satisfaction with newly adopted materials; however, further study ought to be completed to confirm full implementation. Any set of data has its limitations. By recognizing these limitations, leaders can increase their confidence in subsequent decisions based on those data. Furthermore, by assuring that the data is used in valid and reliable ways, decision-making confidence can be increased.

• *Consider additional data needs.* If data suggests that attendance at school-sponsored tutoring programs has decreased over time, additional data probably needs to be collected as to why this has occurred. One may want to collect data on such things as how the program has changed, what transportation issues have arisen for students, *or* whether staffing changes have impacted the type or quality of support services offered to students in the program. Attendance data alone is insufficient for drawing conclusions about the effectiveness of the program. It is necessary to collect and consider additional data before such judgments regarding the program are made. This is often the case, as the data we collect can only provide a snapshot of a much bigger picture. In schools where a culture of data collection exists, these data are strategically collected, analyzed, and used to inform schoolwide instructional decisions. Additionally, schools that use data wisely take caution to maintain a balance concerning the data they choose to collect. The collection of small amounts of purposefully selected, high-quality data will have more affect on student learning than the collection of mountains of "stuff." Similarly, data collection must be paired with a clearly developed analysis and application plan. We have seen more than one school, in an effort to "do data," develop cumbersome forms of data collection policies, only to flounder once they have assembled the collections. Data absent sound policies and practices for its use do little to enhance decision making.

DATA-DRIVEN DECISION MAKING: CONSIDERATIONS AND CONCLUSIONS

The collection and analysis of valid and reliable data in school settings need not be viewed as another task for school leaders. To the contrary, the sustained and strategic use of data to inform decisions is essential to the effective performance of the school's core tasks of teaching and learning. While reaching this level of proficiency requires time and effort, once achieved it will increase the quality of one's decisions and yield ongoing benefits to the larger school organization. When considering data use in schools, the following points are worth remembering:

- *Without data, all you have is opinion.* The process of identifying, collecting, and analyzing data allows educational leaders to replace myth with fact, legend with information, and illusion with reality. Valid and high-quality data can provide the foundation for goal setting and focused instructional and assessment strategies.
- *Data is more than test scores.* Comprehensive data collection and analysis can provide a rich, variegated picture of the school and the people who work and learn in it. One should work to systematize and institutionalize the collection and analysis of data through the school year and across various programs. Work toward developing formal and informal quantitative and qualitative data collection strategies. This should include data related to student and community demographics and perceptions, school instructional programs, and processes (Bernhardt, 1998).
- *Data collection and analysis are best accomplished in coherent ways.* To maintain coherence, leaders must align data collection and analysis efforts with anchors such as school goals, performance criteria, student-learning outcomes, instructional practices, and assessment demands.
- *Development of a continuous improvement cycle is essential to high-quality data collection and analysis strategy.* Start with a focus on a desired outcome, define your inquiry, identify data valid to desired outcomes, collect and organize the data, make meaning of the results, take action, and evaluate the results of those actions.
- *Learn to communicate with data in ways that speak to your audience.* Utilize quality graphics to effectively depict the data, educate your internal and external communities on the relevance and meaning of the data, and seek to provoke thought.

QUESTIONS FOR REFLECTION AND DISCUSSION

- How can understanding the characteristics and conditions of data-based decision making help you to better understand decision making in context?

- To what extent do the data-use practices of your school promote change, professional community, and organizational learning?
- What specific instances have you experienced the use of data to help frame, investigate, or resolve a problem or issue in your school? What characteristics and conditions described in this chapter were present in these processes? In what ways did these characteristics and conditions support or hinder the decision-making process?
- What activities does your school engage in to focus attention and sustained effort on the *strategic* collection and use of data to guide instructional decisions in the school? How do you see these as effective in creating anticipatory plans for future effort?
- When have you seen the use of data *enhance* the decision-making process? In what ways has it helped focus attention on the tough questions of student learning?
- When have you seen the use of data inhibit or adversely affect the decision-making process? What could leaders do to minimize or address this issue?
- How do you view your data-management skills? What are your strengths and limitations? What can be done to address these?

CHAPTER EIGHT

Dispositional Aspects of Effective Decision Making and the Competent Decision Maker

At the heart of successful leadership are ingenuity, perseverance, integrity, and resourcefulness. A competent decision maker embodies all of these dispositions. Attuned to the needs and desires of the school and community, effective educational leaders have imagination in abundance to envision novel solutions to problems both simple and complex. Familiar with the values and aspirations of the communities they serve, effective educational leaders employ a variety of communicative approaches focused on the attainment of organizational goals. These dispositional qualities comprise what might be considered the core of leadership, a core that some people seem to naturally possess.

Many factors determine who becomes a great leader and who is merely adequate. Certainly, experiences, both personal and professional, play a part, as does schooling, training, talent, and temperament. The organizational context also matters. Understanding organizational history and the surrounding political landscape aid decision makers. How one approaches an emerging situation is part of the alchemy as well. However, great leaders were not born with some secret cache of knowledge and skill, nor are they immune to moments of insecurity and fear. The difference is they recognize what is happening around them, focus their thinking, and apply their knowledge base and skill set in original and productive ways. Events both inspire and intimidate them. It is all a question of what happens after a problem arises. How they respond, with whom they share the decision-making experience, and where they go for guidance and support all contribute to successful outcomes.

This chapter seeks to develop these ideas by focusing on the affective and dispositional aspects that are associated with the sound and competent decision maker. In other chapters of this text, we discuss what effective leaders *do* when they are faced with a decision. In this chapter we seek to develop the construct of *how* they might approach each task and situation. We focus our attention on the ways in which a leader's personal style and interpersonal skill can influence the decision-making outcome. Decision making can be enhanced by understanding how we communicate and interact with one another, how our relationships with other people actually work, and how we affect others positively or negatively by what we say and do.

We will not attempt to create an exhaustive list or endeavor to suggest a formula that will create uniformly effective leaders. Instead, we seek to develop an operational *heuristic*, designed to focus the reader on those aspects of their own behaviors and actions that support or hinder their own decision-making practice. Consistent with the notion of a heuristic, we look at the problem of identifying those behaviors, attitudes, and actions that enhance decision-making practice from multiple angles. Our intent is to offer a metaphorical compass with which the reader might identify his or her own particular strengths and areas in need of improvement.

On the notion of heuristics. Developing a heuristic is a particular technique of directing the learner's attention in the problem-solving arena. Originally derived from the Greek "heurisko," heuristics means, "I find." Popularized in the mid-1990s by mathematician George Polva, heuristics offer a way of *thinking about how others think.* When considering his own teaching, Polva realized that he could instruct students in the *process* of solving mathematic proofs. However, he was less skilled at teaching them the *concepts* that allowed them to think as mathematicians, thus decreasing their understanding and advancing the field of mathematics. He recognized that by allowing his students a glimpse into the ways of looking at problems and formulating solutions senior mathematicians employed, he could increase students' potential to deeply understand and solve complex math problems.

Thinking about the dispositions leaders bring to the decision-making process is similar in nature. While we might simply list a set of qualities great leaders are said to exemplify (e.g., courage, focus, competence, initiative, positive attitude, and the like), we, instead, seek to employ an instructional heuristic, describing how others personify dispositional and affective traits that have served them well. We shall focus on these traits within the decision-making context, concentrating on *how* leaders utilize these attributes and in what *ways* these qualities have enhanced decision making and the attainment of organizational goals. By focusing on four distinct arenas of leadership action—developing vision, managing communication, applying ethical thinking, and reflecting on day-to-day actions—we shall explore the application of a variety of dispositional qualities simultaneously, illustrating how they interact in the decision-making context. In this way, we attempt to assist the reader in finding their own way to understanding how decision making is affected by their actions and behaviors.

DEVELOPING VISION

Vision has been alternatively defined as *the ability to see* (not only as in actual sight, but also as in the ability to discern) and as *a process of setting direction* (Baldoni, 2006; Bass, 1999). One can think of organizational vision as comprising the dual tasks of knowing where to go and how to get there. Similarly, one can think of vision as creating the intention and rationale that projects individuals and organizations to high levels of achievement. Consider the following vision statements. Offered first is the vision of a premium ice cream company; second, a luxury automobile manufacturer; and third, the New York City School District.

- "To make, distribute and sell the finest quality all natural ice cream & euphoric concoctions with a continued commitment to incorporating wholesome, natural ingredients and promoting business practices that respect the Earth and the Environment."
- "To be the world's most desired and successful premium car brand."
- "To engage students in the learning process; establish lasting relationships with students; embrace students as they are, not as we want them to be; encourage students to dream about a promising future; elevate our expectations for student achievement; and evaluate our definition of academic success to include differing learning styles and needs."

By clearly developing a vision, each organization has attempted to articulate a desired future. Notably, the Disney Corporation's vision is straightforward—*to make people happy*. It is easy to see the core values that flow from such a vision—creativity, imagination, and ingenuity. It is also easy to see how the corporation's focus on parks, videos and movies, themed toys and plush animals, and children's books and clothing contribute to the reality of making people happy. The Nike Corporation's vision is similarly forthright—to be the consumer's first choice for style and value in performance footwear. Nike's advertising campaign, *Just Do It*, capitalizes on the company's core values—stimulating individual initiative, focusing on hard work and self-improvement, and being part of something special. The Nike product line of athletic shoes, clothing, watches, glasses, and corporate humanitarian effort *ninemillion.org* jointly focus on developing a progressive stance toward sport and play. Had Disney's vision been to make cartoons and Nike's to make sneakers, each business probably would not have grown to be the enormously profitable enterprises they are today.

A compelling vision projects an image of how the organization intends to grow and serves its stakeholders through individual, team, and organizational excellence. On one hand, the vision articulates the values and purposes on which the school organization rests. On the other hand, it is the most inspiring future that can be imagined. The significant issue for leaders in the decision-making realm to recognize is that you cannot go about to create or set a vision separate from one's recognized and demonstrated behaviors. For a leader to do anything else rings false and counterproductive. Think for a moment of organizations of which you have been part. Have you ever had a moment where you have asked yourself, "Who are they kidding?" or "Where do they think they're working?" If you have experienced this sense of disconnect, you have most likely noticed that what the leaders say does not match their actions. As Margaret Mead noted, "What people say, what people do, and what they say they do are entirely different things."

To embellish this example, consider the actions of a leader who begins each school year by announcing to faculty and staff he or she will maintain an open-door policy. Perhaps they even add the statement, "I'm always interested in what you have to say about our progress toward raising student achievement." The statement is clear. The leader has said that he or she wants to know what faculty and staff think. Furthermore, by employing the metaphorical open door, the leader has said they will be open to a variety of comments concerning progress toward school goals. Yet, when faculty tries to approach the principal they find, quite literally, a closed door. Moreover, the principal always seems to be out of the building either at the central office at meetings or attending a seemingly endless series of professional development events. When faculty do manage to catch the principal for a moment, they are often told, "I think this is an important point, be sure to make an appointment so we can talk more about this later." What the leader is doing differs dramatically from what was presented at the onset of the school year.

To complete the scenario, let us also consider what this leader tells others she does. In public, this leader may claim that they have a relentless focus on students and student learning. They may even cite the open-door policy as evidence of commitment. As is often the case, people do not see the contradictions in their statements, actions, and reports of their actions. Had this point been obvious, a noted anthropologist would not need to have surfaced the distinctions. However, the more tightly a leader can align what they intend or insinuate with what they say and do, the more likely they are to be trusted, respected, and effective in their initiation and implementation of change. Nowhere is this more important than in the arena of visioning.

If one is to think of decision making as related to vision as an important and ongoing task of educational organizational leadership, then the leader's charge is to articulate and nurture a shared vision that engages and empowers individuals in order to bring out the best in faculty, staff, and students. However, we do not mean to suggest that vision creation is the sole responsibility of the superintendent or principal. Many school leaders mistakenly think they must develop a vision that others will follow. In fact, the opposite is true. Successful schools and companies have found that the broader the participation of staff in creating a vision, the greater the commitment people will have to it (Collins, 2001; Kotter, 1999). As the age-old adage notes, people will support that which they help to create. For leaders concerned about how they develop the dispositions necessary for the creation of a vision that all stakeholders can share, it is important for them to focus on the purpose their school serves the community.

Leaders can get to the heart of the school's purpose by setting forth a descriptive statement about the school or district they lead. By stating, "We deliver X benefits," or "We provide the community Y advantages," and then repeatedly asking, "Why is that important?" leaders can begin to articulate the fundamental purpose of the school. If a team of teachers, parents, and students are asked to develop answers to the "Why?" question, a sense of shared purpose and vision arises. Schools that set forth purposes that focus on outcomes such as developing youth leadership, engaging students in the learning process, establishing lasting relationships with students, encouraging students to dream about the future, and elevating expectations for achievement begin to realize that their sense of collective efficacy comes from not only helping students to master learning goals but also from contributing to student success.

Consider the case of Jim Alexander. Newly hired to lead a small urban intermediate school, Alexander used the development of a shared vision as a way to orient himself to his new position. Shortly after the start of the school year, Alexander called a faculty meeting. He began the meeting by reminding faculty that he was setting up meetings with each faculty member early in the fall to get to know them better. He was anxious to learn about their sense of the school's history and future directions. Alexander also remarked that he had already met with several of the faculty and was pleased to note that each meeting had been "informative" and "enjoyable." Keeping with the message he had shared with the interview team, he stressed that for him to be a good leader he would need the faculty's support and wisdom. He began the meeting by asking the question, "Why are we here?"

In this way, Alexander demonstrates the dispositions of focus and competence in the context of creating shared vision. His actions both in individual and group meetings demonstrate a genuine openness to the views and understandings of the faculty and staff within the building. He is also approaching the situation with a spirit of humbleness, evidenced in his eagerness to understand the context of the school prior to his arrival. Such an approach increases the potential for him to be embraced as a trusted leader. To understand the dispositions evidenced within his actions, let us examine each one separately: focus *and* competence and consistency.

Focus. The key priority for a leader who wishes to maintain focus is to concentrate on what matters. When Bill Clinton, the nation's 42nd president, hit the campaign trail in 1996, the mantra employed by his campaign staff and speechwriters was, the now infamous, "It's the economy, stupid." Mythology holds that the statement was displayed on poster-sized boards on the campaign bus, in the oval office, and in his personal residence. In the mid-1990s, the nation's economy was relatively stable. The country was enjoying a long period of peaceful relations with other nations. Inflation and unemployment were low, and a much-needed respite from the economic volatility of the late 1980s was occurring. Clearly, much of the success was attributable to Alan Greenspan's managing of federal monetary policy. Widely known for his nuanced management of interest rates, Greenspan's expertise allowed Clinton to focus on the success of the American people and, in part, claim ownership for the nation's prosperity.

By identifying the economy as a priority goal and concentrating on it, Clinton managed to defeat Dole and secure a second term in office. He did so by playing off the strengths inherent in the political, social, and economic climate that surrounded him. His campaign focused a majority of his attention on—and by default—capturing the media's awareness of the nation's prosperity. Additionally, he shared his vision for continued change and reform. Health care, education, and welfare reform were all issues in the campaign. By pairing the strengths with areas of growth and by using the economy as the proxy for the potential of the nation, Clinton maintained a persistent focus on what mattered.

School leaders have much to learn from this example. As researchers have noted (Elmore, 2004), for decades schools have focused attention on the inputs within the educational system, most notably teaching practices and curriculum resources. Simply put, vast amounts of attention have been placed on teaching and the support structures of and for teaching. As the nation has begun to concentrate on outcomes, measured by accountability standards, a shift in focus has taken place. Evidence of student learning has become central to the educational process. Savvy principals might be well served by the exhortation, "It's the learning, stupid." Embracing learning as the encompassing organizational vision, capitalizing on the strengths inherent in the school, and using successes as a springboard for future efforts can create the conditions in which school leaders can begin to realize their goals. However, focus alone cannot sustain a leader; the disposition of competence and consistency are also required.

Competence and consistency. No matter how focused one might be, if they cannot back up their attentions with capable knowledge and action, they will not go far. Competence is generally defined as the ability consistently to do something well. Competent individuals are consistently able to respond to challenges with dependable results. Their competence may be a product of innate talent paired with strict training and practice, as evidenced in world-class athletes, *or* it may be a result of careful study and reflection on patterns and precedents as evidenced by medical researchers or legal scholars. Consider an example from athletics.

From 1999 until 2005, Lance Armstrong dominated the world's largest and arguably most difficult cycling event, the Tour De France. Prior to Armstrong's victories, the record number of wins by a single individual was five tour victories. His seven consecutive tour victories shattered the records of Spain's Miguel Indurain (1991–1995), France's Bernard Hinault (1978, 1979, 1981, 1982, 1985), and Belgium's Eddy Merckx (1969–1972, 1974). Armstrong's athletic success coupled with his dramatic recovery from cancer inspired the creation of the Lance Armstrong Foundation, a charity founded in 1997. Sale of the now ubiquitous LIVESTRONG yellow, rubber wristbands have raised tens of millions of dollars for cancer research and helped Armstrong become a major player in the nonprofit sector.

Armstrong's competence as cyclist is clear. He is uniquely mentally and physically able to withstand the rigors of training and race preparation as well as the emotional stresses and the drama of the 3-week long race. He demonstrates a rare ability to both climb the strenuous mountain stages and attack an individual time-trial course. He knows race strategy and employs tactics with razorlike precision. Every breakaway and assault for the finish line is expertly planned. While it is an impossibility to win every stage, he consistently places in the top 20.

His team has introduced the tour to a variety of technologies designed to increase communication between coaches and teammates as well as technologies to provide comprehensive heart rate, oxygen uptake, and energy expenditure data. No athlete is thought to have analyzed the mechanics of bikes, helmets, clothing, wheels, pedals, and position more completely than he does. Armstrong demonstrates his competence by seeking and analyzing extensive data and employing the conclusions reached as part of the decision-making process prior to each Tour de France. His knowledge of the sport and what it takes to succeed, balanced with his unique physical gifts, have made him famous.

Yet, his competence is not his alone. Just as Clinton's successes concerning the national economy can be credited at least in part to Greenspan's efforts, Armstrong's victories are shared with a well-oiled and constructed team of support riders, mechanics, doctors, and press managers. While the world remembers a single victor, at its core, the Tour de France is a team event. Without a team of equally competent and gifted cyclists and support staff, Armstrong could not have won a single year, let alone his record-setting seven.

We choose Armstrong as an example here to make clear the point that although competence, much like focus and the other dispositions we will discuss in this chapter, must reside in the leader, the leader must also be able to locate those dispositions and capacities in others. Equally important is the role of research and data. Like Armstrong, competent leaders seek information, analyze the findings for applicability to their context and task, and consistently employ the findings in strategic and reflective ways.

The ability to reflect upon what one does well and to build a support structure around them to complement their own strengths and to compensate for their weaknesses increases a leader's opportunities for the successful implementation of the vision. For the Armstrong team of cyclists, first sponsored by the U.S. Postal Service and then the Discovery Channel, the vision was clear—to win the world's most challenging cycling event, not once, not twice, but multiple times convincingly and decisively. In retirement from cycling, Armstrong's current vision of funding cancer research is equally demanding.

Here, again, school leaders have much to learn. The school year, much like the Tour de France, is an endurance event. Go out too quickly and one runs the risk of wasting the energy and capital that will be needed in later weeks. Wait too long to raise the important issues and you will find yourself too far behind to make significant progress toward goals before the finish line in late May or early June. Fail to seek out or ignore important data and critical fissures may develop in the school's practice and policy. Neglect to identify and push toward meaningful and motivating goals and risk falling short of creating real and lasting impact. Developing, implementing, and stewarding the school's vision requires focus, competence, and consistency. Successful decision making relies on demonstrating these dispositions daily and over time.

MANAGING COMMUNICATION

Foundational to quality decision making is the notion that leaders can clearly and competently communicate information, thoughts, ideas, and goals and provide the motivation to achieve individual and shared visions in an effective and appropriate manner (Buchholz & Rosenthal, 2005; Buenger, Daft, Conlon, & Austin, 1996). Known as *communication competence* (Jablin & Sias, 2000; Payne, 2005), the knowledge and skill set that comprises effective communication includes attention to the communicator's ability to knowledgably use many forms of interaction (e.g., written and spoken words, subtle gestures, nuances of delivery, and personal behaviors or organizational structures and systems) to transmit information (e.g., thoughts and emotions) from one individual to another or group to achieve goals (Payne, 2005). Yet, to suggest that communication is merely the exchange of information oversimplifies the construct. Individuals do more than exchange data. People communicate to create meaning about and in relation to the world around them. The intent of the messenger as well as the receptiveness of the listener contributes to the goal of meaning-making within the communicative setting (Weick, 1995). In other words, the goal of communication is the *creation of shared meaning* with the potential to maximize the achievement of one's personal goals as well as those of the organization.

Our earliest form of communication is to cry. Healthy infants begin to cry the moment they are born. In fact, the lack of a first cry often indicates a potential problem. All those present at the delivery understand the first cry—it communicates the infant's ability to breathe on its own and its entrance into the world. From that first cry, infants quickly learn that crying also cues those around them to their needs and wants, discomforts and anxieties. Parents swiftly learn to identify the hunger cry, the wet diaper cry, the boredom cry, or the attention-seeking cry. Although basic or rudimentary, baby's cries do constitute a form of communication competence—information is shared and goals are successfully met. However, as with other forms of communication crying is imprecise. While parents learn to distinguish the difference between the wet diaper wail from the hunger howl, others, even close relatives, may not be able to discriminate the two. Trial and error may eventually result in a satisfactory resolution, but the process of discovery is frustrating for infant and adult alike.

If crying represents our first and most basic attempt at communicating the meaning of our wants and needs, it might be said that we spend the remainder of our lives learning to be understood. Good communicators are perceived as more effective leaders than those of lesser ability (Vince, 2001). In empirical studies, when researchers control for the content of the message (e.g., the information provided is identical), communicators who deliver a message that is rated as more focused, coherent, and comprehensible are also rated as more effective leaders than their less clear counterparts (Parks, 1994). Researchers conclude that it is not only what you say (the quality of the information) but also how you say it (the quality of the message) that matters (Gunderman, 2001; Payne, 2005). In practical terms the research suggests that leaders must attend to both content and presentation when communicating.

Furthermore, we are not equally adept in all communicative situations. Consider your own communication preferences. Do you prefer one-on-one conversations to small meetings? Are you one of the many that has said, only half jokingly, that you would rather die than have to speak in public? Do you consider yourself a great communicator at dinner parties with close friends but horrible with strangers? Is your communication particularly effective when you compose your thoughts in writing but less effective when you must speak informally or spontaneously? Communicating competently with close friends, family members, strangers, or professional colleagues is based on your *ability to interact well with others*. We can then further this definition by clarifying the term "well" to include concepts of accuracy, clarity, comprehensibility, coherence, expertise, effectiveness, and appropriateness of and within the communicative process (Payne, 2005). No matter the descriptor we might choose to define the word "well," it cannot provide concrete measures that allow us to infer if our communicative goals have been met. Communicative competence is measured by determining if, and to what degree, the goals of interaction are achieved (Gamble & Gibson, 1999). As stated earlier, the function of communication is to maximize the achievement of "shared meaning" where the leader and follower(s) both understand the message that has been delivered as well as the intent behind the message.

For our content or information to be considered, the receiver must sense that the message is both genuine and plausible. That is, the receiver must both believe that the content is valuable and important as well as delivered in a manner that inspires their commitment and faith in the messenger. In this way it is important for the leader as communicator to send messages that promote attainment of goals while maintaining social acceptability. Competent communicators attempt to align themselves with each other's goals and methods to produce a smooth, productive, and often enjoyable dialogue. When these elements are achieved, the message is more likely to be internalized by the listener. In turn, the listener is more likely to follow through with tasks, actions, or reflection concerning the message provided. Leaders may achieve communicative competence by employing a number of important attitudes and abilities including commitment and good faith, empathy, sensitivity, and adeptness.

Commitment and good faith. In organizational contexts that lack trust, communication is more difficult than where such trust exists (Bryk & Schneider, 2002; Tschannen-Moran, 2004). We may try to convince, cajole, and manipulate others into doing what we ask, but often only minimal results are attained. A principal might, for example, decide that it is important for teachers to differentiate instruction for students to attain optimum learning. On the surface, the conclusion makes sense, if students are of different ability levels', employing a variety of instructional pedagogies has the potential to increase student learning. If the principal tells or orders teachers to differentiate, minimal compliance may result. Teachers may pretend to employ the strategies by grouping students for instruction, *or* they may ignore the principal entirely. The principal may respond by pushing harder. As a result, resistance may escalate. In the end, the principal may assert his positional power, adopting a compliance strategy by requiring teachers to provide lesson plans to prove they are indeed differentiating. He may win the battle, and teachers may begin to change their practices. However, he will have done so at the expense of the relationship. Competence entails caring about the other person and the relationship, accepting his or her perspective and needs as legitimate, and ensuring that the results of communication are as satisfying as possible to all involved.

Empathy. Empathy is the ability to view a situation from another person's perspective and experience how that perspective feels. In the case above, by telling teachers to do something without offering adequate support the principal lacked empathy for the teachers predicament—how to vary instruction across a wide variety of skill and ability levels while still addressing all the material in the course or subject and maintaining classroom order. He needed to align his otherwise sound recommendation with a realistic appreciation of how teachers might experience the proposal. Leaders must have a realistic understanding of what is possible to achieve with another person. In other words, leaders need to be able to identify which goals they espouse are compatible with the goals of others. By approaching the communicative task from the perspective of empathy, they are more likely to act and to be perceived as acting in good faith by others.

Sensitivity. If leaders are to develop trust and respect among their followers, it is important that they demonstrate sensitivity to those with whom they work. Sensitivity is generally thought to be a state of empathic responsiveness to another when the receiver is in need or distress. Yet, the receiver experientially measures sensitivity. By this we mean that although a leader may think they are acting with sensitivity, unless the person on the receiving end of the exchange perceives those actions as sensitive, those actions will not be welcomed or respected. Much like empathy, sensitivity requires that the communicator approach the communicative task with an appreciation of another's needs and desires concerning the exchange. Leaders may practice sensitivity by employing attentiveness; simply listening without preoccupation sends a message of caring both about and for the individual and the situation. Similarly, adopting a stance of responsiveness also increases sensitivity as the communicator conveys by responding to the concerns and needs of the individual that they understand what is necessary to achieve shared goals.

Adeptness. As leaders become more skillful at using communication to develop relationships with organizational members, they become more adept at managing the communicative process. Several factors contribute to a leader's skilled practice. Among them is social experience. Social experience increases as one participates in a variety of professional interactions. These interactions influence one's communicative choices. We learn, for example, that, although efficient, e-mail can be considered a socially cold way to communicate sensitive information and that face-to-face interaction provides a warmer venue for sharing complex or difficult messages. Through practice, we also learn how to keep calm in difficult situations and our social composure increases. We begin to learn to modulate our disclosures, becoming sensitive to the amount and type of information we provide in any given setting or circumstance. For example, as principals gain experience, their communication with teachers concerning instructional supervision changes. The experienced principal knows that new teachers cannot absorb as much feedback about the subtle nuances of their practice as more experienced faculty might. Therefore, a principal might choose to have a single, longer conversation with more veteran faculty and several shorter, more focused sessions with newer recruits. Clever communicators learn when and how to use humor. Whether it is to ease the tension in a stressful situation or to keep the staff's attention during a meeting, humor can help deliver a message, make the message more memorable, and increase the interpersonal bonds between members. Whether through practice or experience, by increasing adeptness with the communicative process, leaders can improve their effectiveness in the communicative arena while subsequently achieving the objectives of the organization.

APPLYING ETHICAL THINKING

Ethical issues are part of our daily lives. They confront us as we read the morning newspaper, as we draft organizational policy, and as we confront the daily pressures of providing effective and efficient educational opportunities for students. We are personally and professionally confronted with ethical questions concerning the justice of our decisions regarding the abilities of schools to serve an increasingly diverse public, to balance the benefits of strong neighborhood schools with those that assure integration of student populations, and to create culturally responsive settings for students of color and difference. Addressing these issues is difficult. They call on leaders to consider how to think through ethical problems that may lead to challenging issues concerning which factors should be considered and in what ways might we consider the rights, values, fairness, and goodness of our decisions. In the coming section we shall explore the foundations of ethical thinking and decision making, provide a primer on ethical standards, and offer leaders a recommended dispositional stance for approaching the ethical problems of leading schools.

What are ethics? Ethics refer to *personal and professional principles that govern our actions in given situations, a code of conduct* (Ruggiero, 2004; Synder, et al., 2006). They serve to uphold the civil nature of communal, professional, governmental, and societal interactions and exchanges. Ethics govern the moral choices we make in our lives. Considering and understanding our ethical values and choices as well as the responsibility leaders assume for their choices offer us a window into understanding how ethics shape the choices we make.

Our ethical education starts early. As children, we are taught "The Golden Rule" (i.e., treat others as you would wish to be treated). For many of us, this standard of personal acceptability still serves as the litmus test for our behaviors. Another aspect of our early ethical education regards helping children to see how their choices may be viewed by others around them. As teachers, we seek to provide boundaries for students by asking questions that make public how their choices expose their character. Questions such as "Would you want your parents to know about your actions?" "Would you want me to tell your mother?" or "If you knew someone was watching would you have done this anyway?" help to guide students' choices by revealing how their actions might be judged against more communal standards of behavior. In short, ethics allow us to consider if our actions are right or wrong when measured against a normative standard of behavior.

It has been suggested that ethics guide us to be our best selves when faced with temptation (Harris, 2001; Morse, 2006; Ruggiero, 2004). However, ethics are often hotly contested. What one person views as acceptable action may be fair game for another. Certainly, the rash of recent corporate scandals—World Com (off the books loans and overstated cash flow), Enron (manipulating power markets, bribery, and debt hiding), HP (wiretapping and privacy violations), and Arthur Andersen (document shredding)—suggest that ethical violations often involve legal transgressions as well. However, ethics cannot be reduced to simply following the law. A good system of law does incorporate many ethical standards, but law alone does not dictate what is ethical. Beyond what is defined by the power of legal statute, ethics address issues such as the trust society places in its institutions and those that lead them. These issues include one's right to dignity, to be treated well by those charged with our care and safety, and to be told the truth about matters that significantly affect our lives. In this way, ethical action becomes more complex. To address this complexity, we must understand both our core moral standards and how to apply those standards in our personal lives and in the workplace. The identification of one's ethical standards involves understanding the foundations on which standards are set, followed by discerning how ethical standards become applied in specific situations. We shall first consider a variety of theories with which we might consider the nature of ethical standards.

Ethical standards. Over time, as people have sought to determine an appropriate response to a given situation, questions of ethics have been raised. Consideration of these matters is largely the territory of philosophers who seek to provide answers to what often seem to be life's unanswerable questions (e.g., What is the good life? How free are our choices? What is justice?). However, certain understandings concerning ethical actions and standards have been established, and understanding these approaches is helpful in determining how ethics are useful in decision making.

One branch of ethical study focuses on the nature of the choices people make concerning their actions. *Normative ethics* answers questions concerning moral choices—determining what is reasonable behavior and what is not (O'Fallon & Butterfield, 2005; Ruggiero, 2004). Normative ethical dilemmas concern questions of rights and rightness, good and goodness, in an effort to develop a set of valid and reliable ideas that result from an examination of the conclusions derived during reasoned discussion. Normative ethical questions address the simple choices we make about the products we buy (animal tested, or cruelty free?), the transportation we take (SUV, hybrid, or bus?), or the food we eat (organically grown, locally farmed, or factory raised?). Normative ethical questions also address the more complex choices society grapples with concerning issues such as the death penalty, abortion, the environment, biomedical decisions, and social justice, to name a few.

A second branch of ethical study concerns the consistency of the logic within the argument. Known as *metaethics*, this examination of the logical argument determines the quality of the thought within the argument and seeks to surface faulty reasoning (O'Fallon & Butterfield, 2005; Ruggiero, 2004). Some examples of faulty logical reasoning include circular logic (when the conclusion to an argument is already implicitly or explicitly stated), post-hoc fallacy (misunderstanding what causes an event), or ad hominem reasoning (directing attention away from the argument by attacking the person).

An example of circular logic might be the statement, "Having school leaders focus on school reform is useless because it is an inadequate answer to the problems schools face." Since useless and inadequate are synonymous terms, no new information has been proved to further the argument. The discussion is circular in that it provides no argument as to why having leaders attend to reform may well be useless (it goes without saying the authors would not defend this position). A *post hoc* fallacy may occur when the causes of an event are incorrectly attributed to an unrelated incident. For example, if the fire alarm rings as you settle into your fifth cup of coffee, it would be incorrect to assume that your coffee habits caused the fire alarm to ring.

A favorite of political foes, *ad hominem* reasoning or argument diverts attention from the matter at hand by attacking the person who makes the argument. When you hear the words, "My opponent claims to support public schools but has no children," you can be certain *ad hominem* reasoning is being employed, since support for public schools has no relation to one's status as a parent. In this case, the argument is faulty because the two variables—support for public schools and one's status as a parent—are not necessarily linked. One may support public school whether or not they have children of their own. Likewise, one may be a parent of five and still find supporting public school problematic. This shift creates a logical inconsistency in the discussion, misdirecting the focus of discussion from what matters (supporting schools) to what does not (status as a parent).

Ethical thinking concerns both the choices one makes and the judgment and argument that support those choices. However, these broad descriptions of ethical philosophy provide inadequate theoretical grounding for thinking in a complex fashion about the issues one faces. We turn next to exploring the foundations of five modern approaches to ethical thought—utilitarianism, fairness or justice, rights, common good, and virtue—in the hope that school leaders might be able to identify what informs their own thinking concerning the ethical issues that confront them.

The utilitarian approach. Credited to John Stuart Mill (1806–1873), utilitarianism suggests that the study of ethics should be concerned with choices that promote the greatest good and cause the least harm for those affected by the choice. Utilitarianism offers a straightforward measure for promoting the "greatest good for the greatest number." Its application is straightforward as well: first we identify potential courses of action, second we determine the benefits and harm in following each course, and third we choose the course of action that provides the most benefit after all costs have been taken into account. Utilitarianism proves an adequate theory when relative costs and benefits can be determined. The difficultly in employing a utilitarian approach comes when one must balance costs and benefits for more ethereal values such as the value of life, art, happiness, justice, or dignity.

The fairness or justice approach. With its roots in Aristotelian (384–323 BC) thought, the fairness or justice approach to ethics suggests that equals should be treated equally. Implied in this approach is the ability for a decision maker to evaluate the situation on its merits, without bias or prejudice, and determine judgment. The ideal of justice is best applied when unfair advantage is not afforded to one group. Actions are then judged on the basis of fairness and applied without favoritism or discrimination. Of course, the difficultly inherent in this approach is determining what might be fair today as measured against other possible choices and within the context of history. As such, issues of equality and equity are of consideration within the fairness or justice approach. The stance suggests that treating everyone equally may in fact be unjust as reparations for past unfair actions might be required to remedy prior injustices. Similarly, to address equity or fair treatment, one must consider the broad social and societal contexts in which the decision rests.

The rights approach. Focusing on the individual's right to freely choose what is best, the rights approach considers one's right to privacy, truth, safety, dignity, and the like. From an ethical position, the moral action is one that best defends the rights of those involved in a situation. A rights position suggests that an action is moral if all parties' privacy, safety, dignity, and access to the facts of the matter are protected. Immoral actions violate one or more of those tenants, and the more severe the violation, the more wrongful the action.

The common good approach. As we have seen, other approaches to ethical reasoning privilege consideration of the individual when moral or ethical standards are deliberated. The common good approach suggests that moral thought must take into account the community of which the individual is a part when considering ethical outcomes (Rawls, 1971). By suggesting that we share common interests, morality can be determined by deciding which concerns have the potential to benefit the greatest number of society. However, the challenge lies in defining the common good. As an example, let us suggest that all members of society may well agree that excellent schools are of value to society. Furthermore, they may agree that affordable health care is important as well. Yet, after initial agreement, reasonable people may differ concerning which of the two—education or health care—should receive the larger share of scarce resources and which might be sacrificed for the other. The resultant disagreement on the matter weakens society's ability to both identify what might be considered a common good and achieve shared goals. Additionally, the pursuit of the common good may conflict with one's individual right to free choice. In our individualistic society, such sacrifice lies counter to values many uphold. Nonetheless, the common good approach does offer an opportunity to consider the ethical concerns present within the larger society.

The virtues approach. By adopting certain ideals of behavior, the virtues approach to moral behavior contends that morality and ethical action resides in the individual's ability to act honorably. Once adopted, virtues such as sincerity, truthfulness, courage, compassion, integrity, veracity, steadfastness, and trustworthiness form the character of the person. These character traits are then thought to provide a measure of how one should respond to any given situation thus, promoting the individual and the community in which he or she resides. It is difficult to suggest that the pursuit of a virtuous life is not admirable. Yet, as we have seen with other approaches to ethical action, the critique lies in the definition. Who is to say what constitutes honorable action? To what levels must one be truthful? Clearly there is a difference between lying on one's income tax and telling one's spouse they do not look fat. Agreement on what constitutes basic human and civil rights, what is good and what is harmful, how shared a common good must be, are all difficult questions. The importance lies in that we ask them.

APPLYING ETHICAL THINKING TO DECISION MAKING

Considerations of fairness and good, bias and discrimination, dignity, and safety are all important issues for leaders to contemplate when decision opportunities arise. Yet, school and district leaders must first recognize which decisions may contain ethical implications. Recognizing those issues with potential ethical consequences requires leaders to broadly consider the context in which the decision rests and the ways in which the decision may affect members of the school community (Willower & Licata, 1997). We find the adoption of the following dispositional stances to be of help in settings where ethical dilemmas are present.

Apply conscious effort. Deliberation and intentional consideration should be paid to the framing issues of the decision. The adoption of an ethical stance toward the problem can lead one to identify aspects of the issue that may not have been apparent at first blush. A leader may first start by attempting to identify if someone might be wronged as an outcome of the decision. Next, they might clarify the extent to which wrong action might result in damage to an individual or group. By considering if individuals have special needs and if the school has special obligations to those needs, the school leader can identify if issues of fairness or justice are present. Leaders should take time to develop several alternative courses of action and consider which option provides the most opportunity for a good outcome. When considering options leaders may apply utilitarian thinking by asking if there is an outcome that can result in the greatest good for those involved. They may also apply a rights approach by considering the rights of the individual and groups involved and posing the question, "Is there an outcome that is more respectful to the parties involved?"

Adopt a reflective stance. Most decisions do not need to be made immediately. Decisions that address issues of ethics deserve contemplation. Leaders should allow themselves the necessary time to collect the facts and to consider available options. Leaders may choose to employ a fairness approach to the problem by asking, "Is there a decision that is fair to all involved, or will one party be more disadvantaged than another by the choices at hand?" Furthermore, leaders may look to others, not only for guidance as options are considered, but also to determine how your actions might be viewed by across a variety of audiences and stakeholders. Ask yourself if you would be proud to be known as the person who made this decision. By considering the virtue of the choices at hand, the decision may become clear.

Act with clarity and responsibility. Once a choice has been made, clearly provide both the decision and the thinking that underscored the decision-making process. Offer those who are affected by the decision as much insight into your thinking as possible. Take responsibility for what you can. Even if the affected parties may not agree with the decision as it was made, understanding the process and considerations allows for others to abide by the decision. By adopting a stance of conviction, the leader is more likely to gain the trust and respect of those around them. In turn, one's ability to confront other decisions with certainty and confidence in the future is strengthened.

REFLECTING ON DAY-TO-DAY ACTIONS

It is tempting to think about decision making and the dispositions that support its effective practice as singular events in time—that is, as moments of our prac-tice in which we are called to act when faced with difficulties and dilemmas or something we do only after a problem presents itself or a crisis arises. Instead, we would like to return here to a central notion of this text—*decision making lies at the heart of leadership*. As such, our decision-making practice is comprised of the daily choices we make as we interact with those around us. Rather than something we practice infrequently and in response to trouble and difficultly, we would like to examine decision making as a disposition itself, a perspective from which one might approach one's day-to-day reflection on the progress the school organization is making toward goals and the areas of need that remain. We would argue that, in fact, it is the day-to-day decisions that determine a leader's reputation (Daft & Weick, 1984; Harris, 2001) and provide evidence of one's personal and organizational commitment to success (Morse, 2006).

Every day a principal enters the school building, he or she is faced with choices about how they approach their work. They may view the day-to-day tasks of school leadership as *separate distinct actions*. They may view each interaction and its related decisions as a never-ending cyclone of trials that present them-selves, each unrelated from the other and unrelated to the larger purposes of the school. It is easy to understand how one might adopt this position. On any given day, a school leader may be asked to attend a meeting on the upcoming school levy, address several classroom discipline matters, coordinate school testing materials, read to the kindergarten class, observe a new teacher's classroom, and address the band's booster group. In between these actions, he or she will need to field several interruptions concerning other matters such as hall or bus duty, the registration of a new student or calls from parents, central office personnel and community members. As the principal becomes more hassled and hurried, it is easy to see why the principal might begin to see their day-to-day actions as unrelated to their decision-making role. It is also easy to see why the principal might believe that their purpose is to react as situations present themselves, viewing reflectivity and contemplation as nice but unrealistic dispositions in their work environment.

In contrast, a leader may approach those tasks as a series of *coordinated responses* made in concert as one enacts a unified theory of practice. As each situation presents itself, the leader may take a moment to determine the potential this opportunity offers to contribute to the school's larger vision and mission. An approach that views the day-to-day behaviors of the role as the enactment of decision making allows for the practice of decision making to become a disposition itself. In this way, the school leader is always seeking to understand the context of the school, scanning for potential tensions and dilemmas, and collecting informal data on progress toward goals and impending need. Their actions are viewed as predictable and understandable within the context of the school's goals. Consequently, the leader may avoid larger problems and has gained the opportunity to develop trust and respect among faculty, staff, and the community.

When leaders act in ways that develop trust and respect, the leader's reputation within the organizational setting is enhanced (Daft & Weick, 1984; Harris, 2001; Tschannen-Moran, 2004). When leaders act in ways that are clearly visible and their motives are transparent and evident, they model the dispositions of effective decision making, further enhancing their reputation as a good leader. The benefits to the organization are clear. As the leader's reputation is enhanced, organizational members are more likely to support and champion a leader's decisions. They are also more likely to participate in shared decision-making efforts and to offer assistance as needed when difficulty arises. In turn, decision making becomes more fluid as members share common goals and methodology for problem resolution. Furthermore, as a leader's actions become more transparent, a leader's personal and organizational commitment to success is evidenced (Morse, 2006). When organizational members see a leader who is committed to quality decisions made in productive and supportive environments and focused on issues and themes they value as well, the school's climate and culture is improved, setting the stage for growth and progress.

SUCCESSFUL APPLICATIONS IN PRACTICE: QUALITIES OF SUCCESSFUL LEADERS

It is our belief that leaders can develop effective decision-making dispositions. Rather than believing that some principals and superintendents are born with a nature that allows them to approach the decision-making process with patience, skill, and wisdom, we assert that effective leaders grow into these attributes through reflectivity, reflexivity, and practice. If a leader takes a reflective stance toward their behavior, they can begin to see themselves part of a larger organizational whole. By studying what surrounds them daily and working to understand the organizational whole in which they lead, effective leaders can develop a situational awareness and sensitivity to the dispositional aspects of the decision-making process. Central to the development of effective decision-making dispositions are the following ideas:

- *Attend to trivial events as they often shape a situation before it happens* (Gonzales, 2003). As leaders become attuned to the larger organizational whole in which they work and lead, they begin to notice that small, seemingly meaningless events take on momentum and contribute to a leader's eventual organizational success or failure. Consider the hiker that packs lightly for a day hike and then becomes trapped by a sudden change in weather. Lacking proper clothing and food, the potential for tragedy increases. Schools are laden with similar possibilities. Reflective leaders focus daily on what occurs around them asking if these events are contributing to or subtracting from the vision and goals of the school. They then act accordingly.

• *Develop multiple alternatives when issues present themselves.* By generating several choices, leaders are more likely to choose a sound and ethical solution as well as one that can be embraced by the organization's membership. By incorporating a planning process into decision making, the leader engages a long-term view, incorporating the feedback and the perspectives of others. Furthermore, as leaders practice strategic decision making, they increase their ability to employ strategic thinking in their work. In turn, their ability to effectively respond when a quick judgment must be reached is improved.

• *Adopt a stance of perseverance.* We are not sure who said it first, but the old saw is correct, leadership is not a sprint, it is a marathon. In no setting is this truer than in schools. School improvement, student achievement, equity, and equality are all issues that will be with us during our careers. Leaders who persevere, who identify a problem or issue and stick with it, adopting a "relentless focus" (Collins, 2001) on quality, progress, and goals have more success than those who tinker about the edges of worthy prospects. Tenacity rewards those who accept the long-term approach toward decision–making, allowing each decision to contribute to the larger goals and missions of the school.

• *Develop a tough skin.* School leadership is an often-frustrating enterprise. As principal or superintendent, leaders are called on to make the hard choices, to address the difficult questions, and to meet the daily challenges that face the school organization. In as much as we have stressed that decision-making dispositions are about how a person approaches an issue, we also need to stress that, at times, the decisions one makes are not about them (Fessler, Pillsworth, & Flamson, 2004; Meyerson, 1998). Good leaders consider the school context, the ethics of a situation, and a myriad of other considerations before coming to a choice about the best course of action. Reflexive practice suggests that one steps outside themselves and realize that we often act as an agent of our role. When angry staff, faculty, or parents approach the principal, they are approaching *the* person of authority. As an agent of the school, leaders must act in the best interests of the organization by employing his or her knowledge and skills to best remedy the situation at hand. Realizing that it is not personal when a parent lobbies for their student, when faculty press for more and better resources, and when community's demand nothing less than excellence of their schools, can help the leader get out of the way and allow quality decision making to emerge.

- *Learn to deal with ambiguity.* Rarely does a situation quickly and easily resolve itself. Rarely do we have the data we would like to consider as part of our decision-making process. Rarely are choices clear and indisputable. As researchers (Conger, 2004; Coy, 2005; Payne & Joyner, 2006) suggest, vagueness, uncertainly, and doubts are the specters of leadership. Decision makers must realize that even in the best circumstances they will never be able to fully know or understand the complexities of what surrounds them. Ambiguity, either in the form of contradictory data or an issue that may be difficult to understand, can either paralyze or inspire creativity. If we become paralyzed, we freeze; our decisions become tentative and timid, ultimately resulting in ineffective choices. If we embrace the ambiguity of our organizations by employing original and inventive analysis of what surrounds us, we have a chance of discovering the iterative nature of the decision-making process, realizing that our most effective actions are those in which we apply our best thinking and behavior, remaining open to what might come.

QUESTIONS FOR REFLECTION AND DISCUSSION

- How can understanding the characteristics and conditions of dispositions and decision making help you to better understand decision making in context?
- To what extent do you as a leader demonstrate effective decision-making dispositions? Which of the dispositions discussed in the chapter presents the most challenge?
- Do you see yourself as the central figure in all decision making, or as the facilitator to organizational decision making? How can you improve your role?
- What characteristics and conditions described in this chapter were present within your school? In what ways do they support or hinder the decision-making process?
- Do your actions support your intentions? Is there a consistency in regard to your role as leader supported by unfaltering character?
- How do you view your dispositional skills? What are your strengths and limitations?
- As a leader, how are your actions perceived? Are you sensitive to the needs of others?
- How might you develop a plan to enhance your skills?
- When considering ethical decisions, which approach do you most favor? In what ways do you see the applications of ethical thinking in your practice?

CHAPTER NINE

Making Tough Decisions: Issues and Considerations

Leadership as a social and educational phenomenon has been the subject of considerable attention in the literature of business, sociology, psychology, and education. Common to these studies is an attempt to define and type leader behaviors, characteristics, and actions (comprehensive surveys are provided by Bass [1990] and Yukl [2002]). While there may be some difference in the specifics of a definition, most authors conclude that leadership generally comprises the exercise of intentional social influence through which members of a group are steered toward a goal through a process of structured activities, efforts, and individual or shared endeavors (Bass, 1990; Bryman, 1986; Yukl, 2002). The contention of this volume is that *leadership exercised is decision making in practice.* That is, without the challenges of and opportunity for decision making within the organizational setting, leaders cannot exercise power, effectively influence organizational processes, or create change. Think for a minute about a leader you admire. Now think about what aspects of their leadership you find compelling. Perhaps you are drawn to the image of a winning coach as a leader, remembering his or her decision concerning what play to call at a critical point during the big game against a worthy opponent. Instead, you may recall a political figure evoking savvy choices and decisions about international policy and domestic programs. You may recollect a business leader's spirited deal or competitive strategy. In any case, each of these leaders must first, when faced with a knotty problem or impending situation—be it fourth and ten or a corporate takeover—decide what course of action to take. It is for these decisions that we remember and ascribe greatness to our leaders. As such, we contend that the exercise of leadership is found in the decisions a leader makes. How they choose to act given the circumstances they face and what skills they bring to each state of affairs is what separates successful leaders from their less noted counterparts. Clearly, great leaders make more mundane decisions on a regular basis. Winning coaches mentor their teams throughout the entire season, and determined business leaders motivate employees to daily tasks. Yet, we remember those leaders we admire for the decisions they make during times of stress, difficulty, and challenging circumstances. Great leaders are remembered for the difficult decision—the decision on which success rests.

LEADERSHIP AND MANAGEMENT

A foundational argument of this book is that creating more effective decision makers in school settings requires significant change in how we educate prospective building and district *leaders* concerning decision-making knowledge and skill. Embedded in this argument is the notion that effective school administration requires the skill of a strong leader, rather than merely a high-quality manager. This distinction suggests that we are concerned with organizational functions typically attributed to "leadership" such as strategic planning for change and transition, vision formation and mission setting, and adaptive problem solving as well as with organizational functions typically credited to management, such as designing operational systems to carry out strategic planning efforts, organizing routine operations, and supervising the performance of staff. It is easy to see how both leaders and managers make decisions on a daily basis; with leadership decisions potentially encompassing decisions regarding the big picture aspects of an organization and management decisions addressing decisions regarding the day-to-day concerns (Barnard, 1938; Simon, 1976). Much has been made in the educational literature of the distinction between leadership and management (Murphy, 1999; Sergiovanni, 1995) suggesting that whether the principal leads or maintains the school can provide noteworthy insight into a school's effectiveness.

The organizational literature on leadership and management is equally contentious, with some researchers (Bennis & Nannis, 2003) suggesting that leadership and management are qualitatively different and mutually exclusive constructs. Others (Bass, 1990; Kotter, 1996) view each as addressing distinctly different goals and outcomes for the organization with some complimentary and overlapping skill sets. Kotter (1996) suggests that management is differentiated from leadership in terms of the processes utilized and the outcomes sought (e.g., leaders seek to produce change and growth for organizational longevity and managers seek to produce stability and predictability to assure orderly operations and short-term success). In an effort to synthesize these two notions, Yukl (2002) suggests that they coexist with leadership as an essential management role that pervades all other roles of an organization's administration.

For the purposes of this discussion, we suggest that rather than differentiating between these two constructs, a more blended notion of school administration that integrates aspects of both leadership and management is needed. In particular, we argue that schools are distinctive organizational settings in that the administrator is often required to address daily operations as well as long-term adaptive planning and vision. They must, as a regular characteristic of the position, be equally able to manage and lead. Furthermore, the challenges of school leadership include daily, regular decision making as well as incorporating long-term planning and situational adjustments as need arises. Simply put, schools require both excellent managers who address the regular operations of schools and high-quality leaders to face the challenges that exist today for educators. Decision making is an important component of both roles.

THE LANDSCAPE OF TOUGH DECISIONS: SCHOOL CONTEXT AND CHALLENGE

Throughout the past decades, headlines have pronounced a crisis regarding the ways in which schools function, educate, and are held responsible for students' progress toward measurable learning goals. The national conversation regarding schools has focused almost exclusively on two linked areas of study: *internal* (Bryk & Schneider, 2002; Louis & Kruse, 1995; Tschannen-Moran, 2004) and *external* accountability (Darling-Hammond, 2000; Leithwood, Steinbach, & Jantzi, 2002; Sweetland & Hoy, 2000). Decision-making challenges facing school leaders have been unavoidably influenced by these associated concerns.

ACCOUNTABILITY

School accountability as an educational concern has roots as deep as schooling itself. Attention paid to issues of accountability has waxed and waned for years with varied foci (Tyack, 1974; Tyack & Cuban, 1995). However, high stakes accountability as expressed in the decades, since the publication of *A Nation at Risk* (1983), is a relatively new trend. Prior to recent educational legislation, schools were largely autonomous, teachers' work only minimally evaluated, and measures of a quality education were limited to estimating inputs (i.e., number of books in the library, hours of instruction in each content area, square footage allotted to educational purposes, and the like) to the educational process. Measures of outcomes, student learning, and achievement were principally used to determine progress toward locally held goals rather than as a measure of the performance of schools or administrators. With the passage of the No Child Left Behind Act (NCLB) discussions concerning accountability have shifted and now are centered on the implementation of systematic reforms that hold schools and districts accountable for the academic achievement of *all* students. For the first time, educators are being challenged to provide—through annual state report cards—statewide assessment data that is disaggregated by race, income, and other criteria to reveal student performance.

However, accountability is a broader construct than the computation of student performance, including aspects of responsibility, authority, evaluation, and control, and must be constructed in relation to both internal and external communities. That is, some accountability relationships occur among providers and recipients located within the same organization (internal), while other accountability relationships involve recipients of accountability located outside the organization (external). Critical to understanding the decision-making process, this distinction allows the school leader to consider the audience for which any decision has importance.

Internal accountability. Internal accountability is concerned with how norms and values within the organization are honored. This accountability may be directed toward either process (i.e., how something is done) or outcomes (i.e., what results are accomplished). For example, if one is delegated the authority to engage in some activity, then one is responsible, at the least, for conducting the activity "properly"—that is, in accord with prevailing expectations that guide how the activity should be conducted. Similarly, if a particular pedagogical process or curriculum is adopted, an evaluation or study concerning how students benefit (or do not benefit) from the implementation would be expected.

In the most professional settings, internal accountability extends to include a collective responsibility for student learning and academic growth as well as collaborative and cocreated dialogue around student learning and progress (Louis & Kruse, 1995). Consensus within schools about what constitutes effective practice can be internalized and, in turn, is subject to internal regulation and influence. When norms for internal accountability are violated, a loss of trust may result with potential negative consequences for future mutual activity (Bryk & Schneider, 2002; Tschannen-Moran, 2004). Thus, when a school leader considers decisions made within the internal context of the school, norms of internal accountability must be considered and valued, as breaching internal norms may come at great cost.

External accountability. As previously noted, the most demanding form of current external accountability is to the national requirements of NCLB legislation. In practice, local schools are externally accountable to local communities, the district office, and the state in direct and specific ways. Researchers, policy makers, and state legislators have created accountability systems that are both transparent and exacting in their content-learning standards and outcomes, as well as in their measures of student performance. While these differ from state to state, the results are fairly consistent. As noted by Fuhrman (1999), most states require one or more of the following components: a focus on increased student achievement most often measured by statistically derived indicators, public reporting of student progress toward standards and goals, a focus on the school and classroom teacher as the unit of improvement, expectations for continued improvement and growth, identification of under- and overperforming schools, and rewards and incentives as well as sanctions for schools for student performance.

The increasing pressures on schools by the imposition of these standards-based measures has created a context in which school leaders are held accountable far beyond their local community and in more public ways. Decisions regarding the data derived from standardized testing as well as other local report card measures comprise a good deal of the decision-making responsibility school leaders address today. As such, the external context frames much of the current decision-making agenda in schools.

When considered in tandem, the themes of internal and external accountability are present in most of the decision-making events of school leaders. Moreover, these paired themes share several important situational and environmental characteristics. They are essentially chronic concerns characterized by a lack of stability within the school organization. Accountability issues often involve tensions between conflicting moral "goods" or choices and may require considerable resources before even a short-term solution may be reached. In short, issues of accountability create an environment in which "tough decisions" thrive. Such decisions require clear and specific issue analysis and focused attention to the complexities involved before a solution may be contemplated.

TOUGH DECISIONS

As has been outlined in previous chapters in this volume, the identifiable skills in the decision-making process have been well documented. At a minimum, they include four very broad classes of ideas, including (a) identification of problem(s) in need of attention, (b) recognition of alternative solutions to address the problem(s), (c) evaluation of the alternative solutions so that a best choice might be determined, and (d) the implementation and subsequent review of the chosen solution or solutions. This process suggests that decision making may be considered a rational endeavor (Simon, 1993), and if the school administrator is able to follow a prescribed set of activities all will be well with the world. As defined by Simon (1993, p. 393), rationality is "the set of skills or aptitudes we use to see if we can get from here to there—to find courses of action that will lead to the accomplishment of our goals. Action is rational to the degree that it is well adapted to those goals. Decisions are rational to the extent that they lead to such action." Yet, as Simon (1993) and others (Kotter, 1996; Wallis, 2002; Weick, 2002) remind us, rarely does the school leader function in an optimum, rational environment. Schools, like other organizations, are rarely places in which all the needed information is available when decisions must be executed.

Because of the fast pace of schools, often we may obtain the data or information we need after we have been compelled to act. An example serves to illustrate this point. In a well-performing suburban school district, school leaders began to note a drop in mathematics test scores in the area of measurement across district testing in the elementary grades. This puzzled district leaders as they recently had completed a yearlong textbook adoption process and had paid particular attention to the alignment of resources and materials to the state mathematics standards. District leaders decided they needed to collect more data to ascertain what might be the cause of the test score decline.

They began doing an informal survey of district teachers, asking them how they were implementing the new materials, when measurement was being taught in the new program, and if they were using the resources as planned. The feedback from teachers assured the principals that teachers were teaching to the measurement standard well in advance of testing dates, incorporating hands-on measurement tasks, as well as utilizing measurement in word problems and other problem-solving activities.

In follow-up discussions with teachers, the elementary principals asked the question, "So what's different with the new materials?" The teachers responded that nothing had changed in math; however, they were suspicious that the changes in the science program from the prior year might be affecting the measurement scores. In an effort to create more time in the curriculum to address physics concepts new to the state science standards, units that they had previously taught concerning the use of measurement in experiments and labs had been dropped from the curriculum. This explanation made intuitive sense and offered school principals a potential explanation for the score drop. They further investigated this thought by comparing the old science curriculum, the old mathematics curriculum, and the new materials. In hindsight, the principals realized that the bulk of measurement standards and skills had *never* been addressed in the mathematics curriculum. They consequently made the necessary adjustments to both math and science curriculum planning and pacing guides to reintroduce the lost lessons.

These principals made a rational, but flawed, assumption that measurement was a math standard and therefore must have always been adequately addressed within the curriculum. The failure of leaders in this decision-making process was to oversimplify the problem (i.e., math teaching equals math learning), placing it within the bounds of the resources and information they had available rather than contextualizing the teaching of mathematics to include aspects of the wider school curriculum in which such skills might be employed. By the application of overly rational planning—aligning mathematics standards with *only* mathematics resources—the district overlooked the real-world applications of mathematics as they are employed within the world beyond the classroom as well as how they might be applied in testing situations.

While this example may not fall under the umbrella of a "tough decision," it serves to help explain why schools cannot be considered rational systems when decision making is concerned. Instead, we might consider them "irrational" or poorly adapted to goal attainment (Simon, 1993). In short, leaders often lack much-needed information when a decision needs to be made. Conflicts may arise about what is the right decision to make, and other equally problematic organizational issues may be chronically present in the school setting. The application of a linear set of steps to be followed simply cannot serve a leader in today's school organizations, even in the most regular and commonplace decisions because schools cannot be considered places of rationality when decision making is considered. At best, our decisions within schools are bounded by the information and skills we have at the decision-making time (Simon, 1993). At worst, we must accept the fact that schools are fraught with tensions and dilemmas in which satisfactory solutions can rarely be obtained.

Imagine now a set of circumstances where the decisions facing a school leader might be considered "tough": consistently falling test scores over many subjects, grade levels, and years; failure to attain adequate school funding resources; unstable labor relations; major changes in personnel or resources within the school; and demanding parents and community groups. If rational planning and problem-solving models have the potential to fail us in times of relatively straightforward decision-making circumstances, what hope is there for the school leader in facing more complex and wicked situations? The good news is that tough decisions like the ones offered above share similar characteristics and patterns (Simon, 1976, 1981). Once a school leader learns to recognize these characteristics and patterns, his or her chances of achieving a good result even within an irrational system are increased.

Characteristics of tough decisions. Difficult decisions by nature are those decisions that force a leader to dig down deep for inspiration, information, and ability. They are often described as decisions in which the leader claims he or she cannot get a handle on what is going on or cannot figure out where to begin. They are problems requiring solutions that one district leader describes as "rebounding just when you think you're on top of them" as well as problems that "shift while you're working on them—they start out looking like a sheep and become a fox when you least expect it." Always characterized by the presence of internal and external pressures for accountability, tough decisions are commonly both ill-defined and conflict-laden.

The ill-defined nature of tough decisions. As we have suggested, decision making occurs within an organization once a need, problem, or felt difficulty (Dewey, 1944) is identified. Tough decisions often start out as tough problems. They are problems requiring learning for both problem identification and problem resolution; they are not readily or easily defined. Ill-defined problems are ones where it is not clear from the beginning what the problem is and thus what a solution is. Therefore, finding a solution requires determining what the real problem is. In practice, leaders are often required to define or specify the problem prior to addressing a solution. Additionally, specifying and solving the problem may develop along parallel courses with each driving the other as more information is discovered about the issue at hand.

Similar to "wicked problems" (DeGrace & Stahl, 1990; Rittel & Webber, 1973), which have vague, incomplete, contradictory, and changing requirements, ill-defined problems may lack definitive boundaries to label the problem, may be symptomatic of another problem, may provide uncertain avenues for finding solutions, and may require the group to change operating behaviors should a solution be implemented. Wicked problems arise when an organization must deal with something new, with change, and when multiple stakeholders have different ideas about how the change should take place. The hallmark of a wicked, ill-defined problem is divergence. If the rules and regulations regarding the decision keep changing, if faculty and staff, community, and other stakeholders cannot agree and the target is constantly moving, you are most likely dealing with a wicked problem. In schools, wicked problems include (but are not limited to) problems requiring decisions concerning school funding and resource allocation, decisions about the best way to redesign schools so that violence is reduced and social justice is increased, decisions regarding how to strengthen public and community engagement in schools, and decisions relating to how best to close the achievement gap.

THE NATURE OF CONFLICT IN TOUGH DECISIONS.

Decision making and the potential for resulting change introduce the possibility for conflict within an organization. The very notion of impending change can raise feelings of apprehension, fear, and anxiety for many organizational members. Internal norms of behavior may be challenged, the very nature of "how we do things around here" may be contested, and people may view the situation as threatening or jeopardizing to their positional power. The presence of ill-defined, wicked problems only increases the probability that conflict may occur as the opportunities for conflict within the decision-making process are many. Organizational stakeholders may disagree on the aspects of the problem, the best ways to go about data and information collection concerning the issues, and how to address solutions. Knowing how to identify potential areas of dispute and conflict is useful.

The difference between a simple dispute and a true conflict is worth addressing since each must be addressed differently by the school leader (Bercovitch, 2003). In the case of dispute, negotiation between parties is possible since the issues are generally concerns over self-interest (Brown, 2000; Burton, 1990). While a dispute may develop into a more serious conflict, generally disputes are short-term disagreements and relatively easy to resolve. An example within the school setting might be a quarrel concerning class scheduling or an argument concerning the appropriate disciplinary action for student misbehavior. In each case, a process of negotiation might be entered into with all parties readily agreeing to a final solution and course of action. Each party may have to do something they would rather not. Yet, in exchange they will get enough of what they did want to settle the dispute. For example, a teacher may need to teach class during the early lunch hour in exchange for a planning period at the end of the day, or a student might agree to a Saturday detention as punishment for a classroom disruption. In each case, through negotiation, a satisfactory resolution can be reached with no long-term resultant discord.

Conflict, on the other hand, is more intractable and harder to deal with. The issue at hand may include a protracted disagreement, complex problem, or persistent concern. Of particular concern are conflicts that lie at the edge of an organization's boundaries and seem to elude resolution even when the best available techniques are applied. Examples abound in the world around us (e.g., abortion, homosexual rights, and race relations) and in schools (e.g., issues of social justice, external testing accountability, and school funding). Intractable conflict has several characteristics adding to the difficulty of decision making related to these issues. These include the duration of the conflict, the presence of variance in values and beliefs of organizational members, the potential for destructive behavior, and the potential for resistance to conflict management efforts (Brown, 2000; Burton, 1990). Simply put, an intractable conflict is characterized by a process of competition that extends over a period of time and involves dispute over strongly held beliefs (Bercovitch, 2003).

In schools, intractable conflict often occurs when decisions must be made that involve large-scale reform and innovation. In these cases, school personnel and parents are often divided on issues concerning what is best for students. For example, consider the case of Middle Rock High School. Middle Rock is a large high school facing overcrowding. Originally built to house 2,500 students, it now holds over 3,250 students in cramped classrooms and overheated portables with surrounding neighborhoods continuing to grow. District leaders would like to build another high school allowing the school to alleviate their problems of growth. Furthermore, building a new school would allow the district to incorporate some "small school" innovations designed to make high schools more personalized and to improve the learning for students. They believe that opening a new school would provide the perfect opportunity for incorporating changes to curriculum and instruction at the secondary level. The community has resisted the building of a second high school for financial reasons, contending that when the existing building was erected promises were made that a second school would not be required "well into the next century." Furthermore, they are publicly opposed to changes in the way high school students are educated arguing that the district "doesn't know our kids, our values, and our community." Public forums were held to educate the community on the potential changes. Parents claiming that any changes to the high school's program would jeopardize their children's ability to gain athletic scholarships to college mounted strong opposition. Repeatedly, the refrain was echoed that our schools were "good enough" and had a "proven" record of success. According to vocal parent groups, any changes to the school structure or curriculum would only have negative consequences.

The district sought to obtain funding for a new school by placing in the ballot an initiative designed to fund construction costs. The initiative was soundly defeated with 82% of the community voting against the levy. Subsequently, community leaders have called for the resignation of the superintendent and the upcoming school board election promises to be hotly contested as those opposing high school reform have formed a coalition and have announced their candidacy for seats.

As can be seen, the community of Middle Rock is facing an intractable conflict. No form of negotiation will allow each side to obtain what they wish as each side's goals are incommensurate with the other's goals (i.e., change versus permanence). Furthermore, a conflict such as this defies the application of small-scale negotiation skills that are so useful in one-on-one situations because of the large numbers of parties involved in the conflict at this time. At the root of the issue are highly complex, unpredictable issues with thousands of community actors (students, parents, and voters) with a stake in the conflict.

Generally speaking, as conflicts escalate, the number of issues in the dispute tends to increase as well. We can see that, in this case, issues related to prior promises are of importance to some community members, while others see the debate as over issues of athletics, reform, instruction, and curriculum. As we can observe here, a dispute initially may focus on one event or problem (e.g., overcrowding at the high school), which may be very clear, as the dispute goes on and parties bring up more and more related problems (e.g., mistrust of school reform agendas), the number of issues in contention expands as well (e.g., election to school board seats). Complexity may breed polarization adding to the difficulty of decision making in situations of conflict. One or more contributing conditions are typically at play.

Contributing conditions. Distinguishing the characteristics of tough decisions separate from the conditions that contribute to the difficulty is somewhat artificial but necessary for the purposes of explanation. In most circumstances, a tough decision is distinguished by the presence of complexity as well as a variety of contributing conditions such as a lack of trust, scarcity of resources, and environmental turbulence.

Trust. Schools need cohesive and collaborative relationships to accomplish organizational goals. A hallmark of such relationships is trust. Trust connects leaders to followers (Tschannen-Moran, 2004) and acts as organizational glue (Louis & Miles, 1990; Tschannen-Moran, 2004), allowing organizational members to hold confidence in a leader's ideas, actions, and words. Essential to the establishment of trust are predictability, reliability, and competence. Predictable leaders act in expected and knowable ways on which teachers and parents learn to rely. These allow stakeholders to trust in daily decision making and serve as positive memories during times of stress and difficulty. Similarly, reliable leaders act in a consistent and dependable fashion fostering long-term respect for their leadership skills and abilities. As leaders act in predictable and reliable ways, community members begin to see them as competent to do the job well, and in turn, increased trust grows. When facing tough decisions, trust becomes an invaluable resource on which a leader may draw. An absence of trust can have negative consequences for a school leader. When faculty, staff, and parents do not believe they can trust the principal or superintendent, this barrier may undermine the decision-making process.

Scarcity of resources. "I could do it, if I only had . . ." In schools, scarcity can seem ever present. There never appears to be enough time, money, or in-house skill to complete the task of educating students well. Scarcity means not having sufficient resources to fulfill unlimited subjective wants (Barbier & Homer-Dixon, 1996). Alternatively, scarcity implies that not all of society's (or a school's) goals can be attained at the same time; therefore, we must trade off one good against others (Barbier & Homer-Dixon, 1996; Nickel & Fuentes, 2002).

When resources are scarce, organizational members tend to focus on small, short-term issues at the expense and risk of losing touch with larger, long-term goals and objectives. Discussions become mired in issues of what can be done next week rather than "What is our potential?" It is hard for people to dream big when their current realities seem so limited. The difficulty for school leaders when dealing with tough decisions is that scarcity serves to limit the imagination of organizational members just when ingenuity and inspiration are needed most. Issues of scarcity must be addressed at the start of any difficult decision and treated as part of the problem at hand rather than as a barrier to solution.

Environmental turbulence. It is well documented that schools today are different from schools of past decades (Tyack, 1974). If we accept that today's school climate is equally different, we must also embrace the notion that change is inevitable and omnipresent. Part of any change is instability, volatility, and turbulence. Yet disruption and challenge can be viewed as positive forces for innovation and creativity. Even under regular circumstances, turbulence is the stuff of unpredictability—the parent who calls at 4:30 p.m. wondering why their kindergartner was not on the bus, the "packed-house" PTA meeting when the health program is on the agenda, or the state ruling that calls for even more stringent testing across more grade levels.

Turbulent environments are characterized by high levels of dynamism, complexity, and uncertainty (Choo, 2001). They are environments in which tough decisions originate. Turbulence may be produced from any number of sectors: internal and external accountabilities as well as conflict and complexity within the school environment. Leaders, even those considered highly competent, cannot control environmental turbulence any more than they can control the weather. However, they can prepare for turbulence using strategies that are as flexible as possible. Data-collection processes can be planned and executed, and ongoing evaluation of the educational environment within the building and district can be undertaken. Finally, leaders must be attentive to the possibility of still more change and have resources ready to address changes as they arise.

SUCCESSFUL APPLICATIONS IN PRACTICE: QUALITIES OF SUCCESSFUL LEADERS

Under times of duress, successful leaders utilize a variety of overlapping strategies and skills that see them through the tough times. These tactics are employed prior to and during the decision-making process. Successful leaders make use of regular environmental scanning as part of their habitual leadership practice and routine employing careful attention to organizational cues and norms during decision-making processes. They also utilize negotiation skills when appropriate to assure that disputes do not exacerbate or escalate the level and complexity of conflict and build trust with faculty and staff by acting in predictable and reliable ways. Thriving change-leaders apply the lessons learned during tough decisions to future organizational action resulting in new learning that permeates the organization's memory and becomes part of the organization's shared history and narrative.

Environmental scanning. Environmental scanning is the "acquisition and use of information about events, trends, and relationships in an organization's environment, the knowledge of which would assist management in planning the organization's future course of action" (Choo, 2001, p. 2). Leaders within the school organization scan the environment in order to understand the internal and external forces of change so that they may develop effective responses to difficulties that may arise. They may scan in order to avoid surprises, identify threats and opportunities, gain competitive advantage, and improve long-term and short-term planning. To the extent that a school's ability to adapt to its environment is dependent on knowing and interpreting the changes that are taking place, environmental scanning constitutes a primary mode of organizational learning.

Environmental scanning includes the examination of available information (e.g., student grades, test score data, or faculty meeting discussion) and the search for novel information (e.g., parental feedback concerning the homework policy or community leaders' impressions of the curriculum's ability to educate students for the workforce). It can range from a casual office conversation, to the formal evaluation of program or test score data. Environmental scanning allows the school leader to make better sense of the environment that surrounds the school milieu providing for increased "intelligence" about potential difficulties on the horizon.

So what do exceptional school leaders need to do to develop environmental scanning skills? We recommend the following action steps to increase a leader's ability to use scanning techniques to increase decision-making success.

- *Listen hard.* Leaders who invest time and effort to listening to those around them often can predict small changes or disruptions in the environment before they become big. Much like economists who look at obscure indicators (i.e., sales of expensive jeans and the like on the theory that if sales are up in those areas, people must have disposable income to spend) to predict economic growth, good environmental scanners pay focused attention to those school, local, state, and national indicators that have the potential to bring clarity to school level issues. Hard listening can encompass paying close attention to what is being talked about literally in meetings as well as what is "talked about" in the educational news and literature.
- *Include others.* The adage that "two heads are better than one" serves well here. By involving other community members (e.g., teachers, parents, students, and business leaders) in the environmental scanning effort, communication is enhanced, as is the sense of shared effort. By creating advisory

councils, learning teams, or consultative boards, leaders can encourage people to regularly participate in discussions regarding future planning, and as a result schools can develop any number of strategic options that can be used proactively to cope with tough decisions.

- *Develop a clear vision.* Environmental scanning is most effective in an environment of clear direction, where an awareness of organizational direction can be enhanced by new information. Steady awareness of what is occurring within the organization offers the leader an ability to filter out what has little potential to negatively affect the school (e.g., building a new Wal-Mart in the community) in favor of events with greater potential to be of concern (e.g., shifts in the political climate).

Negotiation skills. Negotiation skills have long been considered a staple in any good leader's backpack of communication skills. The ability to negotiate effectively allows a leader to reconcile differences, manage conflict, resolve disputes, and establish or adjust relationships (Cohen, 2003). Fisher and Ury (1981) describe four principles for effective negotiation: (a) separate the people from the problem, (b) focus on interests rather than positions, (c) generate a variety of options before settling on an agreement, and (d) insist that the agreement be based on objective criteria (p. 11). Long considered the seminal work in the area, Fisher and Ury explain that a good agreement is one that is wise and efficient and that improves the parties' relationship by satisfying each member's interests.

People do not enter into a negotiation process unless something is at stake. The issue may be minor (e.g., a playground dispute) or complex (e.g., development of common course assessments). Leaders can use each negotiation opportunity as a way to build trust and a strong foundation for future negotiations where stakes are even higher. The systems involved with internal and external communication are key supports for developing good negotiation skills. Clarity, honesty, and openness contribute to a leader's ability to build solid communication patterns within the school enhancing their ability to draw on these in times of difficulty.

So what do savvy school leaders need to do to build their negotiation skills? We recommend the following action steps to increase a leader's negotiation expertise with the intent of helping the leader increase trust within the school organization.

- *Be hard on the problem and soft on the person.* Develop conversational abilities that allow you to focus your attention on *what* the issues are rather than *who* they involve. Reframe your responses in ways that summarize your understanding of the problem as well as the requests of each party. Invite a trading approach stating things in terms of compromise, "I will, if you will." Display respect for all members of the negotiation, commending each side for what they have previously accomplished. Take time to understand what is at stake, listen more, and talk less.

- *Focus on needs, not positions.* Expand on your ability to define the problem. Invest time in helping all parties identify what they need to feel once the disagreement is resolved. Ask nonthreatening questions to clarify exactly what each party would like to see in a resolution. State these requests clearly and then work on delivering as much as possible to meet each party's desires.
- *Emphasize common ground.* When working to resolve differences, point out how you are aligned with the other person in a common goal. Comments like "We're both looking for what is best" or "We share the goal of providing excellent classroom opportunities for kids," can go a long way to winning over the other party as well as diffusing any anger that might be present. A shared history of effort is worth preserving. It assists in reminding all parties of the positive experiences they have shared and can increase the potential for positive decision outcomes.
- *Be inventive about options.* It is not always possible that everyone can have exactly what he or she wants simultaneously. Consider options that allow for deferred rewards, provide benefits that address other issues, or allow a party to call in the favor at a later date. Remind each party of the investments you have already made toward their goals; it may just be that they do not require anything further at this time.
- *Make clear agreements.* Restate what each party will do and gain. If needed, write out your understanding of what is to come. End each conversation with the invitation to "check back" if the agreed solution does not appear to be working or requires refinement.

Organizational learning. Thriving leaders seek to develop new and deeper understandings of how their school responds to pressure and change. While it may sound trite, successful leaders really do see each new challenge as a learning opportunity, seeking to understand how this decision might provide insights and foundational learning for decisions yet to come. The ability for a leader to incorporate those lessons into the shared memory of the school can be called organizational learning (Leithwood & Louis, 1998; Scribner, Cockrell, Cockrell, & Valentine, 1999). Organizational learning includes lessons learned that are shared among a variety of organizational members and that help to create a sound foundation of experience on which members may draw in the future. Understanding how the explicit and tacit knowledge gained during the decision-making process is processed and stored in the organization's memory is an essential component of organizational learning.

Explicit knowledge is a formal and tangible form of knowledge that is most easily shared between organizational members (Markus, 2001; Tuomi, 2000). Explicit knowledge is systematic. It is easily categorized into words and numbers and can be smoothly transmitted between faculty and staff. This form of knowledge is often found in school publications, documents, meeting minutes, and union contracts. It is decontextualized and static and often separate from the contexts in which it was generally understood. These structures are necessary for an organization to run straightforwardly and efficiently. However, they are not sufficient for growth; nor can they be nimble or adaptive in responding to rapidly changing environments. In environments where attention has been solely focused on the development of structures to support explicit knowledge, it is common for organizations to be blindsided when a unique organizational challenge presents itself.

In contrast, nimble and adaptive responses to difficult times rely almost exclusively on tacit knowledge. Tacit knowledge can be thought of as the knowledge individuals and, to a lesser extent, teams develop over time and experience (Markus, 2001; Tuomi, 2000). It is a highly personal form of knowing, hard to formalize, and therefore, difficult to communicate to others. Tacit knowledge consists of both technical and cognitive skills. It is the "know-how" one needs to get the job done and the experience-based skill set to know what is and what ought to be. Additionally, it is action-centered, learned when one interacts within the school environment over increasingly longer periods of time and through distinctive experiences. It is housed in the memories of individual experiences rather than formal school structures.

As schools seek to become responsive to internal and external catalysts, the ability to explicate the tacit knowledge held by school personnel is required. School leaders must develop social and organizational conditions (such as reflective meetings with the purpose of providing input to the leader regarding progress toward goals) supportive of the creation and sharing of this knowledge based on the tacit knowledge held in the organization. Once surfaced, these understandings and insights can become of use during turbulent times.

So what do excellent school leaders need to do to build organizational learning and memory? We recommend the following action steps to increase a leader's ability to draw on and create the conditions for organizational learning and decision-making success.

- *Develop commonly understood structures and systems* in which faculty and staff share ownership in building and maintaining systems and structures perceived as contributing to the success of all participants. These structures will help foster everyone's success within a school and have the best potential to foster commonly held memory.
- *Recognize the power of tacit knowledge* and build redundant work assignments to enhance organizational depth among those tasks and data structures on which the success of the school rests.
- *Identify and create catalysts for the development of shared memories*—retreats, in-services, and other learning opportunities must be built into the structures of organizations so that information is shared, reflected on, and retained in timely and useful ways.
- *Celebrate your successes* and give credit to those in the past who paved the way for the future by demonstrating how the school builds on what it once was to enhance what it now is and will become.

TOUGH DECISIONS: CONSIDERATIONS AND CONCLUSIONS

Tough decisions do not have to bring school leaders to their knees. In fact, tough decisions have the potential to provide schools and those who work and care about them the opportunity to create exciting new environments for student and faculty learning. Although addressing the tough decision requires thought, effort, and skill, the endeavor will bring continuing benefit to those who are served by expert leadership. When faced with tough decisions, the following points are worth remembering:

- Tough decisions involve issues of leadership and management. The school leader must address the regular operations of the school and be prepared for the challenges that exist.
- Issues of external and internal accountability comprise the decision-making context of schools today. Equally important, they require clear and specific problem analysis and ongoing focused attention so that the leader may be prepared for issues that will arise.
- Tough decisions are ill-defined and conflict-prone. In tandem, these characteristics foster an organizational environment of divergence, dispute, and complexity. The leaders must be prepared for this environment.
- Trust, scarcity of resources, and environmental turbulence are conditions that increase the complexity of the decision-making process.
- Focused attention to both short- and long-term goals through environmental scanning can assist leaders in weathering tough decisions and difficult organizational circumstances.
- Learning and applying skills of negotiation can help leaders to avoid turning small, ordinary problems and minor disputes into larger ones.
- Increasing organizational learning allows school personnel to learn from past experiences and plan for future successes.

QUESTIONS FOR REFLECTION AND DISCUSSION

- How can understanding the characteristics and conditions of tough decisions help you to better understand decision making in context?
- To what extent do the norms and values of your school promote change? Trust? Negotiation? Dissent? Organizational learning?
- What instances have you witnessed when a tough decision needed to be made? What characteristics and conditions described in this chapter were present? In what ways did they hinder or foster the decision-making process?
- What activities do you engage in to focus attention and sustained effort on persistent dilemmas? How effective are these in creating anticipatory plans for future effort?
- When have you seen the use of data enhance decision making? In what ways has it helped focus attention on the tough questions of student learning?
- How are your coping skills? What are your strengths and limitations?

PART IV

Conclusion: Underexamined Issues in Decision Making

CHAPTER TEN

The Educational Leader as Decision Maker: Themes, Inferences, and Conclusions

In approaching this final chapter, we consider the ways in which the knowledge and skill sets we have explored in this text have the potential to make a difference in educational leaders' decision making. By taking into account the variety of decision-making theories, we offer school leaders some final thoughts that seek to bring together the ideas we have unavoidably taken up as distinct notions. As we look back over this book, at least three major themes recur.

First and foremost, our exploration of decision making suggests that leaders who are most successful in their decision making are those who seek to make *organizational sense* and *find meaning* within the problems they wish to solve. Finding meaning within and about one's decision-making processes draws on the alchemy of theory, context, and personal reflection. In this final chapter we explore the ways in which school leaders can think about *prioritizing* their decision-making practice. Thinking about our decision-making priorities offers us a way to integrate the ideas that underscore this text while still providing the reader foundational understandings about sense and meaning making in organizations.

A second theme within this text contends that decision making is a *socially constructed* phenomenon. The politics of the school organization, the context in which the decision must be made, and the data on which a decision may rest all contribute to how members of the school organization construct their understandings concerning a decision. In this way, leaders must seek to understand the social and political context in which their decisions lie and take into account organizational constructs when confronting new or reoccurring issues. Moreover, we submit that *learning* about our decision-making practices is socially constructed as well. Our ability to learn from our decision-making successes and failures and the ways in which we learn influence our future practices.

Finally, we suggest that decision making is an *active and dynamic process*. While we have argued that decision making must be informed by the data and context in which the decision is to be made, it is essentially a recursive and iterative process. Specifically, it is a form of mediated action. Neither the school context nor the data on which the leader draws is static. Fundamentally, in the decision-making process the leader actively mediates what surrounds him by taking into account a myriad of organizational and personal variables focusing her energies on the best potential outcome. Yet, we can almost never say we are finished with any decision. As we have illustrated, decisions are wrought with unintended consequences and new organizational developments that often require us to revisit and reassess our prior choices. In this fashion, successful leaders view decision making as an ongoing active process seeking the best balance between process and progress. We turn now to discussing each of these themes in more detail.

PRIORITIZING DECISIONS

There are perhaps as many ways to prioritize decisions as there are decisions to be made. Repeatedly, we have characterized the building and district leader's role as one that is full of demanding and disparate activity. Even the most industrious educational leaders often find themselves at a loss in choosing which difficult task to tackle next. However, research suggests that unless leaders actively work to prioritize their decision-making energies, their efforts are likely to be uncoordinated and unproductive (Yeo, 2006).

The following figure offers the reader a schema for thinking about prioritizing decisions. We have attempted to create a framework for leaders to consider the potential for a decision to occur as well as the consequences of action. Along one axis, we offer the dyad of probability. In this case, we suggest that events can occur in one of two fashions—either often and somewhat predictability or infrequently and without forewarning. However, in considering how one might prioritize decision-making efforts, probability is a useful but not inclusive category. Clearly, as leaders we would like to think we would prioritize decisions we know we will need to make over those that might present themselves. Yet, is it persuasive to view events that happen often as more compelling than those that happen equally predictability but less regularly. Our attention becomes captured by the regularity of the event rather than the importance of the incident.

In this way, not all events that require decision making are equal. The outcomes of some decisions hold great significance for the school organization, while the implications of others are less momentous. Thus, the consequence of the decision is of necessary consideration. Our second axis addresses this variable. We suggest that events and the decisions they engender are either of high consequence or low consequence. High-consequence events and decisions include decisions related to the long-term attainment of organizational visions and values, whereas low-consequence events consist of more routine decisions and actions. By creating a dichotomy in which the purpose for and consequences of the decision matters, the framework offers leaders greater acuity in thinking about their decision-making choices.

Leaders might ask if the event that presents itself and the decisions it engenders are of low or high consequence to the organization and if it is likely to occur often. Creation of and adherence to thoughtful policy and practice can assist leaders in streamlining the time they spend attending to daily distractions. Building time into meetings and planning to address data and the evaluation of program and policy can stimulate thinking about goals and vision. In this way, decision making may become more balanced and each quadrant of potential activity addressed.

A note before we move on. We do not argue that low-consequence decisions are unimportant. In fact, we concur with research (Bryk & Schneider, 2002; Tschannen-Moran, 2004) that asserts that how leaders address the day-to-day decision making of the school environment contributes to the overall school climate and culture, trust and respect, and community. Nor do we argue that routine decisions are any simpler. However, we do suggest that school leaders overly prioritize their attention to decisions that fall into the high-probability or low-consequence quadrant.

Daily, leaders are inundated with potential decisions. It is seductive to think that each and everyone one requires one's immediate attention. In fact, we find that novice school leaders often spend their time chasing from one activity to another. Knowingly (or unknowingly), they decide to spend their time in a haphazard fashion—attending every meeting to which they are invited, setting up computers, troubleshooting textbook orders, scheduling or covering playground, bus, and hall duties. Exhausted, they proclaim at the end of the day that there is no time for them to attend to anything other than the daily pressures of running a building.

Mired in high-probability or low-consequence decisions, school leaders bounce from event to event, expending energy in unproductive ways, and often abandoning the core work of school improvement in the process (Louis & Kruse, 1995; Louis & Miles, 1990; Rowan, 2002). Moreover, we suggest that high-probability or low-consequence decisions are readily addressed by the development of clear policy and practice designed to underscore consistency, equity, and equality in the decision-making process.

We turn our thoughts now to helping leaders think about ways to coordinate their decision-making efforts. In keeping with our thinking above, we discuss the realm of decision making that encompasses the high-consequence events. We offer two distinct but complimentary categories with which to consider prioritization efforts. The first category suggests leaders maintain a focus on what matters over the long-term—the vision and commitment of the school to those it serves. The second proposes that leaders must pay attention to those decision priorities related to immediate crisis situations and impending deadlines. In each of these high-stakes cases, making the right decision in the right way matters most.

	High Probability	Low Probability
High Consequence	Predictable events with the potential to affect short-term practices, goals and actions and/or long-term goal attainment.	Crisis events with the potential to threaten student or faculty safety, organizational stability and/or long-term goal attainment.
Examples	Testing, strategic planning, school reform and/or restructuring efforts.	School shooting, hurricane, earthquake, death of a school community member and/or district financial collapse.
Low Consequence	Routine disruptions with the potential to distract attention from the core work of the school.	Random disruptions with little probability of lasting effects.
Examples	Classroom, hallway or playground fight, parent conferences, scheduling, book orders, assemblies, and/or field trips.	Weather-related (snow, flood) school cancellation, holiday parties, school events that disrupt the schedule such as field day and fundraising events.

FIGURE 10.1. High and Low Probability/High and Low Consequence Decisions

PRIORITIZING VISION AND COMMITMENTS—LONG-TERM DECISION-MAKING

Leading a school is, quite simply, hard work. Daily, internal and external tensions pull leaders in a variety of worthy and competing directions. As we have suggested, it is challenging for school leaders to not allow themselves to be forced into a reactive posture by high-probability or low-consequence events and decisions. As compelling as daily interruptions and disruptions can be, there are equally persuasive arguments for attending to actions with the potential to address long-term goals and vision.

In the era of school accountability, it is paramount that leaders thoughtfully attend to those aspects of the school organization related to the assessment of student learning and progress. Testing, data collection, and analysis and the decisions that arise from these endeavors are perennial educational issues. Thus, they can be categorized as high-probability events. Our definition here relies on the truth that, although not as common as a classroom disruption, the likelihood is that a school leader will be called on to account for student progress each year. Again, we stress that high-probability events are events that can be predicted to occur in some regular and orderly fashion. Yet, it is the high-probability or high-consequence decision that most often is ignored by school leaders in low-performing schools (Hargreaves & Fink, 2006; Rowan, 2002; Spillane, 2006). With the absence of a clear and shared vision, it is nearly impossible for the leader to attend long-term goals and the high-consequence decisions in which they arise.

As we have previously discussed, a vision in its simplest form is a declaration of a desired future for an organization. In this way, visions are more than carefully worded grand statements. The vision sets forth the values organizational members have agreed to share and a philosophy about how they will go about their common work. When visions are enacted by a change in behaviors by those within an organization, they can serve to provide direction for decision making (Heifetz, 1994; Kotter, 1999). By helping to create an avenue for coherence among and between decision-making opportunities, a shared vision can provide a litmus test for those decisions requiring priority action. By focusing the school leader on what requires his or her primary attentions, adherence to a vision allows a leader the ability to set precedence regarding which opportunities to grasp.

This is not to say that we do not understand the pressing effort of running a school. Clearly, we understand that when a fight breaks out or an angry parent calls it is not the time to be otherwise engaged. We argue that by keeping the vision an always present touch-tone and using it as a measure of what is important and worth attention, the school leader can begin to sort out what requires immediate attention and what might be delegated, delayed, or declined. A school leader we respect puts it this way: "I hold up my goals when I am considering what I'll do. I get asked to do a lot of things. Go to speakers, attend community meetings, visit with area business leaders. . . . Before I accept anything, I ask myself, 'Will this contribute to the kids?' if I can't say yes, I say no." Not surprisingly, objective measures—including state test scores, value added calculations, and ACT and SAT scores—suggest that the students in this school achieve at levels beyond that of other similar buildings in the district. By attending to high-consequence events and allowing those decisions to guide the choices this leader makes about lower consequence events, priorities are straightforwardly and clearly set.

When pressed further to describe his decision-making strategies, this leader added, "For me, where I want to take this school is everything. It's how I define my job. We set a clear vision—to prepare these students for college. It seems simple but it's not. So when I'm working with teachers, with kids, with parents, I always go back to the core question: 'How will this help kids academically succeed?' If I don't get a compelling answer to that question, I don't go forward. I look for real evidence—I want kids to like going to school here, but I want them to learn more. That's my real vision."

Not losing sight of the real vision is an important aspect of leadership. Every year dozens of people lose their lives in mountain-climbing accidents. Often these accidents are due to freak changes in the weather or other unanticipated, uncontrollable events. More often these accidents are due to losing sight of the real vision. Yes, everyone wants to get to the peak, but climbers in the excitement of the climb often forget that summiting is the reward for their hard work, training, and good luck. Summiting is at best a short-term goal. The real vision is about getting out alive. Climbing teams that focus on surviving, as well as summiting, pay attention to more than how far they are from the top. They monitor the weather, pack appropriately, and take corrective action when the conditions start to deteriorate. Quite literally, by paying attention to what really matters, they create the conditions that allow them the opportunity for success.

Similarly, school leaders who pay attention to long- as well as short-term goals experience greater success than those who do not (Yeo, 2006). By keeping sight of what really matters—student learning and achievement—and focusing their decision-making priorities accordingly, leaders can avoid the pitfall of scattered attentions and increase their opportunities for real success. Having discussed the importance of using long-term goals in high-probability or high-consequence events, we turn now to addressing the pressures of decision making in low-probability or high-consequence events.

COMPLEXITY—SHORT-TERM HIGH-STAKES DECISION MAKING

Good decision making is a balancing act. In the prior section we discussed the importance of holding tight to a vision as a benchmark against which quality decision-making might be measured. We also acknowledged the day-to-day pressures every school leader faces. As leaders seek to balance the competing pressures of long-term foci with short-term deadlines and crisis management, the ability to thoughtfully respond rather than impulsively or mechanically react is paramount.

By definition, crisis situations are circumstances in which the consequences are high (Weick, 2002). However, they are extremely rare. The classic high-consequence or low-probability event crises have the potential to threaten the foundations of organizational stability and trust. In most cases, organizations work to prevent crisis situations. Industrial manufacturing plants have safety and accident plans in place. Hospitals and public health agencies have disease management strategies. Schools are increasingly adopting entry and lock-down policies and procedures. Yet, because human behavior is a complex system, when a major incident occurs emergency plans are tested. Why is this so? Think for a minute about this potential set of events.

1. Oliver has an important after school appointment to attend.
2. Just as he was leaving the building he saw the parent of a student in his class.
3. He wanted to meet with this parent so he walked the parent into the building.
4. He stopped by his classroom to share an example of the student's work with the parent.
5. Upon leaving the room, he closed the door behind him, inadvertently locking his car and house keys in the classroom.
6. Not wanting to wait to locate someone to let him into the room, he reasoned he could use the little plastic emergency car key in his wallet.
7. During his search he remembered he loaned the emergency key to his spouse the last time she used the car.
8. Oliver began to search for the custodian to let him into his classroom.
9. The custodian was located but could not assist Oliver for several minutes.
10. Realizing he will be late for the appointment, he reached for his cell phone to call ahead and discovers the battery is dead.
11. Fifteen minutes later the custodian appears and lets Oliver into the room.
12. He races to his appointment. Traffic is snarled.
13. Upon arrival he finds the door locked and the lights off. Having missed his appointment he worries that he will be charged for the missed meeting because he failed to cancel.

Clearly, a missed appointment is hardly a crisis. However, by following the chain of events in our scenario, we can begin to understand how complex systems fail and in what ways we might prioritize decision making in complex events.

So what happened to poor Oliver? Was the problem human error? Poor system design? Faulty planning and procedure? Schedule failure? In a word, yes. Human error contributed to the situation when Oliver forgot his keys and failed to charge his cell phone. The locking system on the door can share some blame in that simply closing the door could lock it. Oliver miscalculated the potential for interruption when he planned his appointment, and then complicated the matter by engaging the parent in conversation rather than using the opportunity to schedule a different, more convenient meeting. Furthermore, slow-moving traffic further complicated his ability to arrive in a timely matter. So is Oliver a bumbling fool? Hardly. Rather, he is the victim of complexity. The system on which he was counting required that a sequence of tightly coupled interdependent actions to occur (get out of school on time, technology would operate effectively, travel would go smoothly).

When a system is tightly coupled, it requires a series of rigidly ordered processes to occur in sequence (B must follow A). Often these processes are time dependent (B cannot occur until A has been completed), and there is only a single path to a successful outcome (A, then B, then C). As in Oliver's case, there may be little flexibility in the system should an error occur. Classical decision-making models would suggest that it would be relatively simple to plan actions within a complex system and assure success. However, as we have all experienced, unfamiliar, unplanned, or unexpected events often occur. When unanticipated events occur, complexity increases. When complexity increases, so does the potential for error.

Known as *normal accidents*, the unraveling of carefully laid plans is an inevitable outcome of complexity (Perrow, 1999). Normal accident theory (NAT) suggests that when a failure occurs in one part of a complex system the potential for failure in other aspects of the system is increased. When unanticipated events occur within a tightly coupled system, a cascading ripple effect may occur and events may spiral out of control before corrective action can be taken. As we build complex systems, we rely on our decision-making and planning efforts to consider the potential accidents that may occur and provide for them by either creating redundancy within the system (two people on the phone tree call each member below) or by generating safety features within the structures we design (the doors are locked and visitors are buzzed into the building).

Therefore, when accidents do occur we believe that we have done all we could have to prevent them. However, as Cutler (1999) asserts, "Accidents do not occur because people gamble and lose, they occur because people do not believe that the accident that is about to occur is at all possible." In this way, decision making related to crisis situations is unavoidably hampered. Prior to the situation we can only plan for what we believe may occur and only those system structures we can imagine failing. As soon as we assert that X will never occur in our school, we have begun down the path of a normal accident.

This is not to say that prevention is foolhardy. For example, it is not necessary for an automobile manufacturer to predict all the ways a car accident might occur in order to provide seat belts and air bags. Neither is it essential for school leaders to know all the ways students may misbehave to draft a discipline policy. By considering the potential problems that may occur and having comprehensive plans to address them, crises, when they do arise, may be dealt with in timely and effective ways. Leaders can find balance by focusing on emergent issues and problems. Working from the host of potential situations that exist they may then evaluate causal variables and factors as well as potential relational interactions between parts of the system. By thoughtfully considering the constraints that exist within the school organization, it is possible to adapt one's decision-making practices to new and improbable situations. Complexity then becomes a planned for and expected aspect of organizational planning rather than a confounding and impenetrable feature.

Improvement in the reliability of school organization decision making in crisis situations requires that leaders accept that the performance of complex systems cannot be forecast with adequate accuracy to assure consistent behavior over the lifetime of the organization. Once leaders consider the potential of the normal accident, the continual monitoring of system performance through measures that provide insight into potential accidents and occurrences can be established, thus diminishing the potential for occurrence. Finally, leaders must accept that "It can happen here." Developing an organizational commitment to continual improvement through learning and action can provide leaders higher confidence in the decisions they make.

DECISION-MAKING PRACTICE AND LEARNING

At its core, learning about decision making is about learning to lead. We have repeatedly argued that decision making lies at the heart of leadership and that leadership is decision making in action. In this final reflection we wish to delve into those aspects of *learning* within and about school organizations that enhance successful decision making.

In this text we have provided a variety of examples of decisions that can be made by the school leader. However, we hope we have made the case that decisions related to the teaching and learning process, those with the most potential to impact student achievement, are the decisions on which leaders must focus. Moreover, we would argue that when such decisions are placed at the heart of school decision making, leaders' may capitalize on the opportunities these decisions present by developing learning within the school organization.

Learning within the organization occurs when organizational practices are critically examined by using the available data that are, either retained, modified, or abandoned. When a practice is considered and *retained*, it is assumed that the available data supports its success. In this case, it might be argued that what school members have learned previously is reinforced although new learning may not occur. When practices are *modified*, those aspects of practice that were thought to be ineffective are changed. Thus, organizational learning occurs as changes are implemented and evaluated. Furthermore, learning occurs as organizational members persist, embracing the new practices, and developing skillful understandings regarding the new ideas. Finally, in the face of compelling data, practices may be completely *abandoned* and replaced by other more promising actions. When school organizations abandon prior practice in favor of new ideas and actions, we would argue that the potential for organizational learning is greatest. It is in these cases where leaders can refocus faculty and staff on the central values of the school. The literature asserts that, when school leaders view their decisions about instruction, curriculum, and assessment as opportunities to focus on student learning and teacher accountability and improvement, those decisions become a key instrument of reform (Argysis, 2002; Leithwood & Louis, 1998; Markus, 2001; Scribner, Cockrell, Cockrell, & Valentine, 1999; Yeo, 2006). While much of the literature on school reform has emphasized organizational changes in the daily practice of professionals, the organizational learning literature suggests that school reform efforts should be concentrated on those practices central to student achievement and success.

Building an organization's ability to learn has been a key element in discussions of innovation in both restructured schools and businesses (see, for example, Blackman, Connelly, & Henderson, 2004; Senge, 1990; Weick, 1995; Yeo, 2006). Organizational learning as a model for decision making suggests that people working within school organizations are part of a community. Within the school community members socially construct meaning concerning the events and actions in which they participate. The learning organization evokes assumptions about the members of the school organization as more participative, more intrinsically motivated, and engaged in decision making with greater personal effort than the other organizational models. Learning is then thought to be less individualistic, more focused on schoolwide goals, and information more systematically obtained. Information previously held by one or even a few members of the school organization gains meaningfulness to other members of the school only within a socially constructed setting. Thus, decision making is enhanced when school organization members share commonly held understandings concerning the goals and vision of the organization. When decisions are aligned with goals and vision, it is easier for members of an organization to understand the purpose of decisions as they are made and to support their implementation.

Such a socially constructed setting may include time for school organizational members to examine data, consider decision priorities, and make strategic choices that draw from the combined knowledge of the assembled members. What characterizes decisions strongly influenced by an organizational learning perspective is the ability for members to take in new information, process it, and share it among the members of the organization in steady and regular ways. What learning organizations share among them is an inventory of prior knowledge about the decisions their school had made concerning teaching and learning.

The model of a school as a learning organization follows assumptions that suggest organizational learning takes place in groups and cannot be reduced to the random accumulation of individuals' knowledge (Argysis, 2002; Elkjaer, 2004; Yeo, 2006). Thus, it is within a framework of systematic collection and focus on information that decisions with the potential to result in learning occurs. In the learning organization, the technical knowledge base—inclusive of content information, teaching methodologies, and innovations in both areas—provides the structure and context for further social bonds to be created. Teachers in schools focused on learning work to learn new things about both their teaching and their content areas and then discuss, share, and critique the new ideas so that all members understand and can use the newly learned information in the decision-making process. Therefore, when one thinks of school change initiatives, the organizational learning perspective suggests that the collective, regular processes of teachers and administrators working together around issues of practice and professional knowledge will provide schools with the capacity for change and development.

Elsewhere it has been argued that team learning enhances the organizational learning process (Kruse, 2001). Pounder (1998, 1999) and Leithwood and Louis (1998) have suggested that the literature on *work groups* can make a contribution to understanding and improving collaboration among teachers, particularly when considering teams devoted to developing and reinforcing shared norms. In particular, Pounder (1999) suggests that teacher teams are strongly similar to work groups in other organizational settings. Work groups "are designed to increase members' responsibility for the group's performance and outcomes, creating work interdependence and opportunities for self-management" (p. 1). In this type of situation, many of the benefits and features discussed previously that accrue appear to transfer to decision-making teams as well (Blackman, et al., 2004; Elkjaer, 2004).

Team learning that results in quality decision making can be thought of as a mutual adaptation to a series of internal or external stimuli inputs (Argysis, 2002; Hackman, 1990; Haimes, 1995). Two aspects of this process challenge members of a decision-making team. The first concerns a shared attention to and understanding of the team's decision-making purposes. Team members are challenged to make explicit the tacit knowledge on which they draw in daily problem-solving and organizational life activity. The ability to make present tacit knowledge requires the ability to craft and share organizational stories that, in turn, influence organizational member's cognitions and attitudes toward their decisions. As stories of how we do things around here become more concrete, they also attract more attention as points of internal learning opportunity and as such are open to more through processing by the group. Such examination affords group members the conditions to reflect on previously unexamined belief structures. When existing belief structures are considered the potential for learning, and approaching decisions in new ways is enhanced. In turn, the potential for successful results is increased as organizational members address the complexity of the issues they face.

Second, team learning challenges individuals to engage in joint action (Wilkinson & Smith, 1995; Yeo, 2006). Engagement in joint action may result in two kinds of adaptation. Less positive, although equally possible, is the unreflective response. In this response group members rely on traditional problem-solving models to respond to the new inputs provided them. In most bureaucratic situations the result is a return to a division of labor, or the parallel play response; in which members divide the actions around and attending to the tasks at hand in uncoordinated ways. A more productive method in which a team may respond to the call of joint action involves the development of a significant learning opportunity.

Often referred to as double-loop learning (Argysis, 2002; Weick, 2000; Yeo, 2006), complex organizations, such as schools, are required to question the basic assumptions governing behavior(s) and commit to examining the values that guide them. Informed by experience and relevant literature, these organizations question underlying assumptions and practices that inform core decision-making policy and not merely the symptoms of poor organizational performance. Organizations using double-loop learning often merge new learning with existing organizational knowledge and emerge with new norms and values which guide new organizational policy, practices and procedures (Argysis, 2002; Elkjaer, 2004; Yeo, 2006). In short, decision-making leaders who are attentive to double-loop learning focus on knowledge with the potential to change the culture rather than knowledge which can be applied within the existing culture. In doing so, each new decision offers the leader an opportunity for learning.

DECISION-MAKING AS AN ACTIVE AND DYNAMIC PROCESS

As we have worked to develop the concepts within this text we have struggled to balance theory with practice, knowledge development and use, learning over knowing and emergent thinking over prescription. When considering a text on decision making, we wanted to develop ideas that engaged the reader in thinking about the theories of practice they employed in their school contexts. We wanted to challenge the reader to consider alternative paradigms of decision practice, ones that stressed the importance of the relationship of the leader to their own knowledge, values, beliefs, and to others within the school. In developing our arguments we sought to describe the artistry of the decision-making practice alongside theoretical and practical examples. In our efforts to balance description with detail, we have, at times, elected to favor broad descriptions leaving the reader to ponder the practical application of theories we have introduced. At other times we have chosen to offer detailed, almost prescriptive, competency-based inventories hoping to provide the reader with enough detail so that they might see themselves and others as leaders enacting these skills in decision-making settings.

At this point it seems reasonable to look back over this text and ask, what is the next course of action for the leader? How do I approach the next decision I need to make? How do I avoid becoming trapped in a losing situation, and how do I enhance my chances for success? The intent of this text was never to provide school leaders with checklists. Rather, it was conceived to assist leaders in developing a deeper understanding of the theories and practices that should inform their thinking. Nevertheless, there are some general comments we would like to offer in conclusion as we think about decision making as an active, dynamic process.

Avoiding bad decisions is a good idea. As ridiculous as a proposition this seems it is worth remembering. Avoiding bad decisions is all about being prepared, acting thoughtfully, and reflecting on one's actions. Repeatedly we stressed the importance of environmental scanning, knowing the internal and external politics of the organization, examining the logic of decisions, and relying on data to inform choices. We have considered those aspects of tacit knowledge and disposition that assist the leader in guessing well. Guessing well allows leaders to predict what they believe may occur and, in turn, make better predictions about potential results. Yet the decision-making environment often changes and our best predictions of what should happen are proven wrong. In these cases the best a leader can do is adapt. By being prepared, focusing on data and the surrounding environment, observing the surrounding milieu, and considering the available options leaders can work to avoid bad choices, decisions that make the situation worse rather than better. Sometimes by focusing on not making a bad decision a good one surfaces.

Start somewhere and never give up. Another way to state this would be to say, find one issue and the will to do something about it. School reform is a difficult business. Innovations rarely live up to their initial promise. Data seldom offer a clear direction for action. In our experience we have repeatedly seen two extremes of administrators. The first suggests nothing can be done. Central office limitations, the union contract, and the school board's inaction are all offered as reasons why a principal cannot act. Not surprisingly, little changes in their school. Their decisions reinforce old behaviors, policies, and practices. What change does occur is incremental, unfocused, and often fails to persist.

The second kind of administrator looks for opportunities and acts accordingly. They form leadership teams, study groups to examine data, and strategic planning councils. They face often near-intractable problems and yet, simply, decide to take action. What separates these two extremes is often inexplicable and puzzling. At times, one of these leaders will say they felt the need to make a difference. Others may say they were inspired by another's story of success. In any case, these leaders decide at a deep personal level to engage with the context at hand and make the hard choices necessary for success. When we talk with these leaders we are always struck by the near universal theme of their stories—they began with one issue about which they believed they could make a lasting, meaningful decision and simply kept moving from there. They found the will to be the leaders they wanted to be. As trite as it sounds, our experiences suggest that the dynamics of decision making are iterative. The simple choice to act, to decide, and to do something fosters increased performance and success in subsequent decisions.

Strive to make sense of the actions that surround you. As decisions arise, leaders must consider a variety of ways to frame their decisions prior to action. By thinking about how each decision contributes to the overall goals and visions of the school community, a leader contributes to organizational sense making. Reoccurring challenges can become more easily recognized and addressed and new challenges can be seen as fitting into an existing problem solving structure. Sense making can be enhanced by approaching decisions by asking the following questions:

1. In what ways is the problem similar to those I have faced in the past?
2. How did the decisions made in those cases serve?
3. What are the consequences of the decision?
4. How might learning be enhanced in this instance?
5. Does this situation encourage communal or team problem solving? What might be learned from the input and views of others?
6. Can this decision be made in such a way as to reinforce organizational goals and visions, norms, and values? How might that thinking be communicated to members?
7. Where is the evidence? Does this decision require data, and where might legitimate forms of data be located to support the decision?
8. How can the decision be tested? Once made, how will the results be evaluated?

As leaders, we can lead a cautious existence, surviving our daily struggles never really confronting the challenges of today's educational arena. Instead we would wish for the reader the will to take the risk and go forward to face the challenge knowing they have done everything they can to meliorate the difficult situations that face schools and schooling today. Our belief is that by embracing decision making as the heart of leadership practice leaders can make a difference in today's schools.

References

Abelson, R., & Levi, A. (1985). Decision-making and decision theory. In G. Lindzey & E. Aronson (Eds.), *Handbook of social psychology, vol. 1* (3rd ed., pp. 231–309). Reading, MA: Addison-Wesley.

Ambady, N., & Rosenthal, R. (1992). Thin slices of expressive behavior as predictors of interpersonal consequences: A metaanalysis. *Psychological Bulletin, 111*, 256–274.

Argote, L., Ingram, P., Levine, J. M., & Moreland, R. L. (2000). Knowledge transfer in organizations: Learning from the experience of others. *Organizational Behavior and Human Decision Processes, 82*(1), 1–8.

Argyris, C. (2002). Double loop learning, teaching and research. *Journal of Management Learning and Education, 1*(2), 206–218.

Argyris, C., & Schon, D. A. (1974). *Theory in practice: Increasing professional effectiveness.* San Francisco: Jossey-Bass.

Aristotle. (1949). *The works of Aristotle translated into English* (W. D. Ross, Ed.). Oxford: Clarendon Press.

Asher, H. (1976). *Causal modeling.* Beverly Hills: Sage Publications.

Babbie, E. (2004). *The practice of social research.* 10th ed. Belmont, CA: Wadsworth.

Bacharach, P., & Baratz, M. S. (1970). *Power and poverty.* New York: Oxford University Press.

Bacharach, S. B., & Lawler, E. J. (1980). *Power and politics in organizations.* San Francisco: Jossey-Bass.

Baldoni, J. (2006). Steady as you go: Achieving a balance vision. *Harvard Management Update.* Article reprint U0608B. http://www.harvardbusinessonline.org

Baldridge, V. (1971). *Power and conflict in the university.* New York: John Wiley & Sons.

Ball, S. J. (1987). *The micro-politics of the school: Towards a theory of school organization.* London: Routledge.

Barals, S. (2003). When choices give in to temptations: Explaining the disagreement among importance measures. *Organizational Behavior and Human Decision Processes, 91*, 310–321.

Barbier, E., & Homer-Dixon, T. (1996). Resource scarcity, institutional adaptation, and technical innovation. Occasional paper. *Project on environment, population and security.* Washington, DC: American Association for the Advancement of Science.

Barnard, C. (1938). *The functions of the executive.* Cambridge, MA: Harvard University Press.

Bass, B. M. (1990). *Bass and Stodgill's handbook of leadership.* New York: Free Press.

Bass, B. M. (1999). Two decades of research and development in transformational leadership. *European Journal of Work and Organizational Psychology*, 8(1), 9–32.

Bem, S. L., & Bem, D. J. (1973). Does sexbiased job advertising "aid and abet" sex discrimination? *Journal of Applied Social Psychology*, 3, 6–18.

Bennis, W., & Nanus, B. (2003). *Leaders: Strategies for taking charge*. New York: Harper Business Essentials.

Bercovitch, J. (2003). Characteristics of intractable conflicts. In G. Burgess & H. Burgess (Eds.), *Beyond Intractability*. Boulder: Conflict Research Consortium, University of Colorado, Boulder. Posted: October 2003. http://www.beyondintractability.org/essay/Characteristics_IC/

Berger, P. L. and T. Luckmann (1966). *The social construction of reality: A treatise in the sociology of knowledge*, Garden City, NY: Anchor Books

Bernhardt, V. (1998). *Data analysis for comprehensive school wide improvement*. Larchmont, NY: Eye on Education.

Bidwell, C. (1965). The school as a formal organization. In J. March (Ed.), *Handbook of Organizations* (pp. 972–1032). New York: Rand McNally.

Blackman, D., Connelly, J., & Henderson, S. (2004). Does double loop learning create reliable knowledge? *The Learning Organization*, 11(1), 11–27.

Blase, J. (1991). The micropolitical perspective. In J. Blase (Ed.), *The politics of life in schools: Power, conflict and cooperation* (pp. 1–18). Newbury Park, CA: Sage Publications.

Blau, P. M. (1964). *Exchange and power in social life*. New York: John Wiley & Sons.

Blau, P., & Scott, W. R. (1962). *Formal organizations: A comparative approach*. San Francisco: Chandler Publishing.

Brown, A. D. (2000). Making sense of inquiry sensemaking. *Journal of Management Studies*, 37 (1), 45–75.

Blumberg, A. (1986). *The school superintendent*. New York: Teachers College Press.

Blumberg, A., & Greenfield, W. (1980). *The effective principal*. Boston: Allyn & Bacon.

Boyan, N. (1987). The description and explanation of administrative behavior. In N. Boyan (Ed.), *Handbook of research on educational administration* (pp. 77–98). New York: Longman.

Boyd, W. (1976). The public, the professionals and educational policy-making: Who governs? *Teachers College Record*, 77 (May): 539–577.

Browne, G. J., & Pitts, M. G. (2004). Stopping rule use during information search in design problems. *Organizational Behavior and Human Decision Processes*, 95, 208–224.

Bruner, J. S. (2006). *In search of pedagogy: The selected works of Jerome S. Bruner*. New York: Routledge.

Bryk, A. S., & Schneider, B. (2002). *Trust in schools: A core resource for improvement*. New York: Russell Sage Foundation.

Bryman, A. I. (1986). *Leadership and organizations*. London: Routledge.

Buchholz, R. A., & Rosenthal, S. B. (2005). The spirit of entrepreneurship and the qualities of moral decision-making: Toward a unifying framework. *Journal of Business Ethics*, 60, 307–315.

Buenger, V., Daft, R. L., Conlon, E. J., & Austin, J. (1996). Competing values in organizations: Contextual influences and structural consequences. *Organization Science*, 7(5), 557–576.

Burdekin, R., Hossfeld, R. T., & Smith, J. K. (2002). Are NBA fans becoming indifferent to race? *Claremont College Working Papers*, 2002-12.

Burns, T., & Stalker, G. (1961). *The management of innovation*. Oxford: Oxford University Press.

Burton, J. W. (1990). Conflict-dispute distinction. In Burton, John W. and Frank Dukes, eds. (1990) Conflict: Practices in Management, Settlement, and Resolution. New York: St. Martin's Press.

Callahan, R. (1962). *Education and the cult of efficiency*. Chicago: University of Chicago Press.

Campbell, R. (1960). *Administrative theory as a guide to action*. Chicago: Midwest Administration Center, University of Chicago.

Carlson, R. O. (1964). Environmental constraints and organizational consequences: The public School and its clients. In D. E. Griffiths (Ed.), *Behavioral science and educational administration: Sixty-third yearbook of the National Society for the Study of Education* (pp. 262–276). Chicago: University of Chicago Press.

Carroll, L. (2000). *Alice in Wonderland*. New York: Harper Collins Publishers.

Carr, W., & Kemmis, S. (1997). *Becoming critical: Education, knowledge and action research*. New York: Falmer Press.

Choo, C. W. (2001). Environmental scanning as information seeking and organizational learning. *Information Research*, 7(1), 2–38.

Clandinin, D. J., & Connelley, F. M. (2000). *Narrative inquiry: Experience and story in qualitative research*. San Francisco: Jossey-Bass.

Cobb, R. W., & Elder, C. D. (1983). *Participation in American politics: The dynamics of agenda-guiding*. 2nd ed. Baltimore: Johns Hopkins University Press.

Cohen, H. (2003). *Negotiate this!* New York: Warner Business Books.

Cohen, M., March, J., & Olsen, J. (1972). A garbage can model of organizational choice. *Administrative Science Quarterly*, 17, 1–25.

Collins, J. (2001). *Good to great*. New York: HarperCollins.

Conger, J. A. (2004). Developing leadership capacity: What's inside the black box? *Academy of Management Executive*. 18(3), 136–139.

Cook, K., & Emerson, R. (1984). Exchange networks and the analysis of complex organizations. *Research in the Sociology in Organizations*, 3, 1–30.

Cook, T., & Campbell, D. (1979). *Quasi-experimentation design and analysis issues for field settings*. Boston: Houghton-Mifflin.

Corwin, R., & Borman, K. (1988). School as workplace: Structural constraints on administration. In N. Boyan (Ed.), *Handbook on educational administration* (pp. 209–237). New York: Longman.

Corwin, R., & Edelfelt, R. (1977). *Perspectives on organizations: Schools in the larger social environment*. Washington, DC: American Association of Colleges for Teacher Education and Association of Teacher Educators.

Coy, P. (2005, March 28). Why logic often takes a backseat. *Business Week*, 3926. Retrieved October 23, 2007.

Cromey, A., Van der Ploeg, A., & Blase, M. (2000). *The call for data-driven decision-making in the Midwest's schools*. Oak Brook, IL: North Central Educational Laboratory.

Cross, R., & Baird, L. (2000). Technology is not enough: Improving performance by building organizational memory. *Sloan Management Review*, 41(3), 69–82.

Crossan, M. (1999). An organizational learning framework: From intuition to institution. *Academy of Management Review, 24*(3), 522–538.

Crozier, M. (1964). *The bureaucratic phenomenon*. Chicago: University of Chicago Press.

Cuban, L. (1988). *The managerial imperative and the practice of leadership in schools*. Albany: State University of New York Press.

Culbertson, J. (1973). *Social science content for preparing educational leaders*. Columbus: Merrill Publishing.

Cusick, P. (1992). *The educational system: Its nature and logic*. New York: McGraw-Hill.

Cutler, A. N. (1999). *Normal accidents: A statistical interpretation*. Warwick, UK: Royal Statistical Society Conference on Risk.

Cyert, R., & March, J. (1963). *A behavioral theory of the firm*. Englewood Cliffs, NJ: Prentice-Hall.

Daft, R. L., & Weick, K. E. (1984). Toward a model of organizations as interpretation systems. *Academy of Management Review, 9*, 284–295.

Dahl, R. (1991). *Modern political analysis*. 5th ed. Englewood Cliffs, NJ: Prentice-Hall.

Darling-Hammond, L. (2000). Teacher quality and student achievement: A review of state policy evidence. *Educational Policy Archives, 8* (1). http://epaa.asu.edu/epaa/v8n1/

Davis, D. (1980). School administrators and advisory councils: Partnership or shotgun marriage. *NASSP Bulletin*, 62–66.

Davis, D. (1987). Parent involvement in the public schools. *Education and Urban Society, 19*(2), 147–163.

DeGrace, P., & Stahl, L. H. (1990). *Wicked problems, righteous solutions*. Englewood Cliffs, NJ: Prentice-Hall.

Deutsch, K. (1963). *The nerves of government: Models of political communication and control*. London: Free Press of Glencoe.

Dewey, J. (1933). *How we think a restatement of the relation of reflective thinking to the educative process*. Boston: D.C. Heath & Co.

Dewey, J. (1938). *Logic, the theory of inquiry*. New York: Holt, Rinehart & Winston.

Dewey, J. (1944). *Democracy and education*. New York: Free Press. (Originally published in 1915.)

Dimaggio, P., & Powell, W. (1983, April). The iron cage revisited: Institutional isomorphism and collective rationality in organizational fields. *American Sociological Review, 48*, 147–160.

Easterby-Smith, M., Crossan, M., & Nicolini, D. (2000). Organizational learning: Debates past, present and future. *Journal of Management Studies, 37*(6), 783–796.

Easton, D. (1965). *A systems analysis of political life*. Chicago: University of Chicago Press.

Easton, D. (1979). *A systems analysis of political life*. 2nd ed. Chicago: University of Chicago Press.

Easton, J. Q., & Luppescu, S. (2004). *Teacher and principal response to the grow network: A preliminary evaluation of use in Chicago public elementary schools*. Chicago: Consortium on Chicago School Research.

Eisner, E. (2002). What can education learn from the arts about the practice of education? *Journal of Curriculum and Supervision, 18*(1), 4–16.

Eisner, E. (2003). Questionable assumptions about schooling. *Phi Delta Kappan, 84*(9), 648–657.

Elkjaer, B. (2004). Organizational learning: The third way. *Management learning, 35*(4), 419–434.

Elmore, R. (1990). *Restructuring schools: The next generation of educational reform.* San Francisco: Jossey-Bass.

Elmore, R. (1995). Teaching, learning and school organization: Principles of practice and the regularities of schooling. *Educational Administration Quarterly, 31*(3), 355–374.

Elmore, R., & McLaughlin, M. (1988). *Steady work: Policy, practice, and the reform of American education.* R-3574-NIE/RC. Santa Monica, CA: Rand Corporation.

Emerson, R. (1962). Power-dependence relations. *American Sociological Review, 27*(1), 31–41.

English, F. (2002). Cutting the Gordian knot of educational administration: The theory-practice gap. *UCEA Review, 44*(1), 1–3.

English, F. (2003). *The postmodern challenge to the theory and practice of educational administration.* Springfield, IL: Charles C. Thomas.

Etzioni, A. (1975). *A comparative analysis of complex organizations: On power, involvement and their correlates.* New York: Free Press.

Etzioni, A. (1986). Mixed scanning revisited. *Public Administration Review, 46*, 8–14.

Etzioni, A. (1989). Humble decision-making. *Harvard Business Review, 67*, 122–26.

Fessler, D. M. T., Pillsworth, E. G., & Flamson, T. J. (2004). Angry men and disgusted women: An evolutionary approach to the influence of emotions on risk taking. *Organizational Behavior and Human Decision Processes, 95*, 107–123.

Firestone, W. (1989). Educational policy as an ecology of games. *Educational Researcher, 18*(7), 18–24.

Fisher, R., & Ury, W. (1981). *Getting to yes.* New York: Penguin Books.

Foucault, M. (1969). *The archaeology of knowledge and the discourse on language.* New York: Harper Colophon.

Freidson, E. (2001). *Professionalism: The third logic.* Chicago: University of Chicago Press.

Freire, P. (1973). *Pedagogy of the oppressed.* New York: Seabury Press.

Fuhrman, S. H. (1999). *The new accountability.* Philadelphia: CPRE.

Gall, M. D., Gall, J. P., & Borg, W. R. (2006). *Educational research: An introduction.* 8th ed. Boston: Longman.

Gamble, P. R., & Gibson, D. A. (1999). Executive values and decision-making: The relationship of culture and information flows. *Journal of Management Studies, 36*(2), 217–240.

Gamoran, A., & Dreeben, R. (1986). Coupling and control in educational organizations. *Administrative Science Quarterly, 31*(4), 612–632.

Gamson, W. (1968). *Power and discontent.* Homewood, IL: Dorsey Press.

Gamson, W. (1990). *The strategy of social protest.* 2nd ed. Belmont, CA: Wordsworth.

Gaventa, J. (1980). *Power and powerlessness, quiescence and rebellion in an Appalachian valley.* Oxford: Clarendon.

Giddens, A. (1987). *Sociology.* Orlando: Harcourt Brace Jovanovich.

Gladwell, M. (2005). *Blink: The power of thinking without thinking.* New York: Little, Brown.

Glick, P. (1991). Trait-based and sex-based discrimination in occupational prestige. *Sex Roles, 25*, 351–378.

Goffman, E. (1961). *Asylums: Essays on the social situation of mental patients and other inmates*. New York: Doubleday.

Goldring, E., & Rallis, S. (1993). The flag bearer and bridger: Managing the environment. In E. Goldring & S. Rallis (Eds.), *Principals of Dynamic Schools: Taking Charge of Change* (pp. 68–87). Newbury Park, CA: Corwin Press.

Gonzales, L. (2003). *Deep survival: Who lives, who dies and why*. New York: W. W. Norton.

Greenfield, T. B. (1975). Theory about organizations: A new perspective and its implications for schools. In M. Hughes (Ed.), *Administering education: International challenge* (*pp.* 71–99). London: Athlane.

Griffiths, D. (1969). Administration as decision-making. In F. Carver & T. Sergiovanni (Eds.), *Organizations and human behavior: Focus on schools* (pp. 73–84). New York: McGraw-Hill.

Griffiths, D. (1978). Contemporary theory development and educational administration. *Educational Administration Quarterly*, 6(2), 80–93.

Gronn, P. (1984). "I have a solution . . . ": Administrative power in a school meeting. *Educational Administration Quarterly*, 20(2), 65–92.

Gronn, P. (2003). *The new work of educational leaders: Changing leadership practice in an era of school reform*. Thousand Oaks, CA: Sage Publications.

Gunderman, R. B. (2001). Patient communication: What to teach radiology residents. *American Journal of Radiology*, 177, 41–43.

Habermas, J. (1971). *Knowledge and human interests*. Boston: Beacon Press.

Habermas, J. (1973). *Theory and practice*. Boston: Beacon Press.

Hackman, J. (Ed.). (1990). *Groups that work and those that don't: Creating conditions for effective teamwork*. San Francisco: Jossey-Bass.

Haimes, R. (1995). Planning for change. In H. G. Garner (Ed.), *Teamwork Models and Experience in Education* (pp. 819–42). Boston: Allyn & Bacon.

Hall, R. (2002). *Organizations: Structures, processes, and outcomes*. 8th ed. Englewood Cliffs, NJ: Prentice-Hall.

Halpin, A. (1966). The development of theory in educational administration. In A. W. Halpin (Ed.), *Theory and research in administration* (pp. 3–21). New York: Macmillan.

Hargreaves, A. (1988). Teaching quality: A sociological analysis. *Journal of Curriculum Studies*, 20, 211–231.

Hargreaves, A., & Fink, D. (2006). *Sustainable leadership*. San Francisco: Jossey-Bass.

Hansen, D. E., & Helgeson, J. G. (1996). Choice under strict uncertainty: Processes and preferences. *Organizational Behavior and Human Decision Processes*, 66(2), 153–164.

Harris, H. (2001). Content analysis of secondary data: A study of courage in managerial decision-making. *Journal of Business Ethics*, 34, 191–208.

Hasenfeld, Y. (1983). *Human service organizations*. Englewood Cliffs, NJ: Prentice-Hall.

Heidegger, M. (1962). *Being and time* (J. Macquarrie & E. Robinson, Trans.). New York: Harper & Row.

Heifetz, R. A. (1994). *Leadership without easy answers*. Cambridge, MA: Belknap.

Hirschman, A. (1970). *Exit, voice, and loyalty: Responses to decline in firms, organizations and States*. Cambridge, MA: Harvard University Press.

Hogarth, R. M. (2001). *Educating intuition*. Chicago: The University of Chicago Press.

Holzer, H. J., & Ihlanfeldt, K. R. (1998). Customer discrimination and employment outcomes for minority workers. *Quarterly Journal of Economics*, 113(3), 835–867.

Homans, George C. (1950). *The human group*. New York: Harcourt Brace Jovanovich.

Howells, J. R. L. (1995). *Tacit knowledge and technology transfer*. Working paper No. 16. ESRC Centre for Business Research and Judge Institute of Management Studies, University of Cambridge.

Hoy, W., & Miskel, C. (2001). *Educational administration: Theory, research and practice*. 6th ed. Boston: McGraw-Hill.

Hoy, W., & Tarter, C. J. (2004). *Administrators solving the problems of practice: Decision-making concepts, cases and consequences*. 2nd ed. Boston: Allyn & Bacon.

Huffman, D., & Kalnin, J. (2003). Collaborative inquiry to make data-based decisions in schools. *Teaching and Teacher Education, 19*, 569–580.

Hughes, E. (1965). The study of occupations. In R. Merton, L. Broom, & L. Cottrell Jr. (Eds.), *Sociology Today (pp. 87–111)*. New York: Basic Books.

Hulin, C. L., & Roznowski, M. (1985). Organizational technologies: Effects on organizations' characteristics and individuals' responses. In L. L. Cummings & B. M. Staw (Eds.), *Research in organizational behavior*, vol. 7 (pp. 48–79). Greenwich, CT: JAI Press.

Hume, D. (2000). *An enquiry concerning human understanding* (T. Beauchamp, Trans.). New York: Oxford University Press.

Jablin, F. M., & Sias, P. M. (2000). Communication competence. In F. M. Jablin & L. L. Putnam (Eds.), *The new handbook of organizational communication*. Newbury Park, CA: Sage Publications.

Jackson, P. (1986). *The practice of teaching*. New York: Teachers College Press.

Jackson, P. (1990). *Life in classrooms*. 2nd ed. New York: Teachers College Press.

Janis, I., & Mann, L. (1977). *Decision-making: A psychological analysis of conflict, choice and commitment*. New York: Free Press.

Jaspers, K. (1968). *Reason and existence* (W. Earle, Trans.). New York: Noonday Press.

Johnson, B. L. Jr. (1997). An organizational analysis of multiple perspectives of effective teaching: Implications for teacher evaluation policy. *Journal of Personnel Evaluation in Education, 11*, 69–87.

Johnson, B. L. Jr. (1998). Resource dependence theory: A political economy model of organizations. In *International encyclopedia of public policy and administration* (Vol. 4, pp. 1969–1974). New York: Henry Holt Company.

Johnson, B. L. Jr. (1999). The politics of research-information use in the education policy. *Educational Policy, 13*(1), 23–36.

Johnson, B. L. Jr. (2004a). A sound education for all: Multicultural issues in music education policy. *Education Policy, 18*(1), 116–141.

Johnson, B. L. Jr. (2004b). Where have all the flowers gone? Reconnecting leadership preparation with the field of organization theory. *UCEA Review 46*(3): 16–21.

Johnson, B. L. Jr., & Fauske, J. (2000). Principals and the political economy of environmental enactment. *Educational Administration Quarterly, 36*(2): 159–185.

Johnson, B. L. Jr., & Owens. M. (2005). Building new bridges: Linking organizational theory with other educational literatures. *Journal of Educational Administration 43*(1): 41–59.

Johnson, R. (2002). *Using data to close the achievement gap: How to measure equity in schools*. 2nd ed. Thousand Oaks, CA: Sage Publications.

Karsten, H. (1999). Relationships between organizational form and organizational memory. *Journal of Organizational Computing and Electronic Commerce, 9*(2–3), 129–150.

Khatri, N., & Ng, A. (2000). The role of intuition in strategic decision-making. *Human Relations*, 53(1), 57–86.

Kingdon, J. W. (1995). *Agendas, alternatives and public policies*. Boston: Little, Brown.

Kohlberg, L. (1984). *The psychology of moral development: The nature and validity of moral stages*. San Francisco: Harper & Row.

Klein, G. (2003). *The power of intuition*. Doubleday: New York.

Kotter, J. P. (1996). Leading change. Boston: Harvard Business School Press.

Kotter, J. P. (1999). *What leaders really do*. Boston: Harvard Business Review.

Kristol, I. (1995). *Neoconservatism: The autobiography of an idea*. New York: Free Press.

Kruse, S. D. (2001), Creating communities of reform: Images of continuous improvement planning teams. *Journal of Educational Administration*, 39(4), 359–383.

Kuvaas, B., & Selart, M. (2004). Effects of attribute framing on cognitive processing and evaluation. *Organizational Behavior and Human Decision Processes*, 95(2), 198–207.

Ladd, H. F. (1996). *Holding schools accountable*. Washington DC: Brookings Institution.

Lashway, L. (2003a). Data analysis for school improvement. *Research Roundup*, 19(2), 1–4.

Lashway, L. (2003b). *Transforming principal preparation*. ERIC Digest 473360.

Lasswell, H. (1958). *Politics: Who gets what, when, how*. Cleveland: Meridian Books.

Lee, J. (2006). *American idol: Evidence of same-race preferences*. Institute for the Study of Labor, IZA Discussion Paper No. 1974. Available at SSRN: http://ssrn.com/abstract=884482

Leithwood, K., & Louis, K. S. (1998). *Organizational learning in schools: An introduction*. In K. Leithwood & K. S. Louis (Eds.), *Organizational learning in schools*, (pp. 1–14). Lisse, the Netherlands: Swets & Zeitlinger.

Leithwood, K., & Steinbach, R. (1994). *Expert problem solving: evidence from school and district leaders*. Albany: State University of New York Press.

Leithwood, K., Steinbach, R., & Jantzi, D. (2002), School leadership and teachers' motivation to implement accountability policies. *Educational Administration Quarterly*, 38(1), 94–119.

Lindblom, C. (1959). The science of "muddling through." *Public Administration Review*, 19(2), 79–88.

Lindblom, C. (1993). *The policy making process*. 3rd ed. Prentice-Hall Foundations of Modern Political Science Series. Englewood Cliffs, NJ: Prentice-Hall.

Lipsky, M. (1978). Standing the study of public policy implementation on its head. In W. Burnham & M. Weinberg (Eds.), *American Politics and Public Policy* (pp. 391–403). Cambridge, MA: MIT Press.

Lobkowicz, N. (1967). *Theory and practice: History of a concept from Aristotle to Marx*. Notre Dame: University of Notre Dame Press.

Lortie, D. (1969). The balance of control and autonomy in elementary school teaching. In A. Etzioni (Ed.), *The semi-professions and their organization* (pp. 1–53). New York: Free Press.

Lortie, D. (1975). *Schoolteacher: A sociological study*. Chicago: University of Chicago Press.

Louis, K. S., & Kruse, S. D. (1995). *Professionalism and community: Perspectives on reforming urban schools*. Thousand Oaks, CA: Corwin Press.

Louis, K. S., & Miles, M. (1990). *Improving the urban high school: What works and why*. New York: Teachers College Press.

Lowi, T. (1995). *The end of the republican era*. Norman: The University of Oklahoma Press.

Lukes, S. (1974). *Power: A radical view*. London: Macmillan.

Majone, G. (1989). *Evidence, argument and persuasion in the policy process*. New Haven, CT: Yale University Press

Malen, B. (1995). The micropolitics of education: Mapping the multiple dimensions of power relations in school polities. In J. D. Scribner & D. H. Layton (Eds.), *The Study of the Politics of Education* (pp. 147–168). Washington, DC: The Falmer Press.

Mannheim, K. (1936). *Ideology and utopia*. London: Routledge & Kegan Paul.

March J. G. (Ed). (1965). *Handbook of organizations*, pp. 972–1032. New York: Rand-McNally.

March, J. G. (1978). American public school administration: A short analysis. *School Review*, 86(February), 217–250.

March, J. G. (1988). *Decisions and organizations*. Oxford: Blackwell.

March, J. G. (1991). How decisions happen in organizations. *Human-Computer Interaction*, 6, 95–117.

March, J. G. (1994). *A primer of decision-making*. New York: Free Press.

Markus, M. L. (2001), Toward a theory of knowledge reuse, *Journal of Management Information Systems*, 18(1), 57–93.

Martin, W., & Willower, D. (1981). The managerial behavior of high school principals. *Educational Administration Quarterly* 17, 69–90.

McClintock, C. (1987). Conceptual and action heuristics: Tools for the evaluator. In L. Bickman (Ed.), *Using Program Theory for Evaluation* (pp. 43–57). San Francisco: Jossey-Bass.

McCroskey, J. (1999). Getting to results: Data-driven decision-making for children, youth, families and communities. What Works Policy Brief. Sacramento, CA: Foundation Consortium.

Mead, G. H. (1934). *Mind, self, and society*. Chicago: University of Chicago Press.

Meyer, J. W., & Rowan, B. (1977). "Institutionalized organizations: Formal structure as myth and ceremony." *American Journal of Sociology*, 83(2), 340–363.

Meyer, J. W., & Rowan, B. (1978). The structure of educational organizations. In M. W. Meyer, et al. (Eds.), *Environments and Organizations* (pp. 78–109). San Francisco: Jossey-Bass.

Meyerson, D. E. (1998). Feeling stressed and burned out: A feminist reading and re-visioning of stress-based emotions within medicine and organization science. *Organization Science*, 9(1), 103–118.

Michels, R. (1962). *Political parties: A sociological study of the oligarchical tendencies of modern democracy* (E. Paul & C. Paul, Trans.). New York: Free Press.

Mill, J. S. (1850). *A system of logic, ratiocinative and inductive being a connected view of the principles of evidence and the methods of scientific investigation*. New York: Harper.

Miller, C. C., & Ireland, R. D. (2005). Intuition in strategic decision-making: Friend or foe in the fast-paced 21st century? *Academy of Management Executive*, 19(1), 19–30.

Miller, E., & Jensen, J. (2004). *Questions that matter: An invitation to philosophy*. 5th ed. Boston: McGraw-Hill.

Mills, C. W. (1956). *The power elite*. New York: Oxford University Press.

Mintzberg, H. (1973). *The nature of managerial work*. New York: Harper & Row.

Mintzberg, H. (1979). *The structuring of organizations*. Englewood Cliffs, NJ: Prentice-Hall.

Mintzberg, H. (1983). *Power in and around organizations*. Englewood Cliffs, NJ: Prentice-Hall.

Moe, T. (1980). *The organization of interests: Incentives and the internal dynamics of political interest groups*. Chicago: University of Chicago Press.

Moles, O. (1987). Who wants parent involvement? *Education and Urban Society, 19,* 137–145.

Moore-Johnson, S. (1990). *Teachers at work*. New York: Basic Books.

Morgan, G. (1986). *Images of organization*. Thousand Oaks, CA: Sage Publications.

Morse, G. (2006). Decisions and desire. *Harvard Business Review, 84*(1) 19–26.

Muir, W. (1986). Teachers' regulation of the classroom. In D. Krip & D. Jensen (Eds.), *School days, rule days: The legalization and regulation of education* (pp. 109–123). Philadelphia: Falmer Press.

Murphy, J. (1992). *The landscape of leadership preparation: Reframing the education of school administrators*. Newbury Park, CA: Corwin Press, 1992.

Murphy, J. (1999). *The quest for a center: Notes on the state of the profession of educational leadership*. Columbia, MO: University Council for Educational Administration.

Myers, C. K. (2005). *Discrimination as a competitive device: The case of local television news*. Institute for the Study of Labor, IZA Discussion Papers No. 1802. Available at *http://www.iza.org/*

National Commission on Excellence in Education. (1983). *A Nation at Risk: The Imperative for Educational Reform*. Washington, D.C.: U.S. Department of Education.

Nickel, M. N., & Fuentes, J. M. (2002). Survival as a success in the face of scarcity of resources. Working paper. Madrid: Departamento de Economia de Empresa, Universidad carols III de Madrid.

Nisbett, R., & Ross, L. (1980). *Human inference: Strategies and shortcomings of social judgment*. Englewood Cliffs, NJ: Prentice-Hall.

Nitko, A. (2001). *Educational assessment of students*. Englewood Cliffs, NJ: Merrill Prentice Hall.

Northcutt, N., & McCoy, D. (2004). *Interactive qualitative analysis*. Newbury Park, CA: Sage Publications.

Nutt, P. C. (1984). Types of organizational decisional processes. *Administrative Science Quarterly, 29,* 414–450.

O'Fallon, M. J., & Butterfield, K. D. (2005). A review of the empirical ethical decision-making literature 1996–2003. *Journal of Business Ethics, 59,* 375–413.

Ogawa, R. (1996). Bridging and buffering relationships between parents and schools. *UCEA Review, 38*(1), 3–7.

Olivera, F. (2000). Memory systems in organizations: An empirical investigation of mechanism for knowledge collection, storage and access. *Journal of Management Studies, 37*(6), 811–832.

Pareto, V. (1984). *The transformation of democracy* (Renata Girola, Trans.). New Brunswick, NJ: Transaction Books.

Parks, M. R. (1994). Communication competence and interpersonal control. In M. L. Knapp & G. R. Miller (Eds.), *Handbook of interpersonal communication* (pp. 589–618). Thousand Oaks, CA: Sage Publications.

Parsons, T. (1960). *Structure and process in modern societies*. Glencoe, IL: Free Press.

Parsons, T. (1967). Some ingredients of a general theory of formal organization. In A. Halpin (Ed.), *Administrative theory in education (pp.* 40–72). New York: Macmillan.

Payne, D., & Joyner, B. E. (2006). Successful U.S. entrepreneurs: Identifying ethical decision-making and social responsibility behaviors. *Journal of Business Ethics, 65,* 203–217.

Payne, H. J. (2005). Reconceptualizing social skills in organizations. *Journal of Leadership and Organizational Studies, 11*(2), 63–78.

Pedhazur, E. J., & Schmelkin, L. P. (1991). *Measurement, design and analysis: An integrated approach.* Mahwah, NJ: Lawrence Erlbaum Associates.

Perrow, C. (1967). A framework for the comparative analysis of organizations. *American Sociological Review, 32,* 194–208.

Perrow, C. (1999). *Normal accidents: Living with high-risk technologies.* Princeton: Princeton University Press.

Petersen, T., & Saporta, I. (2004). The opportunity structure for discrimination. *American Journal of Sociology, 109,* 852–901.

Peterson, K., & Deal, T. (2003). *Shaping school culture.* San Francisco: Jossey-Bass.

Petrides, L. A., & Zahra Guiney, S. (2002). Knowledge management for school leaders. *Teachers College Record, 104*(8), 1702–1717.

Petroski, H. (1985). *To engineer is human: The role of failure in successful design.* New York: St. Martin's Press.

Pfeffer, J. (1981). *Power in organizations.* Marshfield, MA: Pitman Publishing.

Pfeffer, J. (1992). *Managing with power: Politics and influence in organizations.* Boston: Harvard Business School Press.

Pfeffer, J., & Salancik, G. (1978). *The external control of organizations: A resource dependence perspective.* New York: Harper & Row.

Piaget, J. (1977). *The development of thought: Equilibration of cognitive structures* (A. Rosin, Trans.). New York: Viking Press.

Popper, K. (1974). Causality, explanation and the deduction of predictions. In T. L. Beauchamp (Ed.), *Philosophical Problems of Causation (pp. 14–40).* Encino, CA: Dickenson Publishing.

Polanyi, M. (1967). *The tacit dimension.* New York: Anchor Books.

Pounder, D. G. (1998). *Restructuring schools for collaboration: Promises and pitfalls.* Albany: State University of New York Press.

Pounder, D. G. (1999). Teacher teams: Exploring job characteristics and work-related outcomes of work group enhancement. *Educational Administration Quarterly, 35*(3), 317–348.

Ratner, R. K., & Herbst, K. C. (2005). When good decisions have bad outcomes: The impact of affect on switching behavior. *Organizational Behavior and Human Decision Processes, 96,* 23–37.

Rawls, J. (1971). *The common good: Its politics, policies, and philosophy.* New York: Routledge & Kegan Paul.

Read, H. (1944). *Education through art.* New York: Pantheon.

Reynolds, P. D. (1971). *A primer in theory construction.* Indianapolis: Bobbs-Merrill.

Ricoeur, P. (1981). *Hermeneutics and human science: Essays on language, action and interpretation* (J. B. Thompson, Trans.). Cambridge: Cambridge University Press.

Ricoeur, P. (1976). *Interpretation theory: Discourse and the surplus of meaning.* Fort Worth: TCU Press.

Riessman, C. K. (1993). *Narrative analysis*. Newbury Park, CA: Sage Publications.

Rittel, H., & Webber, M. (1973). Dilemmas in a general theory of planning. *Policy Sciences, 4*, 155–169.

Roberts, R. M. (1989). *Serendipity: Accidental discoveries in science*. New York: John Wiley & Sons.

Ross, W. (1942). *The student's Oxford Aristotle*. London: Oxford University Press.

Rowan, B. (1990). Applying conceptions of teaching to organizational reform. In R. Elmore & Associates (Eds.), *Restructuring Schools: The Next Generation of Educational Reform* (pp. 31–58). San Francisco: Jossey-Bass.

Rowan, B. (2002). Rationality and reality in organizational management: Using the coupling metaphor to understand educational (and other) organizations. *Journal of Educational Administration, 40*(6), 604–11.

Rubenfeld, S. A., & Newstrom, J. W. (1994). Caveat emptor: Avoiding pitfalls in data-based decision-making. *Review of Business, 16*(2) 20–26.

Ruggiero, V. R. (2004). *Thinking critically about ethical issues*. 6th ed. Boston: McGraw-Hill.

Salisbury, R. (1969). An exchange theory of interest groups. *Midwest Journal of Political Science*, 1–32.

Sayegh, L., Anthony, W. P., & Perrewe, P. L. (2004). Managerial decision-making under crisis: The role of emotion in an intuitive decision process. *Human Resource Management Review, 14*, 179–199.

Schattschneider, E. (1975). *The semisovereign people: A realist's view of democracy in America*. Hinsdale, IL: Dryden Press.

Schein, E. (1985). *Organizational culture and leadership*. San Francisco: Jossey-Bass.

Schon, D. A. (1983). *The reflective practitioner: How professionals think in action*. New York: Basic Books.

Schon, D. A. (1987). *Educating the reflective practitioner: Toward a new design for teaching and learning the professions*. San Francisco: Jossey-Bass.

Schon, D. A. (1988). Coaching reflective teaching. In P. Grimmett & G. Erickson (Eds.), *Reflection in teacher education* (pp. 19–29). New York: Teachers College Press.

Scott, W. R. (2000). *Institutions and organizations*. 2nd ed. Thousand Oaks, CA: Sage Publications.

Scott, W. R. (2002). *Organizations: Rational, natural, and open systems*. 5th ed. Englewood Cliffs, NJ: Prentice-Hall.

Scribner, J. P., Cockrell, K. S., Cockrell, D. H., & Valentine, J. W. (1999). Creating professional communities in schools through organizational learning: An evaluation of a school improvement process. *Educational Administration Quarterly, 35*(1), 130–160.

Selznick, P. (1957). *Leadership in administration: A sociological interpretation*. Berkeley: University of California Press.

Senge, P. (1990). *The fifth discipline*. New York: Doubleday.

Sergiovanni, T. (1995). *The principalship: A reflective practice perspective*. 3rd ed. Boston: Allyn & Bacon.

Short, P. M., Short, R. J., & Brinson, K. (1998). *Information collection: The key to data-based decision-making*. New York: Eye on Education.

Shulman, L. S. (1986). Those who understand: Knowledge growth in teaching. *Educational Researcher, 15*(2), 4–14.

Shulman, L. S. (1987). Knowledge and teaching: Foundations of the New Reform. *Harvard Educational Review, 57*(1), 1–22.

Simon, H. (1976). *Administrative behavior: A study of decision-making process in administrative organization.* 3rd ed. New York: Free Press.

Simon, H. (1981). *The sciences of the artificial.* 2nd ed. Cambridge, MA: MIT Press.

Simon, H. (1987). Making management decisions: The role of intuition and emotion. *Academy of Management Executive, 5,* 57–63.

Simon, H. (1991). Decision-making: Rational, non-rational and irrational. Address delivered at the annual meeting of the University Council for Educational Administration, Baltimore, Maryland.

Simon, H. (1993). Decision-making: Rational, nonrational and irrational. *Educational Administration Quarterly, 29*(3) 392–411.

Smith, E. (2001). The role of tacit and explicit knowledge in the workplace. *Journal of Knowledge Management, 5,* 311–321.

Smith, J., & Kida, T. (1991). Heuristics and biases: Expertise and task realism in auditing. *Psychological Bulletin, 109,* 472–489.

Snyder, P., Hall, M., Robertson, J., Jainski, T., & Miller, J. S. (2006). Ethical rationality: A strategic approach to organizational crisis. *Journal of Business Ethics, 63,* 371–383.

Spillane, J. P. (2006). *Distributed leadership.* San Francisco: Jossey-Bass.

Spring, J. (2005). *Conflict of interests: The politics of American education.* 5th ed. New York: McGraw-Hill.

Sternberg, R. J., & Pretz, J. E. (2005). *Cognition and intelligence: Identifying the mechanisms of the mind.* New York: Routledge.

Stovall, O. S., Neill, J. D., & Perkins, D. (2004). Corporate governance, internal decision-making, and the invisible hand. *Journal of Business Ethics, 51,* 221–227.

Streifer, P. A., & Schumann, J. A. (2005). Using data mining to identify actionable information: Breaking new ground in data driven decision-making. *Journal of Education for Students Placed at Risk, 10*(3), 281–293

Sweetland, S., & Hoy, W. (2000), School characteristics and educational outcomes. *Educational Administration Quarterly, 26*(4) 703–729.

TschannenMoran, M. (2004). *Trust matters.* San Francisco: Jossey-Bass.

Thompson, J. (1967). *Organizations in action.* New York: McGraw-Hill.

Thorngate, W. (1976). "In general" vs. "it depends": Some comments on the Gergen-Schlenker debate. *Personality and Social Psychology Bulletin, 2,* 404–410.

Tufte, E. R. (2001). *The visual display of quantitative information.* 2nd ed. Cheshire, CT: Graphics Press.

Tufte, E. R. (2003). *The cognitive style of PowerPoint.* Cheshire, CT: Graphics Press.

Tuomi, I. (2000). Data is more than knowledge. *Journal of Management Information Systems, 16* (3), 103–117.

Tversky, A., & Kahneman, D. (1973). Availability: Heuristic for judging frequence and probability. *Cognitive Psychology, 5,* 207–232.

Tversky, A., & Kahneman, D. (1974). Judgment under uncertainty: Heuristics and biases. *Science, n.s. 185*(4157), 1124–1131.

Tversky, A., & Kahneman, D. (1981). The framing of decisions and the psychology of choice. *Science, 21,* 453–458.

Tyack, D. (1974). *The one best system.* Cambridge, MA: Harvard University Press.

Tyack, D., & Cuban, L. (1995). *Tinkering toward utopia: A century of public school reform.* Cambridge, MA: Harvard University Press.

Vince, R. (2001). Power and emotion in organizational learning. *Human Relations*, 54(10), 1325–1351.

Viteritti, J. P. (1986). The urban school district: Toward an open system approach to leadership and governance. *Urban Education*, 21(3): 228–253.

Waller, W. (1932). *Sociology of teaching*. New York: John Wiley & Sons.

Wallis, J. (1996). Economics, hope and leadership. *Journal of Interdisciplinary Economics*, 7(4), 255–276.

Wallis, J. (2002). Drawing on revisionist economics to explain the inspirational dimension of leadership. *Journal of Socio-Economics*, 31, 59–74.

Weber, M. (1946). *From Max Weber: Essays in sociology* (H. Gerth & C. Wright Mills, Trans.). New York: Oxford University Press.

Weber, M. (1947). *The theory of social and economic organization*. New York: Oxford University Press.

Weick, K. (1976). Educational organizations as loosely coupled systems. *Administrative Science Quarterly*, 21(2), 1–19.

Weick, K. (1978). The spines of leadership. In M. W. McCall Jr. & M. M. Lombardo (Eds.), *Leadership: Where else can we go?* (pp. 37–61) Durham, NC: Duke University.

Weick, K. (1979). *The social-psychology of organizing*. 2nd ed. New York: McGraw-Hill.

Weick, K. (1989). Theory as disciplined imagination. *Academy of Science Review*, 14(4), 516–531.

Weick, K. (1995). *Sensemaking in organizations*. Thousand Oaks, CA: Sage Publications.

Weick, K. (2001). *Making sense of the organization*. Malden, MA: Blackwell.

Welter, B., & Egmon, J. (2006). *The prepared mind of a leader*. San Francisco:Jossey-Bass.

West, C. (1994). *Race matters*. Boston: Beacon Press.

Whitehead, A. (1957). *The aims of education*. New York: Free Press.

Whyte, W. F. (1991). *Participatory action research*. Newbury Park, CA: Sage Publications.

Wildavsky, A. (1979). *Speaking truth to power: The art and craft of policy analysis*. Boston: Little, Brown.

Wilkinson, A., & Smith, M. (1995). Team recruitment, team building, and skill development. In H. G. Garner (Ed.), *Teamwork Models and Experience in Education*. Boston: Allyn & Bacon.

Willower, D. (1982). School organizations: Perspectives in juxtaposition. *Educational Administration Quarterly*, 18, 89–110.

Willower, D. (1985). School principals as threshold guardians: An exploratory study. *Alberta Journal of Educational Research*, 31, 2–10.

Willower, D. J. (1991). Art and science in administration. *Education*, 111(4), 497–500.

Willower, D., & Licata, J. (1997). *Values and valuation in the practice of educational administration*. Thousand Oaks, CA: Corwin Press.

Wilson, T., Houston, C., Etling, K., & Brekke, N. (1996). A new look at anchoring effects: Basic anchoring and its antecedents. *Journal of Experimental Psychology: General*, 125(4), 382–407.

Wirt, F., & Kirst, M. (1997). *The political dynamics of American education*. 3rd ed. Berkeley, CA: McCutchan.

Wolcott, H. (1973). *Man in the principal's office*. New York: Holt, Rinehart & Winston.

Yeo, R. K. (2006). Learning institution to learning organization: Kudos to reflective practitioners. *Journal of European Industrial Training*, 30(5), 396–419.

Yukl, G. (2002). *Leadership in organizations*. 5th ed. Upper Saddle River, NJ: Prentice-Hall.

Index